Microsoft PowerPoint Best Practices, Tips, and Techniques

An indispensable guide to mastering PowerPoint's advanced
tools to create engaging presentations

Chantal Bossé

BIRMINGHAM—MUMBAI

Microsoft PowerPoint Best Practices, Tips, and Techniques

Associate Group Product Manager: Alok Dhuri
Publishing Product Manager: Harshal Gundetty
Content Development Editor: Rosal Colaco
Technical Editor: Pradeep Sahu
Copy Editor: Safis Editing
Project Coordinator: Deeksha Thakkar
Proofreader: Safis Editing
Indexer: Pratik Shirodkar
Production Designer: Prashant Ghare
Business Development Executive: Uzma Sheerin
Developer Relations Marketing Executives: Rayyan Khan and Deepak Kumar

First published: January 2023

Production reference: 1200123

Published by Packt Publishing Ltd.
Livery Place
35 Livery Street
Birmingham
B3 2PB, UK.

ISBN 978-1-83921-533-9

www.packtpub.com

To my best friend, life partner, and business partner, Patrice Perras – you introduced me to computers and technology 30 years ago, helping me discover how fun they are to use, even though I hated everything about them when I started. This book would not have been produced without that spark.

To my two sons, Alexandre and Vincent – what I learned by helping you use PowerPoint and prepare your school presentations has also been an inspiration for this book.

– Chantal Bossé

Contributors

About the author

Chantal Bossé has worked in instructional design and training for over 25 years and is the founder of CHABOS Inc., specializing in M365 training and high-stakes presentation design and coaching. She has been a Microsoft PowerPoint, M365 Apps & Services **Most Valued Professional (MVP)** since 2013 and has helped over 250,000 international French-speaking learners on LinkedIn Learning with her courses on PowerPoint, Teams, and communication. She thrives on helping people understand and leverage technology to help them work efficiently and deliver engaging and impactful presentations.

I became who I am because of many people that crossed my path through the years. Thank you to my friends at The Presentation Summit, my PowerPoint MVP peers, the Microsoft PowerPoint development team, and The Presentation Guild. You all have been an enormous source of inspiration and support. And thank you Packt for believing in and supporting me.

About the reviewer

Glenna Shaw has over 2 decades of experience in creating visual communications in the form of presentations, data visualizations, dashboards, demos, prototypes, and system user interfaces. She is a certified **Project Management Professional** (**PMP**) and a Microsoft PowerPoint MVP. Glenna is frequently sought out for her innovative information management solutions using SharePoint and Microsoft Office, as well as her creative visual communication designs. Glenna has been a spotlight speaker at events, a technical editor for books and training courses, and frequently teaches advanced Microsoft Office classes. She is also the author of tutorials on using sensory psychology to improve visual communications on her Visualology blog.

Under the penname *The PowerPoint Magician*, she is the author of the popular PowerPak for PowerPoint series, an innovative collection of lesson and educational game templates.

Glenna holds certificates in accessible information technology, graphic design, knowledge management, information design, and professional technical writing. Glenna was a mental health therapist for 10 years and now applies that background and knowledge of psychology to the art of visual communications.

Table of Contents

5

Using Artificial Intelligence to Improve Your Visuals   91

6

Adding and Modifying Visual Elements   109

7

Adding and Modifying Multimedia Elements   143

8

Working with
Transitions and Animations   173

9

Building Flexibility and Interactivity into Your Presentations   199

10

Using PowerPoint Third-Party Add-Ins   221

11

Practicing Your Presentation Delivery   253

12

Using Presenter View   269

13

Preface

Using PowerPoint is something that many people have done at some point in their business life, and maybe before as students – but creating engaging and impactful presentations is something many users struggle with.

When I was asked to write on PowerPoint applications, it became obvious I also had to discuss more than just the tools. For close to 20 years now, I have seen clients struggle because they did not know about the industry's best practices and did not have formal training to help them discover and use some more advanced and very helpful features. All the people I trained and all the clients I worked with also had a common desire: they all wanted to save time when creating their presentations.

This is why this book is different from most PowerPoint books. You have the choice to go on a journey through the most important tools to help you plan, craft, and deliver visually appealing and more flexible impactful presentations. Otherwise, you can choose to read any chapter or about any topic that will help you learn about features and tools that you didn't know already.

Whatever method of reading you adopt, I can guarantee that you will be more knowledgeable on presentation best practices, PowerPoint features that help you create better presentations more efficiently, and how to improve your presentation delivery by the end of this book.

Who this book is for

This book is for business professionals without any formal design training or experience, but the advice contained in the book could also apply to executives and teachers. These professionals may have had some very brief PowerPoint training in the past, but many will be self-taught. Most will have used PowerPoint before and will therefore already be familiar with the basics.

What this book covers

Chapter 1, *Analyzing Your Audience and Presentation Delivery Needs*, introduces questions that will help you plan and structure your presentation content.

Chapter 2, *Using Industry Best Practices to Design Better Visuals*, helps you learn about important industry best practices to improve your design.

Chapter 3, *Leveraging PowerPoint's Slide Master for Design*, talks about how the Slide Master can be used as a design automation tool.

Chapter 4, Using PowerPoint's Document Masters for Handouts and Notes, covers how to leverage masters, which will help you make your presentation files serve more than one purpose and still be efficient and impactful.

Chapter 5, Using Artificial Intelligence to Improve Your Visuals, helps you understand how the Designer feature can save you some design time.

Chapter 6, Adding and Modifying Visual Elements, discusses how to use graphical elements and customize them to replace text and bullet points.

Chapter 7, Adding and Modifying Multimedia Elements, goes into how to improve your content by using and formatting audio and video elements.

Chapter 8, Working with Transitions and Animations, focuses on generating movement with purpose, which will improve the pace of your content and the audience's understanding.

Chapter 9, Building Flexibility and Interactivity in Your Presentations, explains how to engage your audience by using navigation elements to adapt to their needs or show them special content.

Chapter 10, Using PowerPoint Third-Party Add-Ins, brings in a few ways to boost your content creation productivity and presentation management possibilities.

Chapter 11, Practicing Your Presentation Delivery, points out some of PowerPoint's native tools that will help you practice your presentations so that you have a memorable effect on your audience.

Chapter 12, Using Presenter View, puts forward how this feature and its many tools can help you deliver more engaging presentations and have more control.

Chapter 13, Using PowerPoint Live in Microsoft Teams, has been included to help virtual presenters who use Teams discover many features that will help encourage engagement.

To get the most out of this book

This book will give you step-by-step instructions to help you find the right features and tools and use them. To get the most out of this book, you should try features that are new to you as you read about them. This is the best way to learn about and remember them. If your goal is to learn about how to implement a better presentation creation process, you should read the chapters in order, but reading chapters or picking up topics in any order can be valuable if you are a more advanced user.

Software/hardware covered in the book	Operating system requirements
PowerPoint	Windows
PowerPoint Live/Teams	macOS is compatible in most cases
BrightSlide	
BrandIn	
WeCompress/NXPowerLite	
Slidewise	
Build-a-Graphic	
THOR	
PPTMerge	

If you work for an organization with an IT admin team, you might need to confirm with them if you find that your M365 PowerPoint version lacks some features, or if you want to install any of the third-party add-ins discussed in this book.

After reading this book, if you need a little support or have some questions, please consider filling in this form – https://forms.office.com/r/9kX3bapZdG – which will also give you access to a special LinkedIn private support group. Here is a QR code for your convenience:

Conventions used

There are a number of text conventions used throughout this book.

`Code in text`: Indicates code words in text, database table names, folder names, filenames, file extensions, pathnames, dummy URLs, user input, and Twitter handles. Here is an example: "For example, you cannot have two objects named `!!Shape` on the same slide."

Bold: Indicates a new term, an important word, or words that you see onscreen. For instance, words in menus or dialog boxes appear in **bold**. Here is an example: "If you uncheck the **On Mouse Click** checkbox, you can remove the option to navigate with the mouse or keyboard when the presentation is in slideshow mode."

> **Tips or important notes**
> Appear like this.

Get in touch

Feedback from our readers is always welcome.

General feedback: If you have questions about any aspect of this book, email us at `customercare@packtpub.com` and mention the book title in the subject of your message.

Errata: Although we have taken every care to ensure the accuracy of our content, mistakes do happen. If you have found a mistake in this book, we would be grateful if you would report this to us. Please visit `www.packtpub.com/support/errata` and fill in the form. Any errata related to this book can be found at `https://github.com/PacktPublishing/Microsoft-PowerPoint-Best-Practices-Tips-and-Techniques`.

Piracy: If you come across any illegal copies of our works in any form on the internet, we would be grateful if you would provide us with the location address or website name. Please contact us at `copyright@packt.com` with a link to the material.

If you are interested in becoming an author: If there is a topic that you have expertise in and you are interested in either writing or contributing to a book, please visit `authors.packtpub.com`.

Share Your Thoughts

Once you've read *Microsoft PowerPoint Best Practices, Tips, and Techniques*, we'd love to hear your thoughts! Scan the QR code below to go straight to the Amazon review page for this book and share your feedback.

https://packt.link/r/1-839-21533-X

Your review is important to us and the tech community and will help us make sure we're delivering excellent quality content.

Download a free PDF copy of this book

Thanks for purchasing this book!

Do you like to read on the go but are unable to carry your print books everywhere? Is your eBook purchase not compatible with the device of your choice?

Don't worry, now with every Packt book you get a DRM-free PDF version of that book at no cost.

Read anywhere, any place, on any device. Search, copy, and paste code from your favorite technical books directly into your application.

The perks don't stop there, you can get exclusive access to discounts, newsletters, and great free content in your inbox daily

Follow these simple steps to get the benefits:

1. Scan the QR code or visit the link below

https://packt.link/free-ebook/9781839215339

2. Submit your proof of purchase
3. That's it! We'll send your free PDF and other benefits to your email directly

1
Analyzing Your Audience and Presentation Delivery Needs

I'm sure many readers might think it is odd to start a PowerPoint book with information about how to analyze your audience and presentation delivery needs. After many years as a presentation expert and public speaking coach, I can assure you that the first step in creating an impactful PowerPoint presentation is to avoid opening the application at all costs!

Like most business professionals, you've probably attended many presentations and conferences where using a PowerPoint presentation was almost a requirement. When you think about your experiences as an attendee, how many times did you think about how boring the content was? Or did you start to tune out, checking your emails or social media from your smartphone?

As a presenter, you might have imposed death by PowerPoint on your audiences a few times. If your main reason is always a lack of time to prepare, then I would advise trying to review your preparation timeline. There is no way anyone can plan, prepare, and deliver an impactful presentation in a few days, whatever the duration of it. As a matter of fact, the shorter the duration, the longer it will take you to choose the right content and deliver it in a memorable way.

There is one important reason I have heard many times throughout the years for not putting in more time to prepare presentations: *I don't know where to start*. This is the main reason that I chose to have this topic as the first chapter in my PowerPoint book. You'll know how to plan better presentations simply by following the three main sections in this chapter:

- 10 questions to help you plan your presentation
- Analyzing and sorting your content
- Structuring and developing your message

10 questions to help you plan your presentation

Before sharing my top 10 questions to help you plan your next presentation, let me ask you the first question I ask *all* my clients before they can even start the official planning process: *What are the three most important elements your audience needs to remember or act on after your presentation?*

This question usually triggers a long moment of silence, mainly because too many presenters are not clear on what they want their audience to remember. If that question triggers the same reaction for you regarding your next presentation, then make sure to take some time to think through what three elements need to be remembered or acted on by your audience before you dive into the next question. This will make your planning task even more efficient.

Here is a summary diagram of the 10 questions you should go through before you create your presentations:

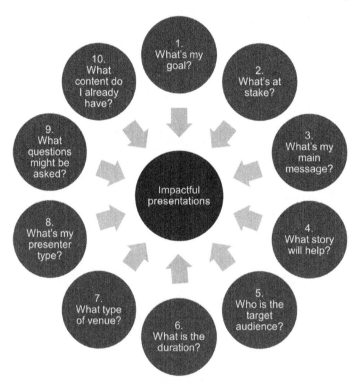

Figure 1.1 – Planning questions summary diagram

Why's the diagram in a circular representation? Because it is an ongoing process leading to more impactful presentations.

Question 1 – what is my presentation's goal?

Presenting for an informative session does not have the same end goal as a project update, a training session, or an investor pitch deck. This is why you need to think through the actual goal of your next presentation. Not only will it improve your audience satisfaction, but you will be able to find more effective visuals for your content when you are clear on the goal you want to achieve.

Let's see a few examples.

An informative session

Even if you think your task is *only* to inform the audience, make sure they will be leaving with clear takeaways. Many years ago, I remember attending an information session for a school trip program. Yes, it was full of nice and enchanting photos of the cities our kids would be visiting, but the trip coordinator made sure we had three clear action steps:

1. Meeting the due dates for payments

2. Meeting the due date for passport validation

3. Attending the vaccination clinic on the specified date

So, even though it was an information session, we all knew we had some specific tasks to accomplish and that there were date limits for each of them. This example can easily be transposed to any business information session. You just need to keep in mind any action steps that the audience needs to accomplish while you are preparing your presentation.

Project update presentation

This type of presentation is usually known to be very repetitive and boring in businesses. The main reason why is that most presenters only keep repeating the same type of information. Instead of simply stating the percentage of advancement or whether the team is on target budget-wise, find three key elements that stand out since the last update. As an example, if a team member found a new way to improve processes and avoid delays, put that information in your project update presentation. Take some time to reflect on why you have had successes or even failures. This will be a much more interesting report than simply stating data.

A client or investors pitch deck

This type of presentation serves the dual needs of helping the audience know about your product or service *and* convincing them to invest in your business or buy your product/service. If this is the type of presentation you need to prepare, you need to think about the advantages of your products or services and identify their perceived value. You need to gain and build your audience's trust before anyone will buy your products or services, and simply listing features and processes won't be enough. Of course, if you present to investors, your financial forecast needs to be realistic!

A corporate training session

Delivering corporate training requires clarity on the objectives of the session. Were you tasked to create training for new hires, or because current employees do not produce quality work? It might also be because there is a brand-new operating system or new applications that people need to get familiar with so they can still accomplish their daily tasks. Taking the time to reflect on whom you will train, for what reasons, and your management's expectations will help you select important topics and decide on the type of content to create to help learners meet expectations.

Question 2 – what is at stake?

Time is the most precious resource in businesses. So, we need to know where we absolutely need to put in more time and effort for the best return on our investment. That is why you need to ask yourself what the impact will be if your presentation lacks preparation and practice. If you are preparing a bi-weekly update, the stakes are not as high as if you are preparing a pitch that can win you a $10 million grant for your project. If you are short on time for your project update, you can always do better at the next one. But if you don't put in more time and effort for the grant pitch, you might wonder whether your presentation made you lose it if you don't get the grant.

In a corporate training environment, the stakes might also be very high. You need to reflect on what happens if your training content does not meet the requirements. What happens to the company's bottom line if employees cannot accomplish the desired tasks? Even if it is difficult to put a precise dollar sign on this, you can think in terms of increased efficiency by taking less time to accomplish certain tasks. If you estimate that your training will help employees gain 1 hour each week, you can then establish a dollar amount by adding hours saved for the whole group and multiplying by their salary to help management see the value of the training.

Question 3 – what is my main message?

This question is most important when you are putting together a presentation that will be a subset or a shorter version of the content you usually present. Knowing your main message helps you to decide what content needs to be kept and what needs to be put aside for the actual presentation. Every presenter I know works with a lot of content and usually thinks everything is important. But when we put our audience's needs or expectations first, while making sure we have the main message as a thread line for our presentation, we soon realize that some content is not as relevant. In the presentation industry, less is more. Choose your content wisely so it will have more impact.

If you are creating training content, your main message also needs to be very clear. Make sure learners see the value of the training for them. I suggest that you think about two main messages for corporate training sessions: one that fits management expectations in terms of productivity or efficiency, and one that fits your learners' expectations, whether they want to save some time on some tasks or understand their role better. There is no magic wand to help you craft messages that will appeal to learners and management. You will need to take some time to ask both parties about their expectations and pain points.

Question 4 – what story can help the audience understand the message?

Human beings love stories. When we look closely, we can even say that most of our decisions are influenced by stories. Have you ever taken a close look at popular advertisements? They all have a story attached to them, just like movies.

This is why you need to find a supporting story for your presentation to make it more impactful. I am not telling you to craft an intricate plot. You just need to look at a personal or client story that supports your content. For example, if you are presenting in front of a room full of potential clients, you could tell the story of a past client that came to you with a specific challenge. Tell the audience how, after using your product or service, the client was able to increase their overall productivity or increase their revenue. If you have permission to name your past client, or even get a testimonial you can use, that would be even better. The important part is to make sure any story you choose supports the main goal of your presentation.

In a corporate training setting, you could try to craft a story around a fictitious employee's journey from before and after the training. Or, you could simply state the actual situation in the work environment versus what it can be after the training and how this will serve the learners too. When I was a trainer in a big telecommunications company for their customer service department, I usually used some client experiences I had when doing the job so they could relate and realize why some content was extremely important. It is okay to use stories in corporate training as long as it illustrates why your teaching points are important and their value when going back to the job.

Question 5 – who is my target audience?

Knowing whom you are presenting to will definitely help you craft a better presentation. The language and examples you use need to be aligned with the level of knowledge your audience might have about the topic. For example, if you are presenting to your peers or industry experts, you can use commonly used technical terms. But if you are presenting at a conference where your audience might be from different backgrounds, the language needs to be simpler. You also need to be aware that any acronyms or industry jargon might be too much for some people. I am not saying to not use them at all. But introducing them to anyone without the proper background could still help them to understand the high-level meaning.

When you are presenting within your company, and you know the topic could be controversial or not be well accepted by some colleagues, make sure to think through what objections they might have. This will help you to prepare content that will help them understand your point, even if they still don't agree with it.

When preparing corporate training sessions, you need to think about who will be attending the training. If they are new hires, you will need to give more detailed information and make sure you avoid using jargon without giving proper definitions. When it is content destined for current employees, you need to consider what their actual level of knowledge might be before the session and what level of knowledge you are expecting after the training.

Question 6 – what is the duration of my presentation?

There is one rule I ask all my clients not to break: *never go over the allotted time*. By sticking to this, you are showing respect for your audience's time and for other presenters coming after you, if you are speaking at an event. Remember what I said previously? More information is not always better. Quality and targeted information brings more value and is more impactful in the long run.

So, keeping in mind the duration of your presentation will also help you estimate how much detail you can include in your content. Also, always include enough time so attendees can ask questions and interact with you.

You might be wondering whether there is a simple way to figure out how much content you can plan according to the allotted time. Through the years, I have shared this rule of thumb with clients to help them out. It is not an exact science, but it worked every time I used it.

> Content planning rule
>
> Plan content for 75% of the allotted time. That means that if your talk is scheduled to be 1 hour, plan content for 45 minutes. You never know when technology glitches might get in the way, or if the event experiences scheduling delays. If you are wondering how this rule can be translated into the number of slides, we will address this burning question in *Chapter 2, Using Industry Best Practices to Design Better Visuals*, on industry best practices.

Depending on your topic, you could even consider having even less content and allowing more time for interactions. When the audience gets the chance to really participate, it will make your presentation more memorable and meaningful. Don't be afraid of finishing early because the audience did not participate as much as you thought. In my 25 years in the industry, I have never seen anyone complain because a presentation finished earlier. Some people will use the extra time for a break before their next obligation, and others will take this as an opportunity to ask you more questions. In either case, everyone is happy.

Question 7 – what type of venue will I present in?

How you will be delivering your presentation is a very important question. Your content design needs to consider whether you will be presenting in a huge venue for 1,000 attendees – that usually means very large screens and some people very far away – a small meeting room, or even a remote virtual presentation that might be watched on regular computer screens, tablets, or mobile phones.

When you are presenting in large venues, you need to be informed of the size of the room and screen, and the lighting in the venue. This will allow using the best font sizes and contrast to make sure everyone in the room will be able to read any words you have on your slides, even from the back of the room. If you will be presenting virtually, you also need to keep in mind the various screen sizes from which your talk will be viewed. The smaller the screen, the less content you can have on slides to keep them readable.

Thinking about where your presentation will be delivered also allows you to plan what type of equipment will be used. When presenting for an event, you might have to use the venue's computer instead of yours. This means you will need to make sure the presentation you design is compatible with the venue's computer – is it Windows or Mac? Also, asking which PowerPoint version is used on the venue's computer will help you to create your presentation file and avoid compatibility issues.

Question 8 – what type of presenter am I?

This question usually triggers some surprised looks! The reason I think this is important is to help presenters reflect on how comfortable they are with technology and equipment and to get them to consider whether they suffer from various levels of public speaking fears.

Being honest about our fears or lack of technological and equipment knowledge is important. It allows presenters to act on and refine elements that will improve their delivery, making them more impactful. Learning how to use a presentation remote when on stage for an event will allow you to get closer to the audience, instead of standing behind a lectern. Getting more familiar with PowerPoint's native tools such as **Presenter View**, **PowerPoint Live**, and **Presenter Coach** will improve your presence and reduce your fear of public speaking. This is why I dedicated the last section of this book to delivering better presentations with PowerPoint's advanced delivery tools. Presentation success is much more than your visuals!

Question 9 – what questions might be asked by the audience?

Through the years, this question triggered many discussions with my clients. Many did not see any value in thinking about potential questions from their audience. I usually replied that the more prepared you are, the less chance you have of being taken off-guard by questions that would have been so easy to prepare in advance.

For example, if you must present a new work process impacting workers in their daily tasks, ask yourself what resistance they might have to this change. Being able to acknowledge their fears and reassure them quickly is much better than having to tell them you will have to check and come back with an answer. If you are presenting your latest revolutionary product, be prepared to answer questions on what advantages your product might have compared to your competitors' products.

Being prepared will give you much more control over how well your presentation will go. It does not mean you need to have answers to every question. Telling someone you will have to check more details and get back with an answer is proof that you are a professional. You just need to avoid having to do this for most questions asked during your presentation so that you don't lose your credibility.

Question 10 – what content do I already have available?

This final question on my top 10 list is essential if you want to be efficient. Through the years, I have seen so many people re-creating content repeatedly, from scratch. Even if you have not done so before, take some time to go through previous presentations you created, and create an image and graphics library you can go to instead of starting the whole process over each time you create a presentation. Know what you have on hand, or what content your organization might have stored on a shared drive, so you can make your content production much more efficient.

Reading through the list of my top 10 questions before creating any slides might have put you in a bit of a panic. If that's the case, breathe and relax! Just keep *Figure 1.1* as a reference for your next presentation planning. Your presentation will improve, even if you take just one step at a time.

Now that you have planned your content, it is time to analyze and sort it. This is what you will learn in the next section.

Analyzing and sorting your content

Making sure your content has a good structure and that your message is clear requires you to take some time to analyze the content you already have. By content, I don't mean only other PowerPoint files you might have created before. Any photos or graphics created for other corporate documents, or even your website, need to be looked at as potentially reusable content. In this section, you will learn how you can start the process and go through the sorting step using one of the printing features in PowerPoint.

What is the best way to start?

I'll repeat myself once again: *the last place to start is on a blank slide in the PowerPoint application.* If you know you have content in other PowerPoint files that could be reused, you should open your files and print the relevant slides in the six-slides-per-page format.

If you have never done that, here is how it can be done. Each of the following steps is represented by the same number bubble in *Figure 1.2*:

1. From the **File** tab in PowerPoint, go to **Print**.
2. Choose the **6 Slides Horizontal** layout from the **Handouts** layouts in the drop-down list.

3. Make sure you are not printing on both sides of the pages.

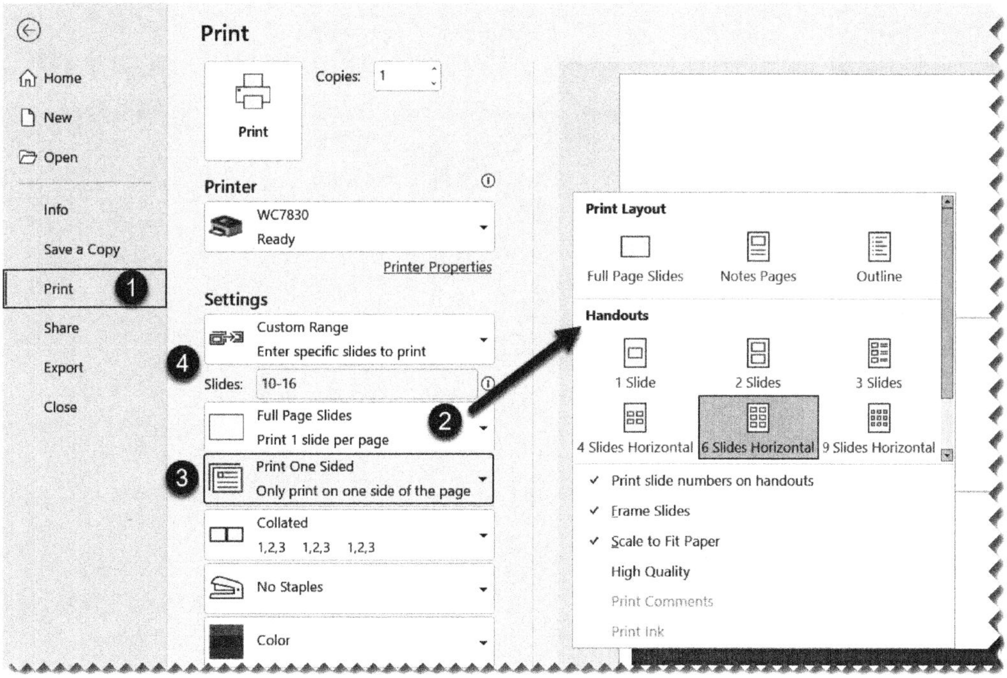

Figure 1.2 – Settings to print six slides per page

4. If you don't need all the slides in your file, don't forget to select them in the slide range field. I want to show you how to create more impactful presentations, but I also want to make sure you don't kill too many trees in the process.

Once you have your pages printed, cut the small slides (*Figure 1.3*) so you can use them to play around with your content sequence:

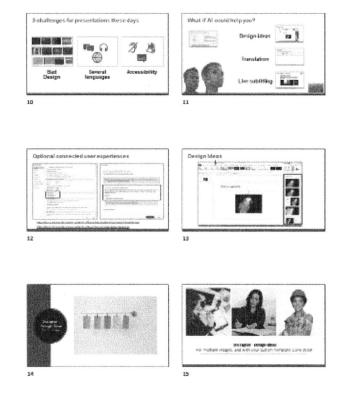

Figure 1.3 – Printout with the six-slide layout

If you find any other type of visual content that could help you make your presentation more visual, then start a blank PowerPoint file in which you can add visuals, with each on its own slide, so you can again use the previous printing tip.

If you have any other idea that came to mind while planning your content, but don't have any existing content for it, just use some plain index cards or any other type of paper on which you can quickly sketch or add keywords.

Sorting the content

Now that you have the printouts of visuals and index cards, you can start organizing and grouping your ideas (see *Figure 1.4*). Many times, people have asked me whether mind mapping software can be used instead of printouts and index cards; the answer is yes. But, working with physical elements that you can manipulate will help your creativity. It usually makes it easier to play around with groupings and start prioritizing what content is important.

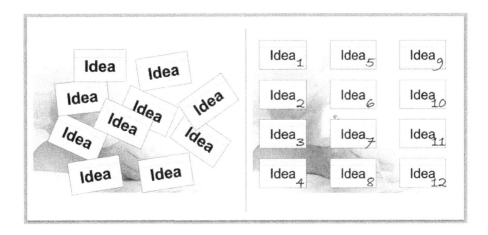

Figure 1.4 – Organizing and grouping your ideas

If you went through the planning questions, you should already be able to start seeing which ideas or content will support your message. It is now time to start grouping ideas into two categories: need to know and nice to have. Maybe you have some interesting content that does not quite fit the actual purpose of your presentation, but could be part of extra content that could be shown on demand. Always keep in mind the most important question I shared at the beginning of this chapter: *What are the three most important elements your audience needs to remember or act on after your presentation?* This will help you determine what content is important for your talk.

Even if you have the feeling that you don't have time to do this, trust me, it will save you a *lot* of time when you start building the content. Many times, I have had to tell people that they need to remove some irrelevant slides from their presentation deck. Most of them replied they did not want to because they had spent many hours building those slides. Putting in the time to plan, sort, structure, and develop your message outside of PowerPoint is how you will avoid spending hours creating irrelevant slides.

Structuring and developing your message

If you have accomplished the planning and analysis tasks from the previous sections, you are in a great position to create a more impactful presentation in less time than you thought possible. Putting aside, or even throwing away, ideas that were slide printouts or index cards is much easier to do than deleting slides you spent hours creating.

Now, you need to structure your message and content. There are many ways to accomplish this and you might even have heard of other models that can be used. Since I want to make this part as easy as possible for any business context, I'll introduce you to the three-part model.

The three-part model

The three-part model might look familiar. This is because it's the structure adopted by movies, novels, and even some ads. It starts with an introduction, flows through three important elements, and then concludes, as shown in *Figure 1.5*:

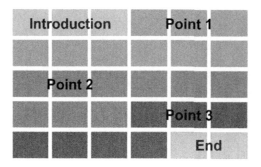

Figure 1.5 – The three-part model content structure

In case you have not realized it yet, it's also the model I've used for this PowerPoint book. I started by introducing the main problems we see in business presentations and how they can affect how impactful your presentation will be, your credibility, and even the level of success, whether it is measured by reviews or sales. The content of the book is divided into three parts: planning and preparation, creating visually appealing content, and delivering better presentations by leveraging the advanced delivery tools in PowerPoint. As for my conclusion, you will be able to read it at the end of the book!

By using this model, you will be able to create your presentation using the following three steps:

1. Plan an introduction that will catch your audience's attention:

    -   Think about a personal story that adds value to the topic you are presenting. Maybe you went through a challenge and overcame it with the elements that you will be discussing in your presentation.

    -   Maybe you have a client case study that shows how their situation was challenging before they came to you, and how your solution helped them.

    -   Think about any surprising statistics from your industry that show how important it is to find a solution.

    -   Ask a disrupting question, knowing that it will get the audience's attention and that you will show them a different way to see things during your talk.

    -   Use anything that can help you show your audience that your message or solutions are linked to an everyday problem or their own lives. Make sure to address any problem or irritating situation they might be going through, its impact on them, and what can be done to resolve it.

2. Choose the three most important points you want to talk about during your presentation:

    - Your content is where you need to show your audience the difference you can make on their problem or challenge.

    - Why three? Simply because human beings can easily remember three main points. When we think about it, we have seen many examples using the number three in our lives, whether in children's stories (three blind mice, three musketeers) or from fast food restaurants with their *combos* that have three components. Increase your chances to be memorable and avoid having more than three main points in your talk.

3. Plan an impactful conclusion:

    - You can summarize your most important three points again, so the audience is reminded, one more time, of what they are.

    - Make sure to have a specific call to action, helping your audience realize that they too can overcome a challenge or solve a problem if they use what you taught them during your talk.

My description of the three-part model is intentionally kept simple so you don't feel overwhelmed or that you cannot apply it on your own. If you give yourself enough time before your next presentation, you will be able to reproduce the steps to improve your content.

Telling your story

Before ending this chapter, I want to talk a little more about using stories in your presentations. If I ask you to think about anything that you have seen or heard that you can still remember after a long time, was there a story attached to it? A specific emotion that comes back when you think about it? I bet this is the case. People remember things much longer when it has a story that either resonated with their daily lives or made them feel a special way.

Some people have saved their businesses because they found the perfect story to help their potential clients realize how important their product or service could be. I have had some workshop attendees tell me that their topic was much too serious to include stories. All human beings will react to emotions, and emotions are triggered best with relatable stories. Unless you are presenting to robots, there is no reason why you should avoid using stories. Of course, make sure your story is relevant to your audience and adapted to their level of expertise or needs.

Tip
When you have found the right story to convey your message, there is another element that you absolutely need to put into practice: *use visuals, not endless bullet points.*

Let me give you an example. A few years ago, I was asked to give a talk on taking advantage of artificial intelligence in the latest version of PowerPoint to help craft better presentations. The script for my introduction was as follows:

- The means of human communication have greatly evolved since the drawings of cavemen.

- From the first art schools, where the teachings were mainly based on the art of public speaking.

- And then the creation of large, majestic libraries filled with books of all kinds.

- After that came the first films.

- Then the introduction of overhead projectors as a means of teaching.

- The technology then took over with desktop software, projectors, Apple TV, tablets, and even smartphones.

- But why do people still talk so much about boring presentations and death by PowerPoint?

Imagine if I had put that script onto slides as bullet points. First, asking my audience to listen to me and read slides would not have given me great results. People usually read faster than they can speak, so they would have reached the end of the bullet list without paying much attention to how I delivered the content. What I did instead was look for a series of nice photos that could relate to my script and go through them while I talked.

This is a screen capture of my presentation introduction (see *Figure 1.6*). After the title slide, each bullet in the previous list is matched to a slide with a photo. Take a look at each slide and read the preceding associated bullet.

Figure 1.6 – Presentation introduction using photos

Can you imagine how different the experience was for the audience? Instead of being forced to read sentences on a slide, they were listening to me and letting their eyes take in a visual, which was much more memorable than words alone.

I now challenge you to go back to your ideas for future PowerPoints and start thinking about visual elements that could replace sentences and bullet points in your presentation. You will then have a starting point for when you go through the chapters discussing PowerPoint features that will help you create visually appealing content.

Summary

In this chapter, we covered my top 10 questions to help you plan your presentation, considered how to analyze and sort your content, and discussed how to structure and develop your message. You now have a better understanding of how to improve your presentation's impact by focusing on the key message, story, and structure.

Of course, reading this chapter won't make you fully comfortable with the process the first time you use it. You might even go through a phase of thinking that it takes too much time and is not worth it. My wish is that you keep on trying, even if it means improving only one element in your planning phase each time. Your overall success won't be determined by how many changes you made in one presentation, but by how many baby steps you took to keep improving your presentations.

I will leave you with a comment I received from a client I worked with not long ago: "This process was eye-opening. It allowed me to think about important information that added value to my message. I now realize how efficient this process is, allowing me to save time during the creation process. Taking that extra time to plan and structure the content also helped me master my content even more and made my delivery practice very efficient."

In the next chapter, we will be moving along our journey to more impactful presentations by learning about industry best practices in terms of font choice and sizes, contrast rules, and how to avoid unnecessary visual elements so that you can improve the look and feel of your slides.

Further reading

To help you learn more about some topics covered in this chapter, here is a list of references you can read:

- To learn more about what audiences have to say about annoying PowerPoint presentations, I suggest you read the results of a survey conducted by my friend and colleague Dave Paradi for almost 20 years now. Have a look at his website here: `https://www.thinkoutsidetheslide.com/free-resources/latest-annoying-powerpoint-survey-results/`.

- If you want to dig deeper into the three-step model discussed in this chapter, you should read *Resonate* by my brilliant colleague, Nancy Duarte. She did an awesome job of researching how the most impactful speeches should be structured. You can even find the e-book on her website here: `https://www.duarte.com/resonate/`.

2
Using Industry Best Practices to Design Better Visuals

Even though presentations have been created millions of times since PowerPoint's initial release in 1990, the presentation industry is much younger. It took many years before some people developed better expertise in terms of what works for the audience and the presenter. Since research on the specific topic of presentations with the help of PowerPoint also had a slow start, we mostly had to use trial and error for a while.

Luckily, the presentation industry has matured, and we now have reliable experts helping us define best practices. Also, the **Presentation Guild**, an organization created by industry experts in 2015, has established professional presentation standards generally accepted by the industry. They guide presentation craftspeople in nine categories: audio-visual, branding, color, data visualization, functionality, images, layout, motion, and typography (see the *Further reading* section at the end of the chapter).

Of course, today's best practices are also influenced by the requirements of making presentations more accessible to people with disabilities. When you are the person in charge of planning and creating all your presentations without any formal design training or a lot of knowledge of what makes content accessible, it can become challenging and stressful.

This is why I have included this chapter before diving into all the content creation and delivery features in the next chapters and sections. I want to help any business professional that wants to create better presentations. The goal of this chapter is not to help you become an expert presentation designer. It's mostly designed to help regular businesspeople apply some basic best practices so they can create better visuals and more professional-looking presentations. Even if you don't have a lot of time, you will be able to review your slides according to the topics shared in the five sections of this chapter:

- Choosing fonts
- Using the right font size
- Learning about contrast

- Decluttering your slide contents
- Standardizing the look and feel of your slides

Technical requirements

The topics discussed in this chapter can be applied to whatever version of PowerPoint you are using. When some features are available only in newer versions, I will let you know.

Choosing fonts

Font choices have evolved very much throughout the years. For those who have been working in **Microsoft Office** for a long time, I'm sure you remember **Arial** and **Times New Roman**! Those fonts have been around for such a long time that users started using anything else that felt new, pretty, or funky just because they were bored. This was not always in the best interest of their audience, I must say. When creating your content, you need to make sure your fonts are readable by audience members wherever they are sitting in a venue, or regardless of whatever device they are using to watch your presentation.

Before diving into the basics, let's clarify a few terms used by the professionals in the industry:

- **Typography**: How letters and text are arranged so it is visually appealing.
- **Font**: This usually refers to the various weights, widths, and styles found in a typeface. An example would be **Bold** or **Italics**.
- **Typeface**: This is a design style for a family of related fonts. As an example, Arial is a typeface constituted of many fonts such as **Arial Black** and **Arial Narrow**.

Since this book's goal is to help regular business users without a formal design background, I will mostly be using the word *font* from now on. After all, most presentation creators will refer to fonts, not typefaces.

Which font category should you use?

If you have scrolled down the list of fonts available in PowerPoint, you have probably noticed there are many to choose from, especially if you are using PowerPoint in **Microsoft 365**. Here are four common categories you will find in that list, all of which you can see a representation of in *Figure 2.1*:

1. **Serif**: This font category was first used for print; it is characterized by small lines that extend the letters (*serifs*). The width of the line for each letter usually varies.
2. **Sans Serif**: As the name implies, there are no extended lines and usually the width of the line will be the same for all letters.

3.   **Decorative**: Again, the name describes this category. These fonts use embellished and stylized letters.

4.   **Script**: This is designed to look like cursive handwriting.

Figure 2.1 – Common font categories in PowerPoint

Font experts might say that there are other categories. Again, for the sake of keeping this book relevant for businesspeople, I have kept the previous list very simple so that it is easier to decide which fonts you should use for your next presentation.

Now that you have learned about four font categories, let's discuss which ones should be used. When Serif fonts were introduced for print, they were considered easier to read because of their serifs. More research has been done on readability and it seems people suffering from different visual disabilities, such as dyslexia, might have more difficulty reading Serif fonts. This is one reason why Sans Serif fonts have become more popular, another being that this category of font also seems to be easier to read for content that is presented on screens.

> Tip
> When creating your presentations, try to use Sans Serif fonts most of the time. If you must use a corporate template that includes only Serif fonts, try to limit the text you are using and, as will be discussed in the next section, use a larger font size so your text is easily readable. If your corporate template uses a Serif and a Sans Serif font, try to use the Sans Serif for body text.

If you feel you must use a Decorative or Script font to convey a particular mood or emotion, try to use them *only* for a few keywords, not full sentences. This is the only way you will be able to assure your text is easily readable.

Font compatibility issues

Through the years, many users have encountered presentation formatting problems when delivering their presentations from other computers. Most of the time, those issues were caused by using fonts that were not present in all versions of PowerPoint. This led my friend and colleague Julie Terberg, from *Terberg Design*, to publish extensively about **safe fonts** (see the *Further reading* section for links). This term essentially means that if you want to make sure your presentations will look good on other computers using other PowerPoint versions or operating systems, you need to stick to a short list of fonts that can be embedded or are present in older versions. However, embedded fonts are not recognized in Office for Mac for **versions 2008** and **2011**.

Luckily for users, the introduction of **cloud fonts** in **Microsoft 365 (M365)** made everyone's life easier. Yes, this does mean that only users with an M365 subscription will be able to choose and insert cloud fonts, which are represented by a small cloud icon with an arrow in the font drop-down list (see *Figure 2.2*):

Figure 2.2 – Cloud fonts are identified with a cloud icon

But since cloud fonts can be embedded, your presentation can be viewed in the newer standalone versions of PowerPoint (**versions 2019** and **2021**) without any problem. There are many more details you should be aware of if you often create presentations that use various styles of fonts. Since this book's goal is not to discuss fonts extensively, I encourage you to visit Julie Terberg's post about cloud fonts mentioned in the *Further reading* section. There is also a frequently updated PDF guide in the article listing cloud fonts with their visual representation and discussing whether they are a good choice for body fonts.

Checklist to help you review font choices

I know that discussing font styles and compatibility might not be helpful enough to feel comfortable choosing fonts for your next presentation. Therefore, I'll share with you a short checklist you can use to review your font choices:

- Avoid stylized and hard-to-read fonts for your titles and content text.

- Use a maximum of two font styles in your presentation. It will make your content more consistent. For example, use one style for titles and another for content.

- Check for potential font compatibility issues, especially if you are creating a presentation for someone else, or if the presentation will be shown from various computers.

- Avoid using title casing in your titles. You should use sentence casing instead.

- Using uppercase everywhere will be more difficult to read. Keep uppercase lettering for when you have fewer words to read.

- Use bold for emphasis only.

- Use italics moderately; my personal choice is to avoid it altogether. Italicized letters don't show as well in presentations and make your content harder to read.

Now that you know more about font styles and how to choose more appropriately, we can proceed with how font size needs to be considered to make your presentations easier to read and make them more impactful.

Using the right font size

When PowerPoint presentations became more common in board rooms and events, we often heard people complaining about having trouble reading text because it was too small. That also highlighted another problem: having too much text on slides! That problem arises because many presenters fear forgetting what they have to say. That is why we have *Chapter 12, Using Presenter View*, and *Chapter 13, Using PowerPoint Live in Microsoft Teams*. You won't have an excuse for putting all your text on your slides ever again.

But back to our font size topic. When you present, your main goal should be that your audience can grasp quickly what is on screen so they can focus their attention back on you quickly. Human beings relate to other human beings, not words written on slides. That is why font size matters. Asking an audience to read your slides in a large venue does not require the same font size as when you are presenting in a boardroom or online.

Selecting the right font size has created many debates through the years. But in the end, the goal should always be to make it as easy as possible for everyone attending your presentation to read whatever text you have on your slides. My personal rule of thumb, whether I'm creating slides for someone else or myself, is as follows:

- **Titles**: Between 32 and 44 points
- **Content**: Between 28 and 32 points

I find these ranges adapt well to most presentation needs, even if I usually adapt sizes during my delivery practice in a venue or a virtual test run. If you present mostly in large venues and meeting rooms, I suggest you have a look at my friend Dave Paradi's post on font size listed in the *Further reading* section at the end of the chapter. He put together tables that reduce the guesswork, making it easy to select your font size according to the size of the room and the screen.

If you are doubting my size rule of thumb, have a look at what various sizes look like when compared to one another in *Figure 2.3*. Of course, the image has been downsized for the book. But it does a pretty good job at showing how difficult it can become to read **Arial 18** points when looking at a presentation on a small screen. It also shows you that using a different font style can also change how its size is perceived.

Lorem Ipsum – Arial 44

Lorem Ipsum – Verdana 44

Lorem Ipsum – Arial 36

Lorem Ipsum – Arial 32

Lorem Ipsum – Arial 28

Lorem Ipsum – Arial 24

Lorem Ipsum – Arial 18

Figure 2.3 – Font sizes comparison

Take some time to test font sizes before your presentation. Take even more time if you are presenting in a hybrid mode, such as having some participants in the venue and others watching from various screen sizes remotely. Now that we have discussed font styles and sizes, the next section on contrast will help us conclude important best practices that relate to fonts.

Learning about contrast

Contrast is what allows us to see different elements easily, such as text on a colored background, or various shapes close to one another. We all have some favorite colors that we would like to use or corporate colors we must respect but, in the end, it always comes down to making sure our audience will be able to see and understand our content.

Some online tools can help you calculate the contrast ratio between the background color and text color, especially now that many countries have put together rules that organizations should follow to make their content more accessible. You can simply do an online search with `contrast checker` as keywords, and you will get a list of various sites that offer the tool. But you can also just apply this basic rule:

- If you're using a **light background**, use text as dark as possible

- If you're using a **dark background**, use text as light as possible

To test contrast in presentations, I usually start my slideshow and move away from my computer screen to assess the readability of the text. I also try different lighting conditions to see whether it changes how the text shows. Even though the contrast example in *Figure 2.4* is in grayscale, we can easily see that the best contrast is with the first line of text, whether the background is light or dark:

Figure 2.4 – Contrast examples with light and dark backgrounds

---

Tip

When choosing background and text colors, always make sure to use the darkest and lightest shades possible between the background and the text. If you use this rule of thumb, you will be able to quickly choose contrasting colors by simply testing their readability at different reading distances. If you want less contrasting colors, I would suggest you take some time to use a contrast checker tool.

Another element you need to consider when assessing contrast is the use of background graphics or textures. As shown in *Figure 2.5*, using texture behind the text decreases readability even though the color is the same for both backgrounds:

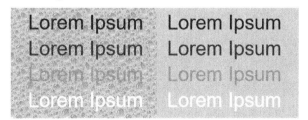

Figure 2.5 – A textured background reduces the readability of text

If the background of your slides must have a graphic of some sort because of a corporate template, make sure it is very subtle. The important element on your slide is your content, not a background texture or graphic.

Choosing colors wisely

Human beings react to colors. It can even influence how your audience will react to your content. Through the years, I have referred many times to the `Colormatters.com` and `Colorcom.com` websites for guidance (see the *Further reading* section) because of the valuable information we can find on their respective sites. In fact, that is where I found research-based information mentioning that color is so important in our lives that our subconscious mind judges many things based on color alone. This is the main reason why you should choose colors wisely for your presentations.

To help you, here is a sample of what meanings or emotions colors can convey (see *Figure 2.6*). It should guide you when choosing what colors should be used for your presentations. As an example, businesses that want to be perceived as trustworthy often use blue, and nature-oriented businesses might want to use green and brown.

Red	Aggressive, strong, passion, intensity
Blue	Trust, authority, peace, dependability
Yellow	Optimism, joy, enlightenment, creativity
Green	Nature, environment, luck, money
Brown	Nature, earth, simplicity, outdoors
Orange	Warmth, enthusiasm, energy, flamboyant
Purple	Intellectual, royalty, refinement, wisdom
Black	Serious, technical, formal, heavy
Grey	Conservative, business, security, distinctive
White	Purity, simplicity, cleanliness

Figure 2.6 – A sample list of some of the color meanings

Digging a little deeper into color meaning would be worth it if you need to present in various countries. Indeed, the symbolism of color might have a totally different meaning from one culture to another.

Whatever the meaning conferred to colors, you also need to keep in mind that certain color combinations need to be avoided at all costs. Here is a short list of pairs to avoid and the reason why:

- **Red and green**: They are hard to read and are problematic for people suffering from color blindness.
- **Red and blue**: They lack contrast and don't project well together.

Red, blue, and green are not the only problematic colors. It would take many more pages of color research information to discuss them all, which is not the main goal of this book. But with the information you have now, you can create presentations that avoid using the most problematic colors together and use the ones that are the most meaningful for your content.

Let's now move on to the next topic, covering how to remove unnecessary content on your slides for your audience to understand your message quickly and remember more.

Decluttering your slide contents

Unfortunately, most people have seen their share of content-heavy and cluttered slides in their life. Even though we all hate this situation, we keep seeing it very often. I sometimes have the feeling that presenters are afraid the PowerPoint application will *explode* if they use too many slides. However, I have had some clients tell me they were restricted to a certain number of slides! This is just a shame because we then end up having to read slides full of content and text.

Let me share a secret with you: *the more content on your slides, the less readable they get, making the content very difficult to remember*. Usually, slides full of content also lead to the use of very small font sizes. You've probably heard, at least once in your life: "I don't know if you can read the figures in this table, but....". If you have a hard time reading the content yourself, why even bother showing it to your audience?

So, what do I mean by cluttered slides? The easiest way to show you is by simply doing a quick **Google** search with the keywords `awful PowerPoint presentations`. The results will be very similar to what you can see in *Figure 2.7*. This is an example I use in my training sessions of a slide that contains too much content and some hard-to-read text. It goes against almost all of the best practices discussed so far.

Figure 2.7 – An example of an awful PowerPoint slide

Any time your slides cannot pass the glance test, meaning that if people can't grasp the main idea you are discussing within 3 seconds, your visuals will have failed. Your main goal should be to limit your slide content to one idea at a time. Dividing what you need to discuss over multiple slides will be much more efficient for your audience.

When clients call me for help with their presentation design, most of the time their initial 25-slide file can end up with 60 or 70 slides. Yes, many of them almost fainted when I told them how many slides their presentation might have! Let's do a bit of math to show you why it does not impact the length of your presentation in a negative way (see *Figure 2.8*):

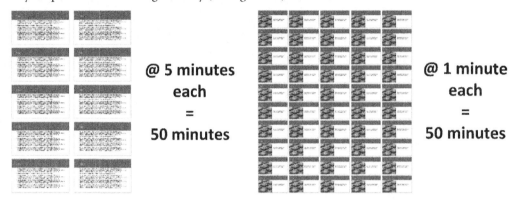

Figure 2.8 – Comparison using 10 slides versus 50 slides in a presentation

If your presentation has 10 slides and you are spending 5 minutes per slide, you have content for a 50-minute talk. The problem is that when you spend more than 1 or 2 minutes per slide, the audience can quickly lose interest. When you divide each point of your content so it is shown on its own slide and add a relevant visual element to it, you will spend much less time per slide, creating a more interesting pace. Back to my example in *Figure 2.8*, if we were to divide the content into 50 slides that we spend about 1 minute on, we would still have 50 minutes of content but the rhythm at which we create a visual change would be much more interesting. Start thinking about your slides as if you were creating a movie. Less time spent on each slide creates a more visually appealing and more memorable presentation.

Here is a list of quick steps you can use to help you remove content from your slides:

1. Start by dividing your content into more slides and make sure you keep one main point or idea per slide.

2. Remove any information present in more than one place on a slide. For example, if the title of your slide is the same as the title of your chart, remove the one for the chart. When you have repetitive words, try to change how you present the content, so you have only one instance of the same word.

3. If possible, remove slide numbers, the date, and the name of the presenter from your content slide. Put that information on the title slide and bring it back on the last slide. This will free up some space to let your content stand out.

4. With regard to the company logo and legal information being on each slide, I know that is a big request in many corporations, but you should also try to avoid them. If the reason is that the slides will be printed, then you will have a solution to offer after reading *Chapter 3*, *Leveraging PowerPoint's Slide Master for Design*, and *Chapter 4*, *Using PowerPoint's Document Masters for Accessible Handouts and Notes*, where I will show you how to be aligned with your marketing and legal departments and still be able to reduce the amount of clutter on slides.

If I had to summarize this section on decluttering in one simple sentence it would be: *less is more*. If you take the time to have less content on your slides but make sure it has a lot of value, you will get better results. You will have less chance of losing your audience to boredom and their favorite app on their smartphone, and you will increase your chances of success.

Removing unnecessary elements from your slides should now be easier to do. It's now time to discuss how the look and feel of your presentation can be made more consistent and look more professional.

Making the look and feel of your slides consistent

The human eye has the superpower of seeing even the smallest of details and that can derail our concentration. This means if your titles seem to be jumping around from one slide to the next, your audience will notice it. There is the same problem if you have been using different font sizes for titles or content across your presentation, or if you have used various alignment styles throughout your presentation.

What does consistency look like? Here is a list of elements that will help you achieve it:

*   Using a maximum of two font styles for titles and content
*   Placing titles and content placeholders in the same position for identical layouts
*   Using a specific color scheme that is applied consistently throughout your presentation
*   Formatting titles and content elements with the same font size and font type and the same alignment
*   Keeping enough whitespace or blank areas on your slides helps the audience to understand your content

I am also sharing a screenshot of a short presentation I did a few years ago to show you an example of how slides can be made consistent (see *Figure 2.9*). As you can see, titles are placed in the same position on all similar slide layouts, using the same font style and size. A thin rectangle is used at the bottom of each slide to recall my corporate colors without using my logo on all the slides.

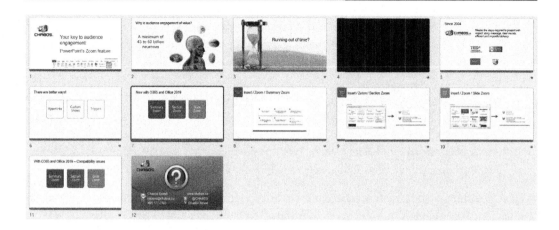

Figure 2.9 – Example of how slides can have a consistent look

Making your slides consistent also means creating layouts that can be reused for similar types of content. You can plan to have slides with a short list of bullet points, some with one image and text, others with full-slide images with a banner over them, and so on. The possibilities are endless if you give your creativity a chance. Of course, you might be starting to think you will never have enough time to create consistent slides if you must create each slide one by one. No worries, that is why *Chapter 3, Leveraging PowerPoint's Slide Master for Design*, is next. You will get familiar with what I call the best design automation feature in PowerPoint.

Summary

In this chapter, we covered how to choose font styles and sizes to help you make your content readable, and how to make sure your background versus text contrast is good. We also discussed how to remove unnecessary content on slides and how to make them look more consistent.

I have not discussed every design best practice in this chapter. But you have learned about the most important elements that can be quickly used to greatly improve your content. As I mentioned in the previous chapter on planning and structuring your content, the most important thing is not to let fear get in the way. Making better presentations is an ongoing process. For existing presentations, start by changing one or two design elements every time you are reviewing your content before an event or meeting. For new presentations, plan more time so you can use what you have learned when you are creating the content; you might as well do it better the first time!

In the next chapter, we are getting hands-on with PowerPoint. You will be learning about layouts, placeholders, theme fonts and colors, and configuring your layouts. By getting to know the **Slide Master**, you will be able to automate most of the design parts of your slides.

Further reading

- The presentation industry standards of the Presentation Guild: `https://presentationguild.org/certifications/presentation-industry-design-standards/`

- If you are using PowerPoint versions older than Microsoft 365 or Office 2019, Julie Terberg's following post will be helpful: `https://designtopresent.com/2018/06/14/an-update-on-safe-fonts-for-powerpoint/`

- Julie Terberg's article on cloud fonts, and access to her PDF guide: `https://designtopresent.com/2019/03/31/a-guide-to-cloud-fonts-in-microsoft-office-365/`

- Dave Paradi's tables on choosing font sizes according to venue and screen sizes: `https://www.thinkoutsidetheslide.com/selecting-the-correct-font-size/`

- To learn more about color symbolism, or even its importance in design or marketing, have a look at the Color Matters website here: `https://colormatters.com/`

- If you are interested in why color matters in your presentations, visit the Colorcom website for interesting statistics on marketing: `https://www.colorcom.com/research/why-color-matters`

3
Leveraging PowerPoint's Slide Master for Design

PowerPoint's **Slide Master** is a design feature that is still overlooked by so many presentation creators and presenters. This is the main reason why I have seen so many presentation files where content has been created by hand *on each slide*. No wonder people have been complaining all this time that slide creation takes so much time!

Therefore, the use of slide masters is one of the first topics I go through in my training sessions. If you are still creating your slides by deleting the placeholders you see on the blank slides and get busy adding text boxes and other types of content manually, this chapter will help you gain hours of your life back. I usually even make this bold statement to users: if you use the Slide Master feature, you'll automate up to 90% of your presentation design tasks. You'll stop re-creating basic design on each slide to focus on adding your content.

The goal here is not to show you how to build a robust corporate template. If that is what you need, you will find a resource in the *Further reading* section from my friends Echo Swinford and Julie Terberg – *they* are the template gurus in our industry and you should read their book if you need to create functional templates for your organization. Instead, I will focus on the main functions in the Slide Master feature that will help you to create your presentations quickly when you don't have a corporate template or if you need to adapt an existing one. In this chapter, we will focus on the following topics:

- Understanding layouts and placeholders
- Choosing fonts and colors
- Configuring standard layouts
- Adding custom layouts

Technical requirements

PowerPoint's Slide Master feature can be found in all versions of the application. The topics discussed in this chapter can be applied to whichever version of PowerPoint you are using, although you might encounter some differences if you are not using PowerPoint in its **Microsoft 365** subscription model.

Understanding layouts and placeholders

Through the years, I have seen many people start a new presentation and tell me they did not like the text boxes on the first slide, so they just deleted them to start from scratch. Unfortunately for them, they did not know that doing so would make them work much harder than necessary to create their slides. This also makes it even harder if they decide to change the overall look of their presentation. This huge mistake usually happens because users don't know about two fundamental features in PowerPoint: **layouts** and **placeholders**. So, let's show you what they are and how they will help you create your content faster.

Layouts

When you start a new presentation with PowerPoint's blank default template, your new file already includes a **title slide**. But there are more layouts available in the **Home** tab (**1**). To access these, in the **Slides** group (**2**), click on the **Slide Layout** (**3**) drop-down list (*Figure 3.1*):

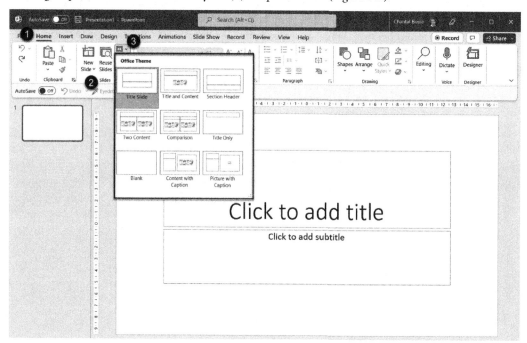

Figure 3.1 – Finding the Slide Layout button from the Home tab in PowerPoint

As you can see, a new blank presentation file already has nine default layouts you can choose from to organize your slide contents quickly:

- **Title Slide**

- **Title and Content**

- **Section Header**

- **Two Content**

- **Comparison**

- **Title Only**

- **Blank**

- **Content with Caption**

- **Picture with Caption**

Whenever you are on a slide for which you want to organize the content differently, your first move should be to go to the **Slide Layout** button to change the layout of the slide. By using existing layouts, you are making sure similar elements on your slides will be placed in the same position across all your slides, creating a more consistent look, as discussed in *Chapter 2, Using Industry Best Practices to Design Better Visuals*. If the standard layouts don't suit your needs, keep on reading because we will address that need in an upcoming section on **custom layouts**.

If you want to add a slide with a different layout than the previous one, then it will be more efficient to simply choose the layout you want from the **New Slide** (**2**) drop-down list in the **Home** tab (**1**) (*Figure 3.2*):

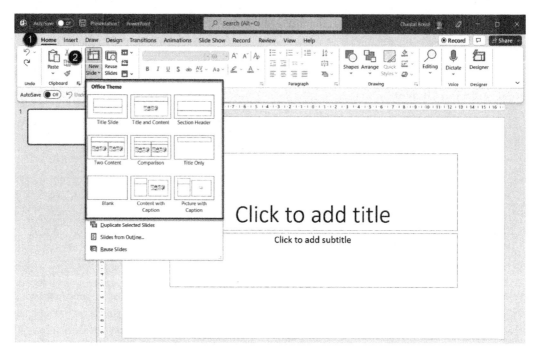

Figure 3.2 – Using the New Slide button to choose a specific layout

> **Tip**
> When applying a new layout to an existing slide, if your content is not changing as expected it might be because the slide was created using text boxes instead of the placeholders described in the next section. If that is the case, simply copy the text from the text boxes and paste it into the right placeholders. You can then delete the text boxes and proceed with the layout changes with better results.

Placeholders

Layouts would not be useful without **placeholders**; these are the default boxes that you see on slides when you have applied a layout. At first glance, they might look like regular text boxes, but they are not. Placeholders are coded and managed differently than other slide elements by PowerPoint. The first way to differentiate them is the prompt text we see before adding any content (*Figure 3.3*):

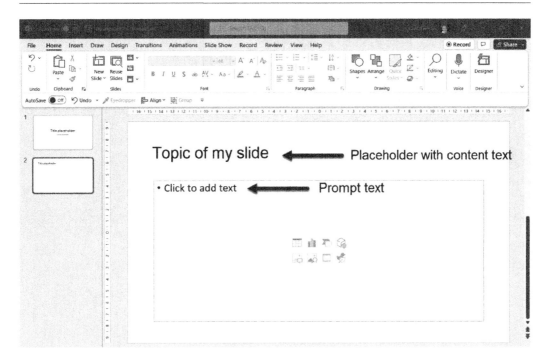

Figure 3.3 – Placeholders have prompt text before adding content

It is important to note that replacing placeholders with text boxes can make presentations inaccessible to people using screen readers. Knowing about placeholders is the first step to helping you navigate the functions we find in the Slide Master feature that we'll cover in our next section.

Accessing layouts and placeholders through a slide master

Now that you have a better understanding of layouts and their placeholders, we can introduce the Slide Master feature, the first of three types of masters discussed in this book (Document and Notes masters will be discussed in *Chapter 4, Using PowerPoint's Document Masters for Accessible Handouts and Notes*). The way I have been describing the Slide Master feature for many years is this: PowerPoint's design automation tool that allows you to determine the overall look and feel of your presentation. It allows you to create a visually consistent look without having to create each element on every slide.

The way to access the slide master is by clicking the **View** tab (**1**), then clicking the **Slide Master** button (**2**) in the **Master Views** group (*Figure 3.4*):

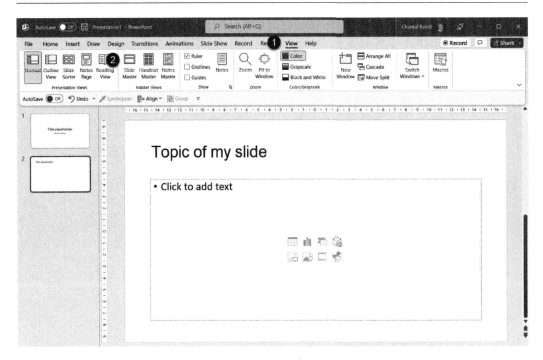

Figure 3.4 – Accessing the Slide Master feature through the View tab

After clicking on the **Slide Master** button, you will be shown a brand-new tab also called **Slide Master** (**1**). This view can be considered the backend of your presentation. Think of it as the place to create your visual standard for all your slides, whether they are placeholder positions, graphic elements required on all slides, and even font styles and colors, which will be discussed in the next section. Any visual element you want to find on all slides can be customized in **Slide Master** (**2**). Then, you can adapt these elements in the layouts (**3**), which are shown as the smaller thumbnails linked to the **Slide Master** feature (*Figure 3.5*). We will discuss how to do this in the sections on standard layouts configuration and adding custom layouts.

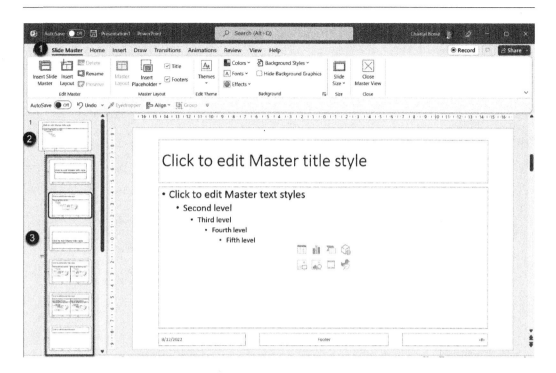

Figure 3.5 – The Slide Master view showing the master and the layouts

> **Tip**
>
> When you have accessed the **Slide Master** view, don't forget that you need to click on the **Close Master View** button to get back into PowerPoint's normal view to add content to your slides. Any time you want to make changes to the overall look of your slide master or layouts, go back to the **View** tab and click on **Slide Master**.

Now that we have explored what layouts and placeholders are and we know how to access a slide master, we will explore some of the features of the slide master, starting with how to choose fonts and colors.

Choosing fonts and colors

Since the introduction of **Office 2007** by Microsoft, users started to see the presence of **themes** in their applications. Just to keep the description short, we can say that themes help to define the overall look of a *document* in terms of colors, fonts, effects applied to shapes, and so on. As you might have noticed, I put emphasis on the word *document*. That's because a theme can be applied throughout your Office applications, making your **Word**, **Excel**, and **PowerPoint** documents look more consistent. Microsoft supplies some free themes that can be found in the **Themes** list in the **Slide Master** view. If you want to learn more about themes, you should check out Echo Swinford and Julie Terberg's book *Building PowerPoint Templates v2*, listed in *Further reading*.

Using one of Microsoft's themes to create your presentations can help speed up the design process, if one suits your needs. But I would still advise you to make some changes so that your presentation will be more aligned with your organization's look. One thing you might want to do is change the colors and the pair of fonts. This process is the same if you decide to start with a template of your own or a new blank presentation.

Selecting the color palette

Since I usually start my presentation process in the **Slide Master** tab, that's also where I set my colors. From the **Slide Master** tab (**1**), simply click on the **Colors** button (**2**) to open the list of Office color palettes supplied by Microsoft (**3**), as shown in *Figure 3.6*:

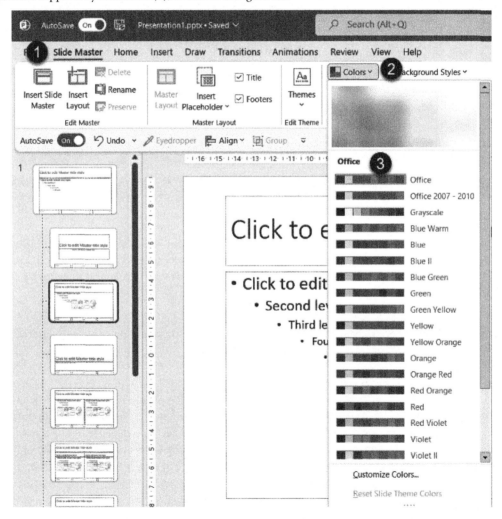

Figure 3.6 – Steps to select a color palette from the Slide Master tab

The other way to access color palettes in PowerPoint is through the **Design** tab (**1**), using the dropdown for background variants (**2**), and selecting **Colors** (**3**), as shown in *Figure 3.7*:

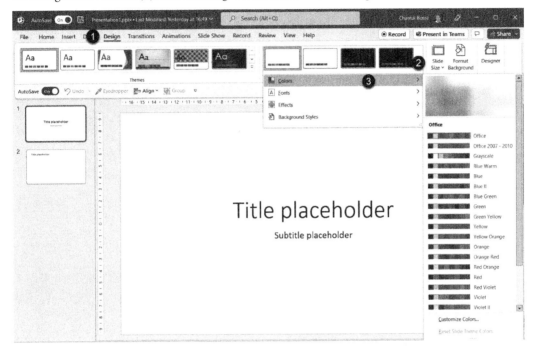

Figure 3.7 – Accessing color palettes through the Design tab

Selecting any palette will help you create a consistent look throughout your content because you then have the color swatches available for font color, shape fill, and outline. Even though Microsoft provides a nice list of color palettes, if the standard Office choices don't exactly fit your corporate colors, you can customize them. This is what we will be discussing in our next section.

How to customize a color palette

If you need to customize some colors in a palette, you need to first open the **Colors** drop-down list (**1**) and click on **Customize Colors...** (**2**) (*Figure 3.8*):

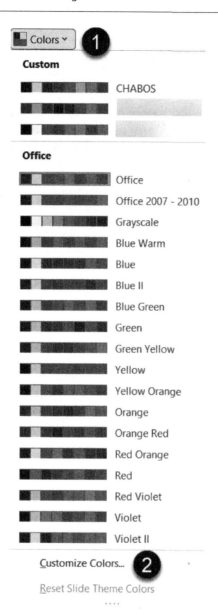

Figure 3.8 – Accessing the Customize Colors... function

You will get the **Create New Theme Colors** window (*Figure 3.9*) allowing you to adjust any color by clicking on any of the colors in the theme (**1**), then choosing the **More Colors...** option (**2**) to get to the **Colors** window. This is where you will be able to choose a **Custom** color (**3**) from a color model (RGB and HSL), a hex code, or from the swatches in the **Standard** tab (**4**):

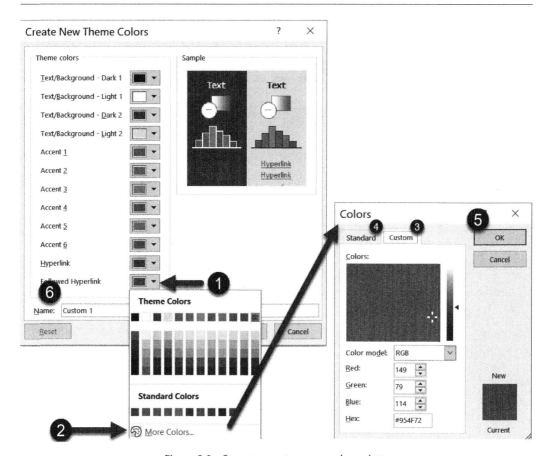

Figure 3.9 – Steps to create a new color palette

When you have finished adjusting a color, click the **OK** button (**5**) to confirm your choice and repeat the process for any other color you want to change. The only thing left to do when you have completed all color changes is to give a relevant **Name** (**6**) to your new custom palette and click **OK** to confirm. After confirming, you can see your new custom color palette (**1**) in the **Colors** drop-down list in the **Variants** group (*Figure 3.10*):

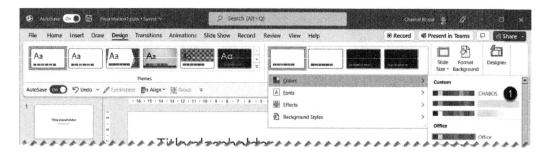

Figure 3.10 – Custom color palettes listed in the Custom section of Colors

Things to be aware of when changing colors in a palette

PowerPoint's color palettes are always set up in three sets (*Figure 3.11*):

1. Four swatches labeled as **Text/Background - Dark 1**, **Text/Background - Dark 2**, **Text/ Background - Light 1**, and **Text/Background - Light 2**.

2. Six **Accent** colors.

3. Two colors for **Hyperlink** and **Followed Hyperlink**.

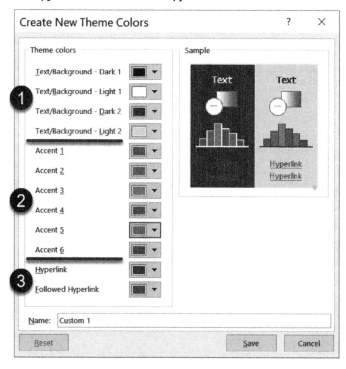

Figure 3.11 – Text/Background, Accent, and Hyperlink color categories

Since my goal is to help business users create their presentations more quickly, I will give you the basic elements you need to be aware of to make colors work in your presentations. For detailed information, I will again refer you to *Building PowerPoint Templates v2*, listed in *Further reading*.

For the first four colors labeled as **Text/Background**, **Dark 1** and **2**, and **Light 1** and **2**, you need to keep in mind that they are used to automatically change the text color to a background style allowing optimal contrast. When a template or theme is built properly, you will usually have **Text/Background - Dark 1** as black, and **Text/Background - Light 1** as white, giving the best possible contrast between text and background. For the **Dark 2/Light 2** colors, you need to make sure their contrast level looks good in the **Sample** preview, as can be seen in the previous figure (*Figure 3.11*).

If you make any changes to the text/background colors, you should test what your content looks like when changing your background style. To do so, you can either use the **Background Styles** button in the **Slide Master** tab (**1**) or go through the **Design** tab (**2**) and click the **Variants** group to get to the **Background Styles** option (*Figure 3.12*):

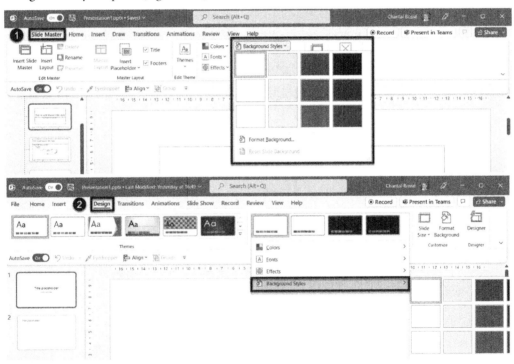

Figure 3.12 – Accessing the background styles from the Slide Master and Design tabs

For the accent and hyperlink colors, make the necessary changes and have a look at the sample preview to make sure your colors have enough contrast with both the dark and light backgrounds. You should also look at the side-by-side effect of your contrast colors, especially if you will be adding charts and using a colorful style in your presentation. If you want to know how your color palette may look for your audience, create a few content slides, open up slide show view, and move back from your computer screen to look at them. You can do the same for your virtual presentations by starting a virtual meeting with your preferred tool and having a look at how a few content slides look when sharing your screen. Viewing your content while imagining you are in your audience's place will help you to correct contrast problems or colors that don't render well.

Selecting title and body fonts

Have you ever had the problem that every time you create a new element on your slides, you have to manually set the font to the one you have chosen as a corporate font? This is usually because you have not set your theme fonts in your file or template and PowerPoint uses its default theme fonts, or the ones previously set as a default. Here is how to solve this issue and help you save a lot of time too.

When in the **Slide Master** tab (**1**), click the **Fonts** button (**2**) to open the list (*Figure 3.13*). There is an **Office** category (**3**) showing you how titles (larger text) and body text (smaller text) will look. You can create your own custom theme fonts by selecting **Customize Fonts...** (**4**) at the bottom. You will then be able to choose the **Heading font** (**5**) and **Body font** (**6**) to match your organization's choice. You can also give it a **Name** (**7**), making it available in the **Custom** category (**8**) at the top of the **Fonts** list. You can also access theme fonts when in the **Design** tab by clicking the more arrow in the **Variants** group.

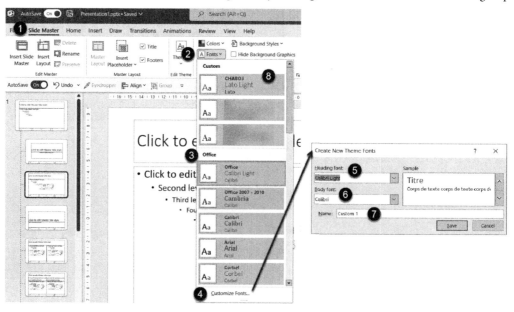

Figure 3.13 – Selecting theme fonts while in the Slide Master tab

To help you choose your fonts, you may want to revisit the *Choosing fonts* section in *Chapter 2, Using Industry Best Practices to Design Better Visuals*. Even though you would need much more information to become a color and font expert, with what was covered in this section you have enough understanding of the basics to help you create better presentations in a more efficient way. We can now move on to configuring the standard layouts found in the Slide Master feature.

Configuring standard layouts

We already mentioned that in the **Slide Master** view, the **Slide Master** is the larger thumbnail and the smaller ones that follow are the layouts. Another element you need to be aware of is the highlighted thumbnail (**1**), which shows you the layout of the slide you were on when you opened the **Slide Master** feature (*Figure 3.14*). You can hover over any thumbnail to show a tooltip (**2**) that tells you on what slide(s) the layout is being used.

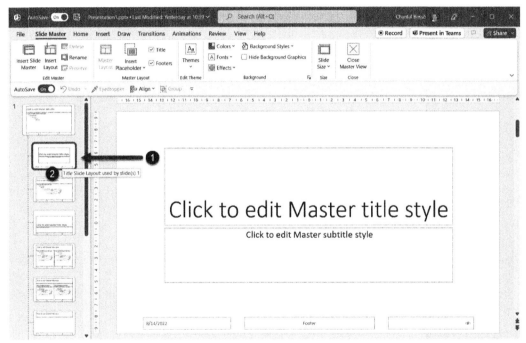

Figure 3.14 – The Slide Master view showing the layout applied to your current slide

Before making changes to any of the layouts, you should make title and content placeholders formatting changes and position adjustments you want to see applied in all of the layouts in the slide master (**1**), as shown in the first thumbnail in the view (*Figure 3.15*). Doing so replicates the changes to the layouts. I have created an example where I changed the font color and size and modified the vertical alignment of the text to the top in the title placeholder of my slide master (**2**). I also changed the font size of three levels of bullets and modified the bullet for the first level (**3**). In the title and content layout, my changes were reproduced automatically (**4**).

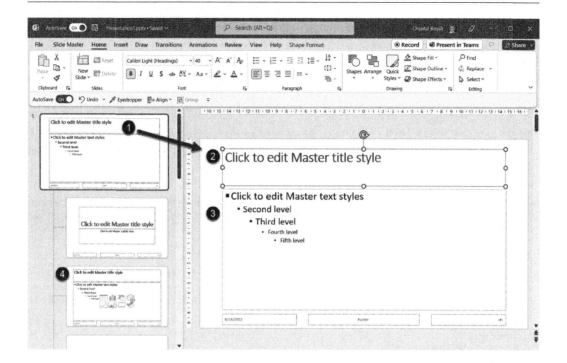

Figure 3.15 – Formatting changes made in the Slide Master replicate in layouts

Some layouts will not get the exact same changes because of their use. For example, the title slide's layout will get the same font style and color but won't get the same font size as the regular titles since it is common practice to use bigger fonts on the title slide. Adjustments can be made on other placeholders after you are done on the Slide Master. Just keep in mind that doing so breaks the placeholder's association with your slide master, meaning the next time you make a change in the Slide Master it won't replicate in placeholders modified on the layouts.

Try it yourself

The best way to understand the previous explanation is to try it yourself. Follow these steps:

1. Open a new blank presentation and go to the **Slide Master** view.
2. Change the font size and color of the title placeholder on your slide master.
3. Select a layout and change the color of the font in the title placeholder.
4. Go back to the **Slide Master** tab and change the title font color again.
5. Now, have a look at your modified layout. The new color change did not replicate.

You need to keep in mind that you should review all of your layouts every time you decide to change something in the slide master to make sure the changes look like what you have in mind.

Changes you can make and should avoid

Whether in the Slide Master or in the layouts, we already mentioned that we can adjust font sizes, font colors, and text alignment within the placeholders. Make sure you always keep in mind the best practices we discussed in the previous chapter. You can also resize and move placeholders so that you can create the look that suits your organization's needs. You can also add any shape or graphic element that you want to see on all slides, or just on specific layouts.

But there is a list of things that could create more problems than you bargained for depending on your situation:

- **Deleting placeholders on the Slide Master**: Doing so breaks the link to the layouts and prevents the possibility of making font size and color changes in one place. Just don't do it!

- **Deleting placeholders on standard layouts**: Doing so can cause a lot of problems when bringing together some slides with the same layout from another presentation, or when applying the template to another presentation. PowerPoint won't be able to map the placeholders thus making you work harder to put everything in its place.

- **Deleting standard layouts you are not using**: This might cause similar problems to the ones mentioned previously, especially when handling content from files that don't use the same template.

- **Renaming standard layouts**: Doing so will create problems when PowerPoint is trying to map content coming from a layout with a standard name with a template that does not have such a layout anymore.

When you decide to do a bit of cleaning in your layouts, you will also realize that some elements cannot be deleted, such as layouts already used by some slides, or placeholders on a layout that are used by a slide in the file; that is by design.

So, if you are not satisfied with some of the standard layouts provided in PowerPoint, what should you do next? Simply add some custom layouts, which is the topic of the next section and also includes some functions to help you create them.

Adding custom layouts

Even though adding custom layouts can be done at any time, I prefer to do it after I have taken the time to configure and format the standard layouts. The reason is simple: you can then simply duplicate a standard layout as a starting point, rename it, and make all the necessary changes to it. Here is how you do it:

- Right-click the layout you want to start with and choose **Duplicate Layout** (*Figure 3.16*):

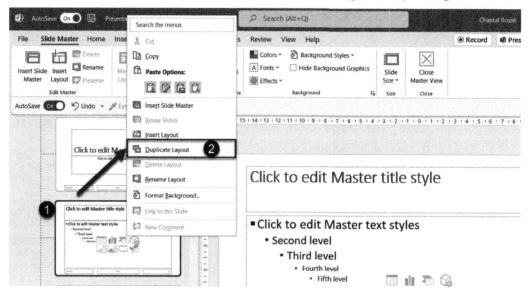

Figure 3.16 – Duplicating an existing layout

- Right-click the second layout that was created (**1**) and choose **Rename Layout** (**2**) to get to the renaming window (**3**). Change the name to one that describes the layout you are creating and click the **Rename** button (**4**) (*Figure 3.17*):

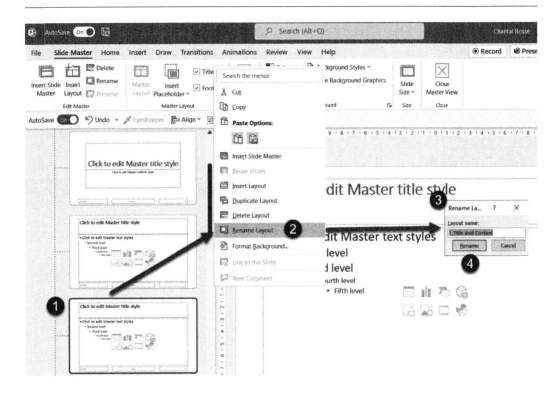

Figure 3.17 – Renaming a layout

You now have a new layout that already has the same title placeholder as your other layouts. Let's see an example of a custom layout that I often use in presentations when I want a full slide image with a semi-transparent placeholder for my title or headline. From the newly created layout (*Figure 3.18*), you need to do the following:

- Select the content placeholder and hit the *Delete* key on your keyboard to remove it (**1**).

- Click on the **Insert Placeholder** button to open the list (**2**).

- Select the **Picture** placeholder (**3**). Your mouse cursor will look like a *plus* sign, meaning you can draw the placeholder just as you would draw any shape or text box on a slide.

> **Note**
>
> If you choose a **Content** placeholder to have easy access to pictures on your computer and stock images, the placeholder will be resized according to the picture you use. The **Picture** and **Online Image** placeholders keep their size and adjust the picture you are using to fit the space. Be aware of this difference if you want to avoid resizing images every time. You can consider creating two separate layouts: one using the **Picture** placeholder for when you want to access an image from your computer, and the second with an **Online Image** placeholder for when you want to access Microsoft's stock images.

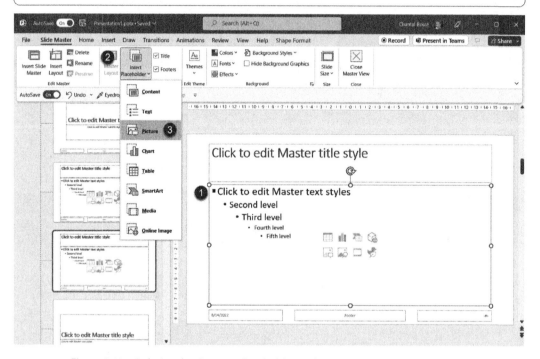

Figure 3.18 – Deleting the Content placeholder and inserting a Picture placeholder

- Make sure the placeholder is the size of the slide (**1**) (*Figure 3.19*). Right-click the placeholder (**2**) to change its order by using **Send to Back** (**3**). This way you make sure you have access to the title placeholder. Inserting a placeholder also brings up the **Shape Format** contextual tab, from which you can access the **Send Backward** button.

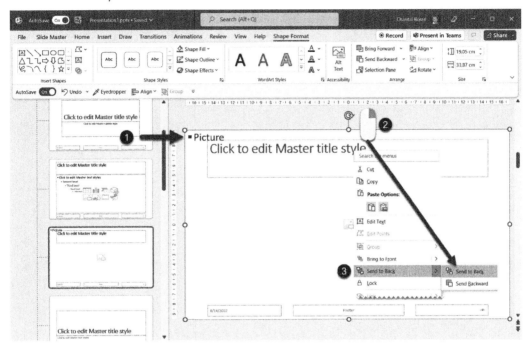

Figure 3.19 – Full-slide Picture placeholder sent to the back

- You can then proceed to adjust the size of the title placeholder. I like to make it the same width as the slide to give it a banner-like look (**1**) (*Figure 3.20*). Then click on the dialog launcher (**2**), which is the small arrow in the bottom-right corner of the **Shape Styles** group. It opens the **Format Shape** (**3**) pane.

- Click on the **Size & Properties** (**4**) icon.

- Open the **Text Box** section (**5**) so you can adjust the margins. The left and right margins can be around half an inch (**1.5 cm**). The top and bottom margins can be adjusted on the slide later when you know how much text you have in the placeholder:

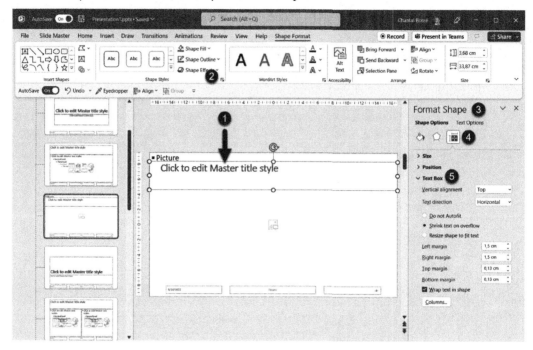

Figure 3.20 – Adjusting the title placeholder and its margins

- Click on the **Fill and Line** icon (**1**) and open the **Fill** section (**2**) (*Figure 3.21*). Choose a solid fill color – usually, black or dark gray looks nice on any picture (**3**). After that, adjust the transparency (**4**). I usually start around **30%** and make sure my font color is contrasting (for example, white):

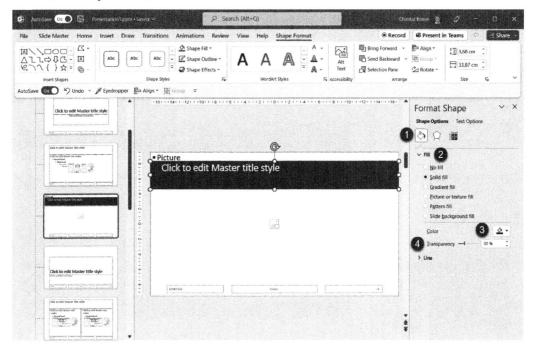

Figure 3.21 – Adding a semi-transparent fill to the title placeholder

You can see how your layout will look by using the **Close Master View** button in the **Slide Master** tab and adding a new slide with your new custom layout. Add your title or headline to the slide, then click the picture icon in the middle to browse for a picture you want to add. In *Figure 3.22*, you'll see an example of this new custom layout with a title and an image:

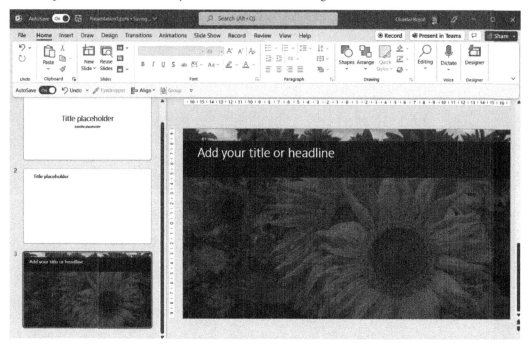

Figure 3.22 – Full-slide image with a title banner

If you have already gone through the planning stage of your presentation, you might have some ideas on what layouts might work for your content. Just create whatever makes sense for the time being. You can always come back to your slide master and change or add extra layouts as you go. I know this tip might not be aligned with some design practices, but I am giving steps that will help you in your usual business settings, which means that you are probably stuck with impossible deadlines. Anyway, there is no such thing as a perfect presentation or design because we always find something to improve in our previous presentations. As I mentioned before: one step at a time is better than no improvement at all.

> **Tip**
>
> If you are using a template that includes many custom layouts that are not used within your presentation, it is okay to delete them if you need to manage the file size. The more layouts you have in your template, the larger the file size. When deleting unused custom layouts from your file, remember that you will need to start your next presentations from the original template to get them back.

When you don't have a corporate template to start with and feel overwhelmed by the thought of starting from a blank presentation, have a look at the templates provided by Microsoft in **File | New**. Browse the list or use keywords relevant to your topic and open a few templates to explore their slide master. Inspire yourself with some of the layouts that might work for you. Unfortunately, many templates provided break a few of the best practice rules, but if it helps you have a starting point, you will be able to fix some issues you might find.

I can also suggest a low-tech means to inspire you for your slide layouts: *The Better Deck Deck* by my friend Nolan Haims. You can find information in the *Further reading* section.

The rest of this section will focus on tips and tricks to help you with common Slide Master problems.

Reordering your slide layouts

When using layouts regularly, the list might not present itself in an optimal order. You can simply reorder them by clicking and dragging the layouts in the **Slide Master** view (**1**), so you have them sorted in a more efficient way (*Figure 3.23*):

- Click and drag any layout to the best position (**2**). According to a Microsoft list of shortcuts available to create presentations, you should be able to use *Ctrl + Up* or *Down* arrow keys to move thumbnails. If you are using an operating system in another language other than English, these might not work. See the *Further reading* section for a link to the Microsoft article.

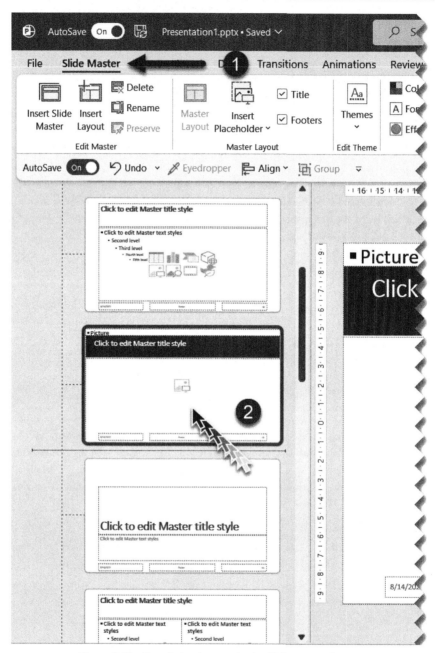

Figure 3.23 – Reordering layouts in the Slide Master feature

The **New Slide** and **Slide Layout** lists will be sorted the way you want them (*Figure 3.24*):

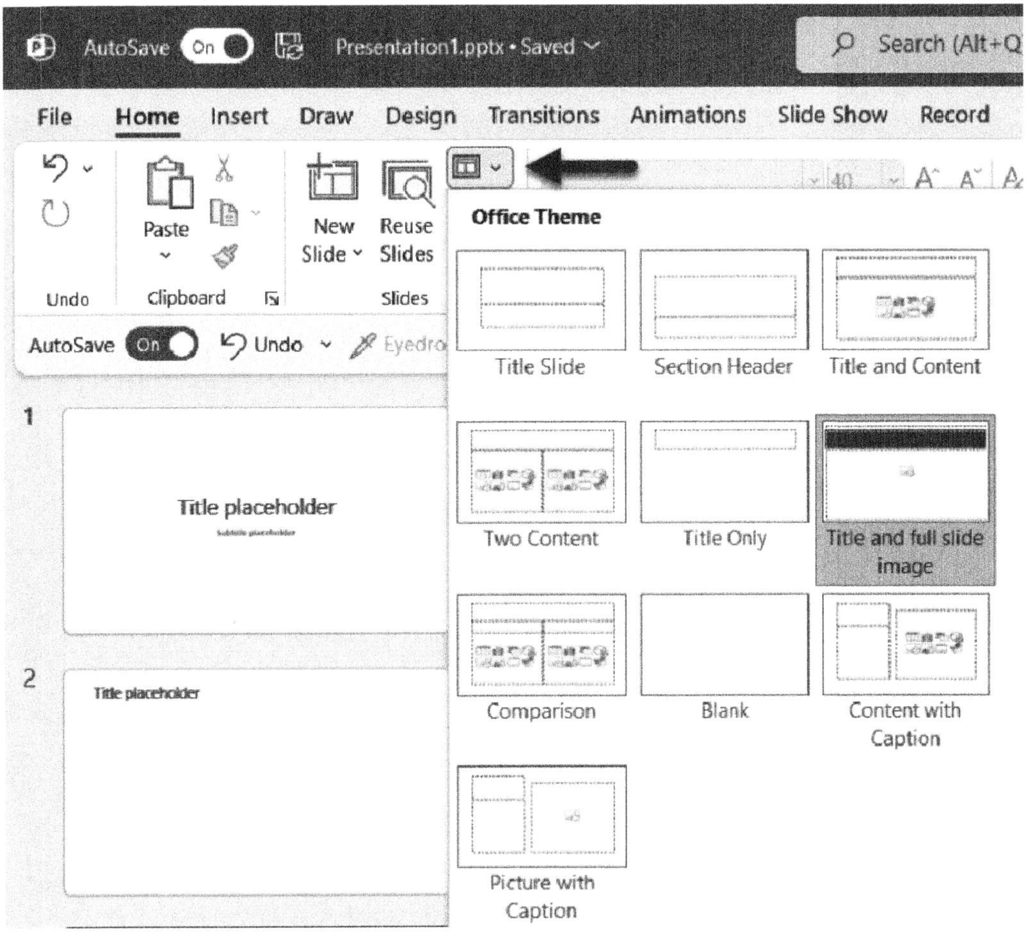

Figure 3.24 - Reordered list of slide layouts

This is not something you should be doing for all your templates. But if you find that you are wasting a lot of time on a very long list of layouts, consider this tip to help you save some time when designing.

Renaming your template to avoid Office Theme labeling

If you have started your template from a new blank presentation, then your slide master will be named **Office Theme**. It is not a huge problem, although it might confuse others using the template you created. You simply need to rename the master by right-clicking it and choosing **Rename Master**. You could give the master your company or department name (*Figure 3.25*):

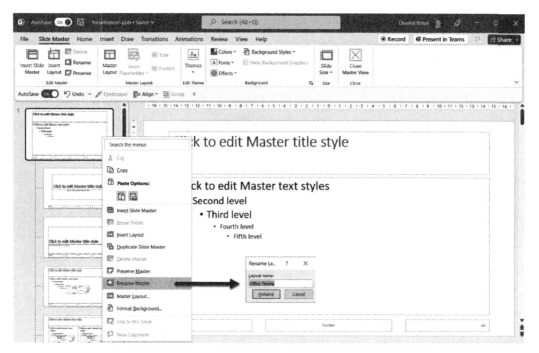

Figure 3.25 – Renaming a slide master

If you have used a template from the list supplied by Microsoft, you should also consider renaming your slide master to avoid even more confusion.

Using the Hide Background Graphics feature

When creating your template, we have discussed that you need to start formatting the slide master first, then the layouts. Depending on what graphic elements you have added to the slide master, you might end up with an issue such as a shape or logo that has been added onto your slide master but not placed properly for the title slide layout design you had in mind, or any other layout for that matter. This is where the **Hide Background Graphics** checkbox comes to the rescue!

In *Figure 3.26*, you can see that the section layout has a colored shape at the bottom (**1**) and the title layout does not (**2**). The only reason for this difference is that the **Hide Background Graphics** checkbox has been used (**3**):

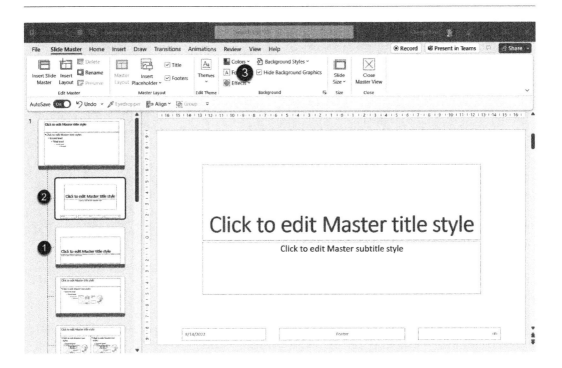

Figure 3.26 – Using the Hide Background Graphics checkbox

So, next time you have unwanted graphic elements from your slide master, use the **Hide Background Graphics** checkbox to help you change the design of your layout without having to first hide them manually.

Using a Microsoft stock image with a picture placeholder

When using a picture placeholder on a layout, the only icon available to fill it opens the **Insert Picture** window to browse your computer. But you can use Microsoft's stock images in one of these two ways to bypass the limitation:

- Add any image from your computer, then right-click the placeholder (**1**) and use the **Change Picture** (**2**) | **From Stock Images...** (**3**) options to access that library (*Figure 3.27*):

Figure 3.27 – Using the Change Picture feature

- After adding the layout, select the picture placeholder (**1**), go to the **Insert** tab (**2**), then click on the **Pictures** (**3**) | **Stock Images…** options (**4**) to access the library. As soon as you choose an image, it will fill your placeholder (*Figure 3.28*).

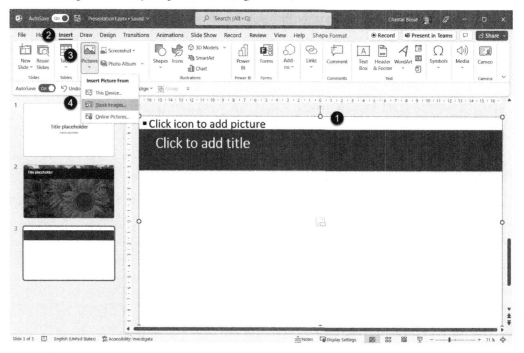

Figure 3.28 – Selecting the picture placeholder and using Insert | Pictures | Stock Images…

> **Important information**
>
> As a licensed Microsoft 365 user, you can use any stock content provided in the library if it is part of a presentation file or any other Microsoft Office file type. All the content is royalty-free and no attribution is required. You cannot reuse any content on its own. Have a look at Microsoft's terms of use listed in *Further reading*.

The picture placeholder is a great way to make your presentation more impactful, whether you use some of your own images or Microsoft's stock images. Let's move on to the missing footer placeholder topic in the next section.

Retrieving missing footer placeholders

If you open the **Slide Master** of a presentation file and realize that the footer placeholders (such as date, footer, and slide number) have been deleted, you can and should add them back so you can control their display more efficiently.

When you are on the **Slide Master** tab, right-click your mouse (**1**) and select **Master Layout...** (**2**) to display the **Master Layout** window. You can then add back all footer placeholders by checking the boxes (**3**). You can also select **Master Layout** on the ribbon (**4**) to access this window (*Figure 3.29*):

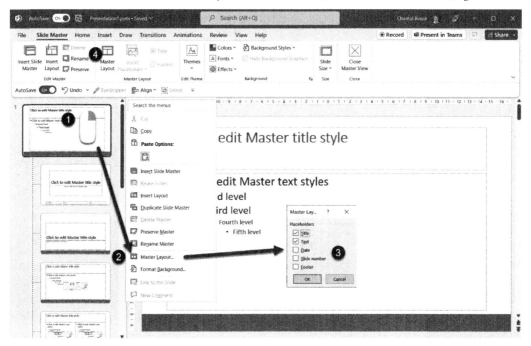

Figure 3.29 – Adding footer placeholders to your slide master

If this does not solve the issue of the footer placeholders being missing from some of your layouts (**1**), then you need to check the **Footers** box (**2**) on the specific layout (*Figure 3.30*):

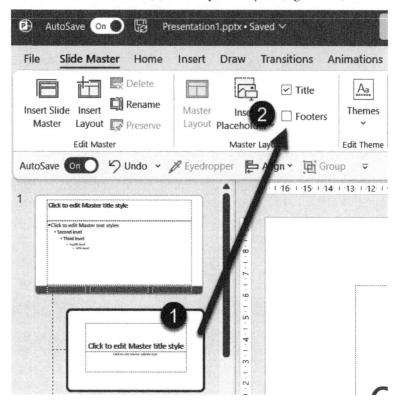

Figure 3.30 – Adding footer placeholders to a layout

Now that you know how to retrieve the footer placeholders, let's move on to a new feature that helps you lock objects or placeholders.

Using the lock feature for placeholders or objects

Any graphic element or regular text box added to a layout in the **Slide Master** view won't be editable when you go back to **Normal** view. This is to protect any content that needs to be displayed on slides without being editable. But for many years users have asked for a feature that allows them to lock placeholders in their templates to avoid having them moved by users. A locking feature was introduced in May 2021 to help users lock slide objects, although it does not yet work as expected in the **Slide Master** view, at the time this book was written.

To access the locking feature, you can either right-click any object on a slide and click **Lock** or **Unlock** in the contextual menu. But I think it is more interesting to do it from **Selection Pane**, a feature often unknown to many users that offers a few other tricks you should know. To display the **Selection Pane**, you need to select the **Home** tab (**1**) | **Editing** group (**2**) | **Select** (**3**) | **Selection Pane…** (**4**) options (*Figure 3.31*):

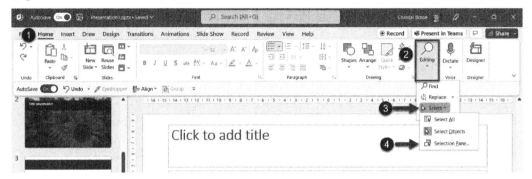

Figure 3.31 – Steps to display the Selection Pane

Once it is displayed, you will have access to the list of objects on your slide labeled with their generic name created by PowerPoint. In the example in *Figure 3.32*, we can see that on slide number five we have only two empty placeholders (**1**). To lock an object, you simply need to click the *lock* icon to close it (**2**). As you can see in the figure, the content placeholder (**3**) has been locked. If we try to select it on the slide, its border will be full without any handles allowing resizing or movement.

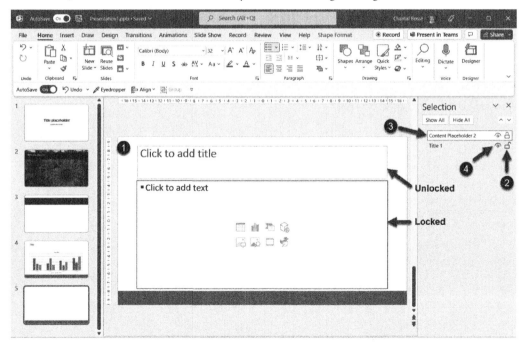

Figure 3.32 – Features available in Selection Pane

If you leave the **Selection Pane** open and go into the **Slide Master** view, it will display the same locking possibility but won't necessarily have the effect we would think. Your objects will be locked in the **Slide Master** view but will remain movable and resizable in **Normal** view, at least at the time this book was written. So, if you want to protect placeholders from being moved or resized when editing the template, lock them in the **Slide Master** view. If you want to protect objects from being accidentally moved on slides while adding content, then lock them from the **Normal** view.

Since we are talking about the **Selection Pane**, let's explore other features there that will become useful later when we discuss animations in *Chapter 8, Working with Transitions and Animations*. If you look back at *Figure 3.32*, you see a small eye icon (**4**) that allows you to hide or display objects on your slide. When we want to create more complex animation effects, it is common to overlay more than one object, which makes it very difficult to select only one. If you double-click on the name of an object (**3**), you will be able to rename it. Renaming objects should become a standard procedure if you want to keep your sanity with multiple complex animations – it is the quickest way to find objects that need special animations.

Using this short list of tips to help you with common problems when dealing with the **Slide Master** and its layouts and the topics to create custom layouts in your template, you will be able to automate your content creation to save some precious time. If you are wondering how you will be able to create layouts that will serve the purpose of presenting and printing your presentation, then you need to read *Chapter 4, Using PowerPoint's Document Masters for Accessible Handouts and Notes*. There are ways to make your PowerPoint file work harder without making the slides do all the work.

Summary

In this chapter, we discussed layouts and placeholders so that you would understand their role in the **Slide Master**. We also covered how to choose theme fonts and colors, and how to format your standard layouts and create new ones.

Of course, many more topics could have been included in this chapter if the main goal had been the creation of a robust corporate template. With what you have learned, you will be able to have a decent template to work from and save yourself a lot of time creating your slides afterward. Even if you have a feeling that it will take you too much time, I can guarantee you that it is all worth it. You will be able to reuse slides and create new presentations very quickly the second time around.

In the next chapter, you will be learning about the document and notes masters so you can make your PowerPoint file serve more than one purpose without overcrowding your slides. We will also explore the various ways you can print or create PDFs from your documents.

Further reading

- To learn how to build robust PowerPoint templates, refer to Echo Swinford and Julie Terberg's book *Building PowerPoint Templates v2*

- Get more information on *The Better Deck Deck*, by Nolan Haims: `http://thebetterdeckdeck.com/`

- Microsoft article on PowerPoint keyboard shortcuts: `https://support.microsoft.com/en-us/office/use-keyboard-shortcuts-to-create-powerpoint-presentations-ebb3d20e-dcd4-444f-a38e-bb5c5ed180f4`

- Microsoft's stock images terms of use: `https://support.microsoft.com/en-us/topic/what-am-i-allowed-to-use-premium-creative-content-for`

4

Using PowerPoint's Document Masters for Accessible Handouts and Notes

We previously stated that PowerPoint's **Slide Master** was often overlooked by users, but I must say that the **Handout Master** and **Notes Master** are features that are mostly unknown to many users. This is unfortunate because most of the time, they allow users to make their PowerPoint files work harder in much less time than having to create separate files for their presentation and document needs.

PowerPoint's two document masters work in a similar way to the **Slide Master**. They allow you to determine the overall look of documents you might want to produce for your audience, so you are on brand while avoiding the obligation to create Word documents.

Again, our goal is to help you format the **Handout Master** and **Notes Master** so you can quickly produce documents from your presentation file. This means there will be no need to create multiple files before your next presentation. Your PowerPoint file will be configured so you can deliver your talk and see your presentation notes, use a formatted **Handout Master** to create a simple document with slide images and lines to take notes, and create a more elaborate document that includes a slide image and text for your audience with the **Notes Master**. In both cases, you will be able to easily print the documents or export them as a `.pdf` file. So, in this chapter, we will discuss the following topics:

- Configuring the **Handout Master** for a simple document
- Configuring the **Notes Master** for a complete handout
- Making your presentations accessible
- Printing your documents
- Exporting your document as a `.pdf` file

Technical requirements

PowerPoint's document masters can be found in all versions of the application. The topics discussed in this chapter can be applied to whatever version of PowerPoint you are using, although, you might encounter some differences if you are not using PowerPoint in its **Microsoft 365 (M365)** subscription model.

Configuring the Handout Master for a simple document

The **Handout Master** allows you to create a branded look for your simple document needs. Although many users don't know about that specific master, many have used its view when printing handouts that have six slide thumbnails per page for their audience. Let's see how you can format it so your printouts or .pdf files will be branded and your audience sees your company information on each page.

To access the **Handout Master**, you need to use the **View** tab (**1**) and choose **Handout Master** (**2**) (*Figure 4.1*):

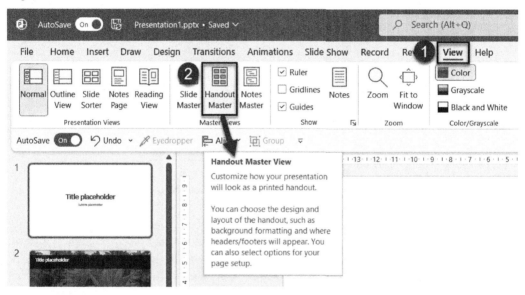

Figure 4.1 – Accessing Handout Master

> **Tip**
> Whenever you are unsure about what a button will do, take time to read the tooltip provided each time you hover over one so you will get a brief description, such as the one provided in *Figure 4.1* for the **Handout Master** view.

You then get the **Handout Master** view tab where you will be able to make all the necessary formatting changes (*Figure 4.2*):

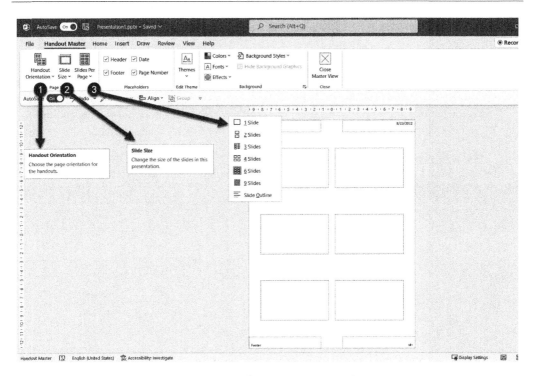

Figure 4.2 – Handout Master page settings

Let's start by discussing the first three buttons on the ribbon:

1. **Handout Orientation**: You can decide to format your handout so that the content is displayed in portrait or landscape orientation. You need to keep in mind that if you change page orientation in the **Handout Master**, it will also apply in the Notes Master, which we will discuss in the next section.

2. **Slide Size**: Although this option shows in your **Handout Master** view, be aware that if you change it here, it will change the size of your slides in your presentation.

> **Tip**
>
> If you are still wondering whether you should consider using the standard 4:3 slide size that was the default in older PowerPoint versions, I would say that you simply need to evaluate where your presentation will be displayed most of the time. In most in-person and virtual settings, your audience will be watching your presentation on devices that usually show content with the modern widescreen 16:9 aspect ratio. The widescreen format also has the advantage of giving more space for your content, helping you create better visuals that have enough empty spaces between components on slides.

3. **Slides Per Page**: This option lets you choose how many slide thumbnails you want to be displayed on your page. As you can see in *Figure 4.2*, there are more display options than the famous **6 Slides** per page one. The trick is to choose the one that suits your needs *before* you do anything else. The reason is quite simple: changing the number of slides per page does not create different branded layouts. You will need to manually adapt any extra graphic elements that were added according to the display you choose. Whatever the layout you choose, the slide thumbnail areas cannot be moved or resized—they show as rectangles with a dotted-line border.

After changing any page settings, we can decide whether we want to keep or remove any placeholders from the page and configure any of the options in the **Background** group (*Figure 4.3*):

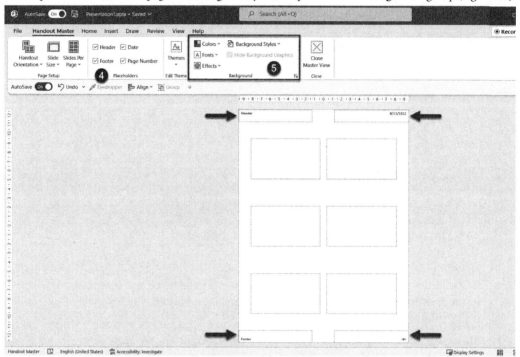

Figure 4.3 – Handout Master layout and background settings

4. **Placeholders**: This group allows you to remove or add any of the placeholders. If you deleted one of them directly on the **Handout Master** page, you could simply add it back by checking the corresponding checkbox. All four placeholders can be moved or resized, and the text formatted. We will see how to include header and footer content later in this section.

5.   The **Background** group: This is where you will be able to choose your color palette and fonts to be aligned with your choices in the presentation. Unfortunately, even if you created and applied a custom color palette or font pair in your slide master, it will not be applied automatically in the **Handout Master**, but you will be able to easily apply them from both lists. If you do not remember how to create custom colors or font pairs, have another look at *Chapter 3, Leveraging PowerPoint's Slide Master for Design*.

Now that we have covered the basics of the handout layouts, we will see, in the next two sections, how to add graphic elements to help you give a corporate look to your handout and properly add any header and footer to your document.

Adding graphic elements to your Handout Master

From the **Handout Master**, you can add any graphic element you want after selecting the number of slides displayed on a page. Explore what is available in your **Insert** tab and be creative! You can reproduce any look you usually have in your organization's Word documents if you want.

Here is a fictitious example of what your **Handout Master** could look like (*Figure 4.4*):

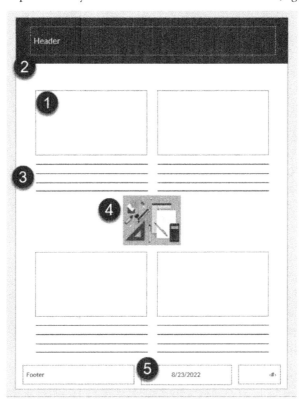

Figure 4.4 – Example of a formatted Handout Master

Here are the steps to add graphics to your **Handout Master**:

1. We have first selected the **4 Slides** per page layout.

2. Then, we changed the font size and color of the header and resized the placeholder to cover most of the width of the page. We also added a colored rectangle and used the **Send to Back** feature available either in the **Home** or **Shape Format** tab.

3. We added four horizontal lines under each thumbnail to accommodate notes. A productivity tip to draw the lines is to create the first four lines, then select them all, press the *Ctrl + Shift* keyboard keys, then click and drag to the right to create the second set of lines. Now select both sets of lines and again press the shortcut keys while dragging toward the bottom of the page.

4. We then added a Microsoft stock illustration. For that, go to the **Insert** tab on the ribbon, then click on the **Pictures** button and select **Stock Images....** In the stock library window, you have several tabs to choose from at the top. In our example, we navigated to the **Illustrations** tab. This illustration could easily be replaced by any company logo or any visual relevant to your content.

5. Finally, the date placeholder was moved to the bottom of the page and formatted.

Adding your header and footer content

Just like in the slide master, you should not add your content in the master view. To properly add your handout header and footer information, you need to go to the **Insert** tab | **Header & Footer** | **Notes and Handouts** options (*Figure 4.5*). You can then decide to add a date that will be updated automatically or fixed. The **Page number** checkbox is checked by default, a good choice since we are creating a document, not slides.

In our example, we also added content in the header and footer placeholders that were already represented in their exact place in **Preview**. The only thing left to do was click on the **Apply to All** button so all our pages would be displayed in the same way:

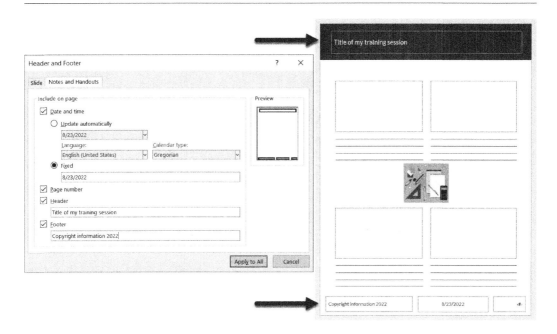

Figure 4.5 – Inserting header and footer information in your handout

As you can see, creating a professional-looking handout does not need to take a very long time. You only need to choose elements that represent your content well while being aligned with your corporate look or branding guidelines. However, if you need to create a document that has more than just picture thumbnails of your slides, the next section on the Notes Master will be valuable to you.

Configuring the Notes Master for a complete handout

The **Notes Master** allows you to create a branded look for documents that need an image of the slide and notes beneath it. The notes are captured from the notes pane beneath each slide in the **Normal** view. Most of the time, notes are used for the presenter, but that does not mean they cannot be used for your audience. There are some workarounds that allow you to create a file that can contain notes for the presenter and notes for the handout, but let's start by going through the changes you should make in the Notes Master.

To access the **Notes Master**, you need to use the **View** tab and choose **Notes Master** (*Figure 4.6*):

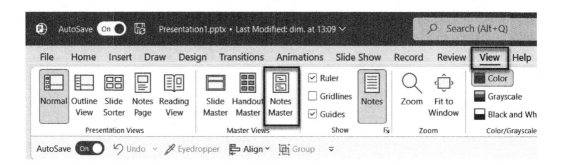

Figure 4.6 – Accessing Notes Master

You then get the **Notes Master** view, from which you will be able to make all the necessary changes to customize your document's look (*Figure 4.7*):

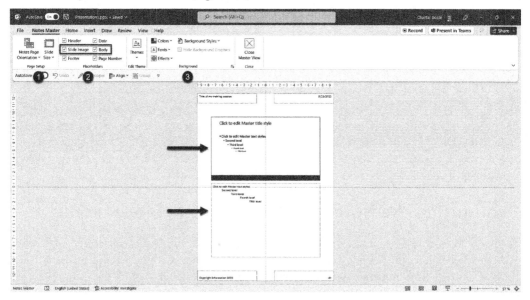

Figure 4.7 – Notes Master view

1. In the **Page Setup** group, you can change **Notes Page Orientation** or **Slide Size** just like in the **Handout Master**. If you change the page orientation, keep in mind that it will also change the orientation for your handout and will probably significantly change the look of it if you had added any graphic elements. As for the slides, it's the same comment: changing this setting will change the size of your whole presentation and it's probably not what you want.

2. The **Placeholders** group looks similar to the handout's, although we now have a checkbox for **Slide Image** and one for **Body**. As you can see, beside the arrows in *Figure 4.7*, those two placeholders take up most of the space on the page. The nice advantage is that they can be moved and resized, helping us create a custom look for our documents.

3. One thing you will notice when in the **Background** group is that even if you have chosen **Colors** and **Fonts** options in **Handout Master**, you will need to do it again in this view. Just select any custom color palette and font pair you created already to apply them to your Notes Master.

Now that we have covered how to access the Notes Master and its functions and layout, we can proceed to learn how you can customize it.

Customizing your Notes Master

All placeholders in the **Notes Master** view can be moved, resized, and formatted. You just need to select any of them and make changes with any available formatting tools, whether in the **Home** tab or the **Shape Format** contextual tab that becomes available when you click on a placeholder. Unfortunately, even if you have customized your **Handout Master** already, you will need to start over in the **Notes Master**. If having the exact same look for both masters is not important for you, just go ahead and make all the necessary changes. If it is and you want to save time, keep reading.

Have another look at the formatted **Handout Master** in *Figure 4.4*. You can see we have increased the width of our header, added a colored rectangle under it, moved the date to the bottom, and changed the font formatting in all placeholders. Nothing was kept in the **Notes Master** view, except the header and footer information—if you forgot how to add header and footer information, go back to *Figure 4.5*.

We're always in favor of trying to outsmart PowerPoint, but if you delete the placeholders and open the **Handout Master** view to copy them from there, it won't work! It might look like you have the same information, but the next time you change your header and footer information, it will not update. Instead, the following are the steps you could use to save time if you already formatted the **Handout Master** (*Figure 4.8*):

1. Open the **Handout Master** view, select graphic elements, copy them, and close the view. Open the **Notes Master** view and paste them there.

2. Make the necessary adjustments to the **Slide Image** and **Body** placeholders in terms of position and size, and make sure the pasted graphic elements are also sized and layered properly:

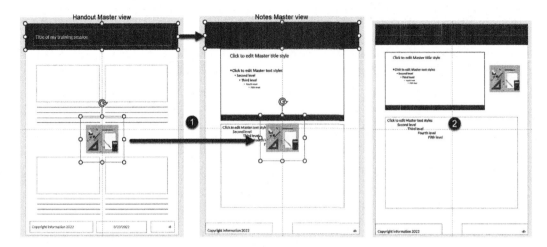

Figure 4.8 – Copying and pasting graphic elements from Handout Master to Notes Master

3.   Then, you can redo text formatting from scratch. You could use the format painter to capture text size, color, and alignment in your **Handout Master** placeholders to apply it to the placeholders in Notes Master, but that means you need to open and close both master views successively. In the end, it might not save you much time.

4.   Adjust the font size for the body placeholder according to your needs. If you are producing a document for your audience, a 12-point font size is usually easy to read by everyone and makes it easier to fit all the text that supports the slide.

Adapting your presentation file for a handout and delivery notes

There may come a time when you need to have your own presentation notes and create a complete handout for your audience or participants. Some might be tempted to make a copy of their PowerPoint file, so they have one for the delivery and one for the document. It does work, but if you know you'll need to update the content often, it can become a hugely time-consuming task. Instead, you might want to consider trying these two hacks we use from time to time.

Making copies of your slides in a new section

The first hack simply requires making copies of your presentation slides in a new section that you label as Handout and making sure the section is the first one in your presentation deck. When you select those *Handout* slides, you can then print the selection or create a .pdf file that will have page numbers starting at #1. If you hide the slides in that section, you will start your slideshow directly from the first slide in your **Presentation** section.

Here are the steps to accomplish this:

1. Add a section before your slides; right-click just before your first slide and click **Add Section**. Then, give it a name; you could use Presentation. Click **Rename** to confirm (*Figure 4.9*):

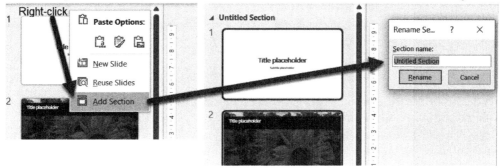

Figure 4.9 – Adding and naming a section in your PowerPoint file

2. Creating a section also has the advantage of helping you select all your presentation slides simply by clicking the **Presentation** section name. You can now copy (*Ctrl + C*) the slides and paste them (*Ctrl + V*) directly before the section in the slide navigation pane. You then get a section with the same name; right-click it to be able to select **Rename Section** (*Figure 4.10*). As you can see, this menu offers you many other options to help you manage your sections, and getting familiar with them will help you improve your efficiency:

Figure 4.10 – Renaming a section and other options

You are now ready to add notes for your audience for the slides in the first section, and your own notes for the slides in the **Presentation** section. You can also remove any slides you don't want in the handout. The advantage of this is having only one file to manage and being able to easily adjust the content of any slides with a simple copy/paste between sections.

When you want to deliver your presentation, make sure to use the **Hide Slide** command for your handout section so they don't show during your slideshow.

> **Important note**
>
> When using this trick, you should avoid showing slide numbers during your delivery because the numbering will start from the slide number following the hidden slides. If you are wondering how you will keep track of your slides during delivery, you can read *Chapter 12, Using Presenter View*. This feature will help you keep track of your delivery without having slide numbers.

This method is easy to reproduce and easy to handle for anyone that might have to work on the file. However, if you are the only one using the file and are now more familiar with the various masters, you could try the next hack.

Hacking the Notes Master to produce presenter and audience notes

When you are in the **Notes Master** view, the **Slide Image** placeholder is automatically populated from your slides, and the **Body** placeholder from the notes you add beneath your slides when you are in the **Normal** view. If you need space for your notes while you are presenting, and information for your audience when you print or create a .pdf file, you need to trick PowerPoint to do it.

We'll use the following steps to do that:

1. Open the **Notes Master** view and move the **Body** placeholder to the left or the right of the canvas, in the gray area (*Figure 4.11*), then close the **Notes Master** view:

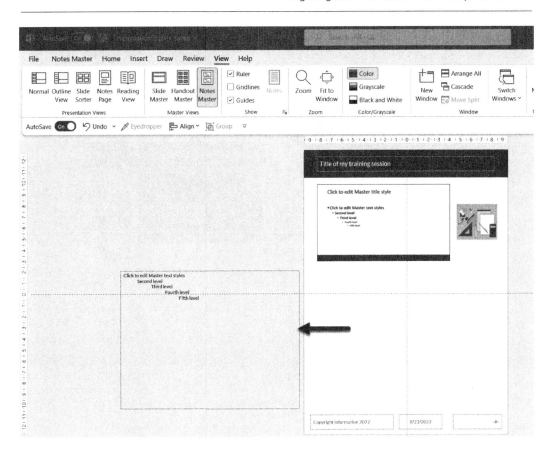

Figure 4.11 – Moving the Body placeholder outside the Notes Master

2.   You could start entering your personal notes in the **Notes** pane under your slides when in the **Normal** view, but you can simply change to the Notes Page view by going to the **View** tab and clicking on **Notes Page** in the **Presentation Views** group (*Figure 4.12*). You will see the **Body** placeholder from Notes Master with either your own notes or the **Click to add text** prompt, over the gray area. You now have a blank space under the slide image on the page to add your handout text. If you use a **text box**, it will resize according to the text you include in it. If you draw a shape, you can then define the exact size and position and remove the fill and outline, aligning the text in the upper-left corner of the shape. If you want to provide lines for people to take their own notes, you can add a simple one-column table with no left and right borders:

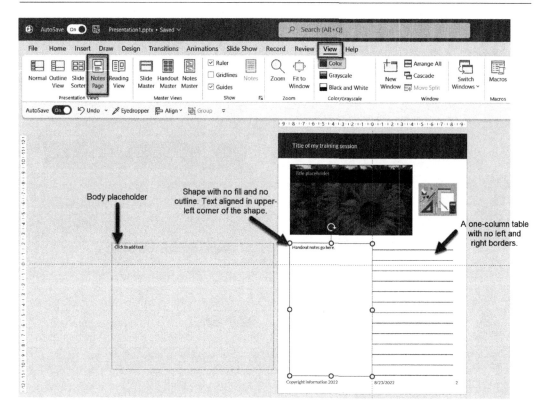

Figure 4.12 – Customizing your document in the Notes Page view

3. Of course, whatever design you create on one page in the **Notes Page** view will need to be copied and pasted on all other pages, or you can create a variety of layouts depending on the information you need to include under each slide image.

As you can see, you can easily create only one presentation file that will serve the double purpose of being a visual tool for your delivery and a complete handout for your audience. If you want to see what it will look like, *Figure 4.13* shows the **Notes Page** view, **Presenter View** in the slideshow, and **Print Preview** of a slide that has been adapted to various uses:

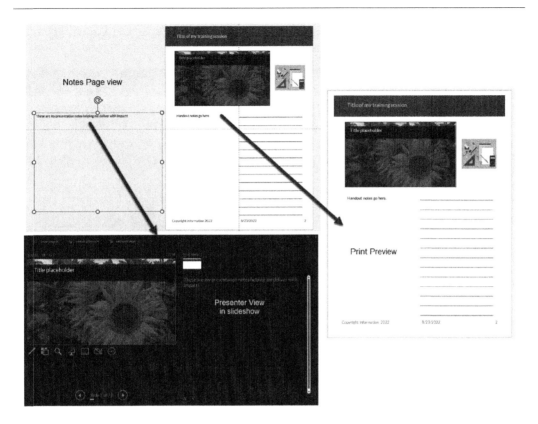

Figure 4.13 – Notes Master hack results

If you are wondering what **Presenter View** is and how to use it, it will be covered in *Chapter 12, Using Presenter View*.

Using the handout and note masters helps you create accessible documents, but there is also a feature in PowerPoint that helps you verify accessibility problems for your slides, which we will briefly cover in the next section.

Making your presentations accessible

Making documents and presentations more accessible is making sure users with a disability can access your content with the various devices they can use, such as **screen readers**. Whether your country has laws or official guidelines or not, there is no reason to shy away from making your documents and presentations accessible because Microsoft has included a great feature to help you do it: **Accessibility Checker**. This feature was made available as far back as **Office 2010**, although it was less user-friendly at the time. If you are using any of the more modern versions (Office 2016, Office 2019, Office 2021, or Office for M365), you will get a much nicer interface that helps you track where are the accessibility problems and how to solve them.

To display the **Accessibility** pane in your presentation, you can click on **Accessibility** in the status bar (**1**) to open the **Accessibility** pane and tab (**2**) (*Figure 4.14*):

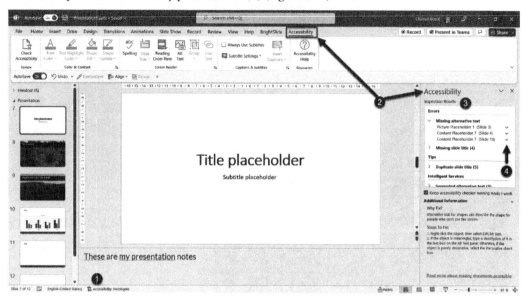

Figure 4.14 – The Accessibility pane in PowerPoint

The **Accessibility** tab gives you more tools on the ribbon, and in the **Accessibility** pane, you will have a list of results (**3**) that can be grouped into four categories:

- **Errors** and **Warnings**: When you see elements in **Errors** or **Warnings**, it means that people using screen readers won't be able to understand your content at all, or it will be very difficult to make sense. Those two categories should be inspected closely, but you don't have to guess what needs to be done. You just need to click on the small arrow to open the list for one category to see which slides need attention and click on the small arrow on the right (**4**) to get a list of recommendations and have that specific slide displayed.

- **Tips**: The **Tips** category doesn't highlight problems but suggests adjustments that will greatly improve the experience with screen readers. In *Figure 4.14*, we see that it mentions **Duplicate slide title**. It might not seem like a problem for people that can read text on your slides, but imagine having to listen to a screen reader repeating the same slide title over and over with different content read out loud every time. It could become very confusing! That's why the Accessibility Checker lets you know about those instances too.

- **Intelligent Services**: In the case of **Intelligent Services**, they are a series of various features powered by **Artificial Intelligence** (**AI**). You need a Microsoft 365 subscription to make them available and be connected to the internet. To check for that option, you need to go to **File** | **Options** | **General** | **Privacy Settings**. There is a **Turn on optional connected experiences** checkbox in the new window that opens. You can also follow the various links provided by Microsoft for additional information. In terms of accessibility, they can help you add alternative text for images and visual elements. Always review any suggested alternative text because AI is not always perfect. I also suggest you have a look at the Microsoft article on how to write effective alternative text in the *Further reading* section.

- **Additional Information**: Finally, in the **Additional Information** section at the bottom of the **Accessibility** pane, you will always get details on why you should fix the element you selected and how it can be done. The **Read more about making documents accessible** link at the bottom will open the **Help** pane, giving you valuable information on how to make your presentations accessible to people with disabilities. I encourage you to explore those resources since our goal is only to introduce you to the **Accessibility** feature, not dedicate a full chapter to the topic. I also suggest you visit the Microsoft Support site articles shared in the *Further reading* section to learn more about accessibility features that need to be considered in various document types.

Let's move on to how you can print the documents after you have configured your masters and checked for accessibility issues.

Printing your documents

You might be wondering why I would cover how to print documents, especially since most users have been doing so for a very long time. Even though everyone knows how they can print from the **File** | **Print** options, or *Ctrl + P*, many have overlooked some nice features hidden in PowerPoint's printing options that you should know about. Those are the ones I will cover in this section.

When you are in the **Print** options view (*Figure 4.15*), you can change so much more than the number of copies and the printer properties:

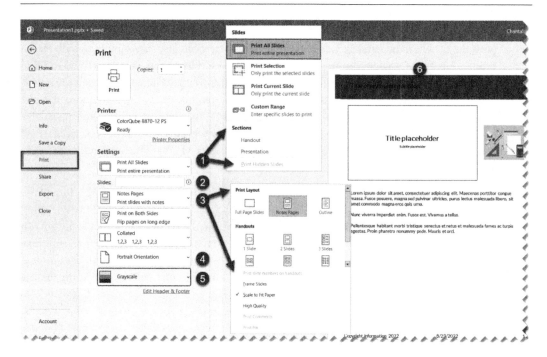

Figure 4.15 – PowerPoint's Print options view

Let's review important settings that you might have missed all those years:

1. Selecting what you need to print might be something you are aware of already, but when we look at the bottom part of that drop-down list, we have two hidden gems. The first one is the possibility to print specific **sections** in your presentation. If you have put in place the previous strategy of making a copy of all your slides in a separate section to produce your handout, you can easily print that section only with this setting. If you have decided to hide some slides but want them in a printout, the **Print Hidden Slides** command will be active so you can include them.

2. In the slide range field, remember that you can select specific slides or a slide range. For example, if you want to print slides 2, 4, and 6, you will enter 2 ; 4 ; 6 in the field. For a range of slides, such as 2 to 6, you will enter 2 - 6.

3. You can choose your printing layout, selecting between **Full Page Slides** and **Notes Pages** or selecting one of the **Handouts** layouts. Don't forget to have a look at the options at the bottom of that list for any element you want to include or setting that you want to use for your printed document.

4. Changing your document orientation between **Portrait** and **Landscape** is straightforward. However, you need to keep in mind that if you change your document orientation here, it changes the orientation of the Handout or Notes Masters too. When you have included any images or illustrations on your master, doing so will inevitably distort them in the process.

5. A word on **Grayscale**: if you are printing on a monochrome printer (black and white), you will get better results using grayscale, but it also means you should review what your text contrast looks like in the preview. When we look at **6** in *Figure 4.15*, we can see the title is hardly visible. If this is happening, follow the steps given in *Figure 4.16*.

I encourage you to explore your **Print** settings more closely to make sure you are producing the best-quality documents you can get.

Troubleshooting text contrast in grayscale

I mentioned the possibility of text color contrast problems when printing in grayscale. It can be that your titles show in a dark color on a dark background, or the text in placeholders or text boxes doesn't show well, and it can also be some shapes that have a dark border when you don't expect it. The following sections will show you how you can solve those problems.

Problems when printing handouts or notes documents

Contrast problems with text in handouts and notes documents usually come from either of the document masters because slides shown on the page are images in grayscale, not the actual slides. We'll fix this problem, as shown in this screenshot (*Figure 4.16*):

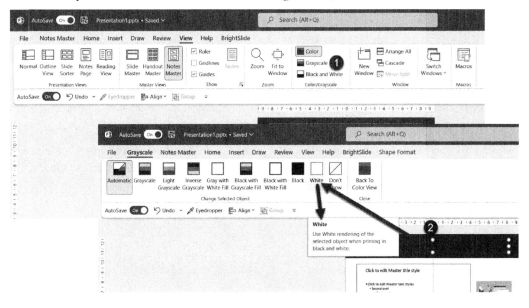

Figure 4.16 – Changing settings in Grayscale to correct a document printing contrast problem

To correct the problem, you need to go through these steps:

1. Open the document master view (**Notes Master** or **Handout Master**). Then, open the **View** tab and click on **Grayscale**.

2. The **Grayscale** tab becomes active. Select the object with poor contrast and change its color with one of the commands on the ribbon. In our example, **White** gave me the best results. As you can see in the tooltip, it is only a setting adjusting colors when printing in black and white. Click **Back to Color View** to close the **Grayscale** tab.

After closing your document master view, you can now go back to printing. All the text elements you fixed will now show the proper contrast in the print preview.

Problems when printing slides

If you need to print full-page slides, I recommend that you review the print preview for all your slides. Depending on how the content was created, you might run into text contrast problems when printing in grayscale. If you stumble on any slides that do have text contrast problems, go back to the **Normal** view, and repeat the two steps described earlier to access the **Grayscale** view. You will then be able to see objects that need color adjustments for printing purposes.

You now have a better overview of what printing options you can adjust to get the best-quality documents. However, since many people have reduced printing documents to help save trees, the next section will help you with the various PDF export settings you have available within PowerPoint.

Exporting your document as a .pdf file

Even though the PDF export feature has been available for many years within Office applications, many users still overlook some settings that might help them produce various types of PDF documents.

You first need to go to the **Backstage** view using the **File** tab. From there, you can use the **Save a Copy** (cloud file) or **Save as** function (local file), or use the **Export** function to start creating a PDF document from a PowerPoint file (*Figure 4.17*):

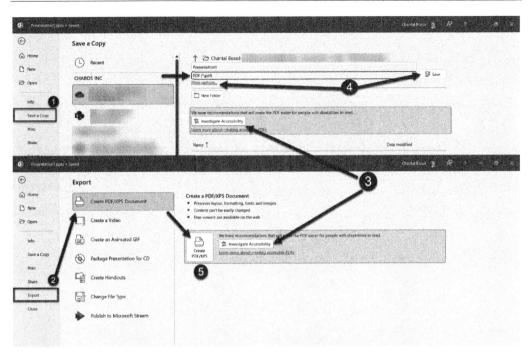

Figure 4.17 – Creating a PDF from a PowerPoint file

1. You can use the **Save a Copy** command and select **PDF** in the file type drop-down list.

2. There is also the possibility to use the **Export** command, then the **Create PDF/XPS Document** option.

3. In both cases, you might see an **Investigate Accessibility** button if any elements are missing to create an accessible PDF.

4. When you click on the **Save** button while in the **Save a Copy** section, it automatically creates the .pdf file in the same folder as your PowerPoint file if you have not changed the destination. That may seem like a quick and efficient way to do it, but it will automatically create a document with full-page slides. To be able to change the document format, you need to click on the **More options...** link below the file format.

5. Clicking on the **Create PDF/XPS** button when in the **Export** section will give you much more flexibility with one click of the mouse.

After going through the previous steps, you will get the **Publish as PDF or XPS** window, which will give you access to extra publishing options with the **Options** button (*Figure 4.18*):

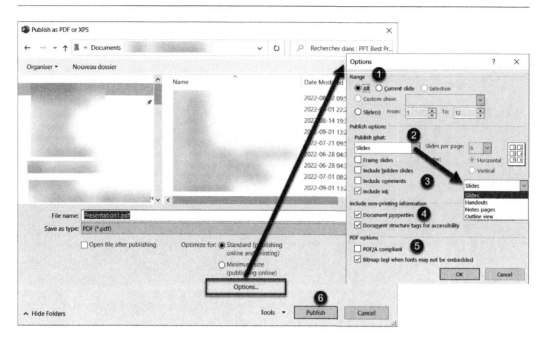

Figure 4.18 – PDF publishing options

Let's go through the list of options you might want to adapt to your needs:

1. In the **Range** section, you can decide which slides you want to have in your .pdf file. If you created any **custom shows** in your file, you could also select one to create a specific .pdf file.

2. The first element you can configure in **Publish options** is whether you want to create a .pdf file of your **Slides**, **Handouts**, or **Notes pages**. When choosing **Handouts**, the grayed-out options will become active, allowing you to choose the number of slides per page and the order in which they will be printed.

3. The following four checkboxes give you the option to print some specific elements, such as any hidden slides, comments, or ink notes you added.

4. The **Include non-printing information** section usually has the options selected by default. You should leave it as is to ensure people can track how the .pdf file was created in the properties and make your document accessible to screen readers with the structure tags.

5. In the **PDF options** section, the first option should be added to make sure your .pdf file will remain readable in the future, whatever the application used or its version. The second option is selected by default to make sure any fonts you have used will display properly even when they can't be embedded.

6. When you have verified all the options, the only thing left to do is click on the **Publish** button.

You now have a better understanding of how to create better documents from your presentation file and make your content more accessible. In *Chapter 5*, *Using Artificial Intelligence to Improve Your Visuals*, we will dive into the great features powered by AI that will help you create great visuals for more impactful presentations.

Summary

In this chapter, we discussed PowerPoint's document masters to help you create handouts and notes from your main presentation file, and how to print them and create PDF documents. You now have enough knowledge to be able to leverage those masters so you can create professional-looking documents and visual slides for your delivery.

I will repeat myself from the previous chapter on the Slide Master: even if you have the feeling it will take you too much time, I can guarantee you that it is all worth it. Taking some time to format your document masters properly will save you time in the long run. Having everything you need in one properly formatted file will also save you the headache of having to manage various separate files.

In the next chapter, you will be learning about great design features that leverage AI to speed the presentation creation process with design ideas. When it comes to creating image layouts, visual lists, and timelines, or creating presentations without a template and bringing perspective to your data, you will see how the designer can become your new best friend.

Further reading

- Additional information on the Accessibility Checker: `https://support.microsoft.com/en-us/office/improve-accessibility-with-the-accessibility-checker`

- Information on how to write alternative text: `https://support.microsoft.com/en-us/office/everything-you-need-to-know-to-write-effective-alt-text`

- Microsoft Intelligent Services: `https://support.microsoft.com/en-us/office/work-smarter-with-intelligent-services`

5

Using Artificial Intelligence to Improve Your Visuals

In this chapter, we'll be creating visually appealing content with a very interesting feature available in the modern version of PowerPoint (**Microsoft 365**): **artificial intelligence** (**AI**). Microsoft's development teams have made it possible for their suite of applications to comprehend what users are trying to do and suggest solutions to help speed up the process of certain tasks.

Even though there are many features leveraging AI, this chapter will focus on **PowerPoint Designer**. Basically, Designer is a feature that will analyze what you are doing and automatically suggest professional-looking design ideas.

By now, it must be clear that my goal is to empower business users that need to create visually appealing and impactful presentations in less time. Introducing you to Designer will help you reduce the time to create various presentation elements. In this chapter, we will discuss the following topics:

- Creating great image layouts with Designer
- Using Designer to create visual lists and timelines
- Using Designer ideas to start a presentation theme from scratch
- Bringing perspective to your data with Designer

Technical requirements

This chapter requires having a Microsoft 365 subscription and **optional connected experiences** turned on. Since the subscription model means the application is updated on an ongoing basis and the frequency of updates might be controlled by your IT department or whether you opted in to **Microsoft's Insider Program**, please read the requirements section of the *Microsoft Support* article mentioned in the *Further reading* section.

Creating great image layouts with Designer

For as long as I can remember, I have heard users complaining about not knowing where to start when they were tasked to create presentations. Even if I have explained a simple process to plan your content, it does not mean you will find it easy to create your visuals. That is when using the latest version of PowerPoint with the Designer feature will be an advantage.

Setting up Designer

Before we dive into the great design ideas we might get when adding images to slides, let's make sure Designer is active in your application. Being part of Microsoft's connected services that leverage AI while being connected to the internet, you might want to check some of PowerPoint's options. You need to access the **File | Options | General** options and have a look at the **Privacy Settings** (**1**) and **PowerPoint Designer** (**2**) sections (see *Figure 5.1*).

In the **PowerPoint Designer** section, there are two checkboxes (as of **Version 2209, Build 15619**) allowing you to decide whether you want design ideas to show automatically and whether you want suggestions for new presentations. If those options are grayed out, you need to click on the **Privacy Settings...** button:

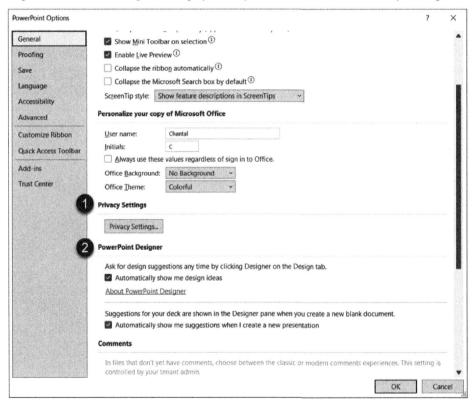

Figure 5.1 – Accessing PowerPoint options

In the new **Privacy Settings** window that opens, you should find a **Turn on optional connected experiences** checkbox (*Figure 5.2*). If it is not available, you will need to check with your IT department. You can follow any links provided in that window to learn more about those settings.

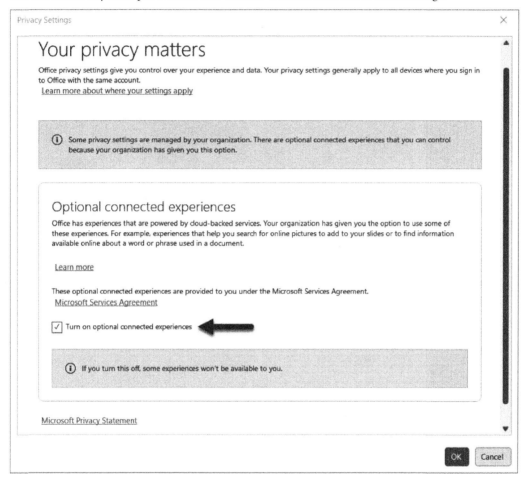

Figure 5.2 – Turning on optional connected experiences

Using Designer with images

Let's start adding some images to a blank slide to see Designer in action. In *Figure 5.3*, I added an image from **Microsoft's Stock Images** library and the **Designer** pane (**1**) opened automatically with design ideas for one image on a title slide. Scrolling to the bottom of the list allows access to the **See more Design Ideas** button (**2**), giving you more layouts to choose from. To apply a design to your slide, you simply need to click on the layout of your choice (**3**):

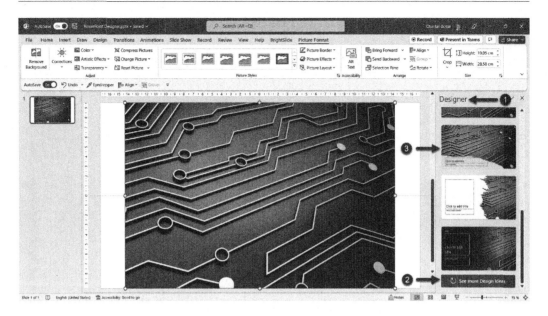

Figure 5.3 – Designer offering design ideas for one image on a title slide

> **Tip**
> If the **Designer** pane did not open, you can use the **Designer** button that can be found on the
> far right of either the **Home** tab or the **Design** tab.

When you add a second image to a slide, Designer will give you new layout ideas you can apply,
always taking the applied slide layout into consideration. In *Figure 5.4*, a second image was added to
the **Title Slide**. As you can see, the new layouts use the two images in various ways, always keeping
the Title and Subtitle placeholders:

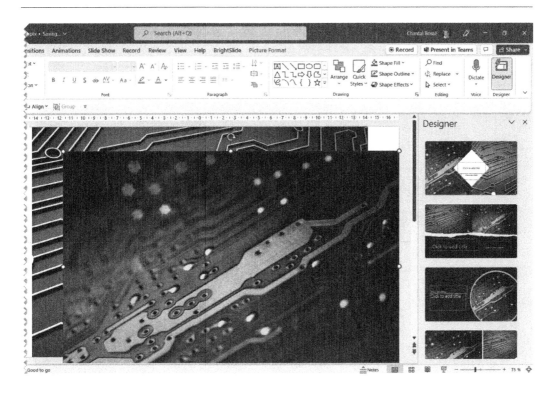

Figure 5.4 – Adding two images generates new image layouts

If you decide to change the layout of a slide when it already has images on it, Designer will simply adapt ideas to the new layout. In the following example, the **Title Slide** layout was modified to **Title and Content** (**1**), and the design ideas were automatically adjusted (**2**) (*Figure 5.5*):

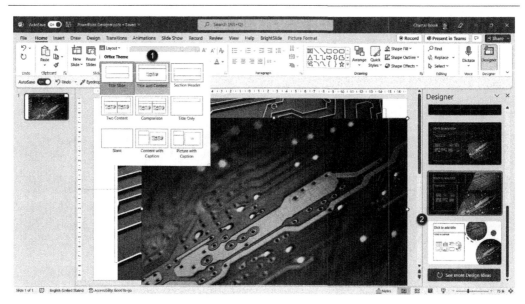

Figure 5.5 – Changing the slide layout generates new design ideas

At the time this book is being written, it is possible to add up to 6 to 10 images on a slide and obtain very interesting layouts from Designer. The maximum number of images on a slide depends on their size (*Figure 5.6*):

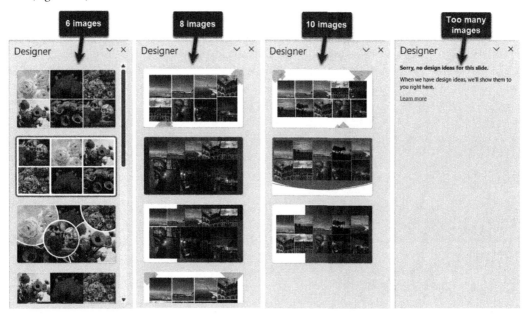

Figure 5.6 – Number of images Designer can handle on slides

Having Designer handle your image layouts means they are cropped automatically. If you are not satisfied with some cropping results, there is a way to make adjustments yourself. In the following example (*Figure 5.7*), a Designer layout was chosen for six images. If I wanted to adjust how the first image is cropped, I'd need to select it, open the **Picture Format** tab (**1**), and click on the **Crop** button (**2**). The mouse cursor becomes a four-way arrow when placed over the image, allowing you to move it to put focus on some gray areas hidden by the automatic crop (**3**). When you are happy with the new crop, just click anywhere outside the image or on the **Crop** button:

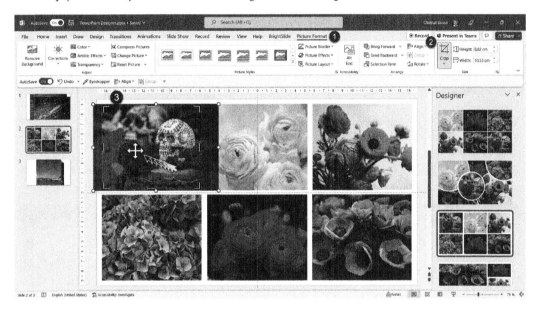

Figure 5.7 – Changing the crop of an image

I must say the AI behind Designer keeps improving as months go by. Not only does it support more images on a slide, but it can also pick up dominant colors to help design layouts adapted to the overall color scheme and is even able to recognize a human face on an image to avoid cropping it in an awkward way. If you must use a corporate template, Designer will even supply layouts that are aligned with your template settings.

With Designer, you can now create great-looking image layouts in just a few clicks. If you are using Microsoft's Stock Images, any graphic element or videos supplied in the library can be used. In *Chapter 6, Adding and Modifying Visual Elements*, we will also see how we can customize elements from the Stock Images library. In the next section, we will see how Designer can read words on your slide and provide visual design ideas.

Using Designer to create visual lists and timelines

Many times, I have heard clients tell me they just did not have time to search visuals, so they simply added text or keywords to their slides. But now, every Microsoft 365 user can get help from Designer being able to search your words to match them with relevant images. There is no more excuse to have only text on your slides! Let's see a few examples of how well Designer can translate your words into visual elements.

Design ideas from a list

Creating a list of bullet points is something we have been doing for a very long time in PowerPoint. For this example and the following ones, I will also show you how Designer keeps the design ideas on brand by using slides that have a simple colored rectangle at the bottom in its template.

In *Figure 5.8*, we have a **Title and Content** layout with a list of three short sentences (**1**): **Update your software**, **Update your system**, and **Restart your computer**. Depending on your settings, the **Designer** pane (**2**) might open automatically but if it does not, you can click on the **Designer** button (**3**) on the far right of the ribbon in the **Home** tab to open the pane. Depending on your Microsoft 365 version, if you don't see it there, you can instead go to the **Design** tab (**4**), also at the far right of the ribbon:

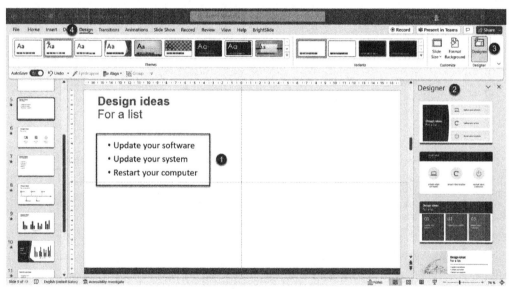

Figure 5.8 – Design ideas for a list of bulleted text

As you can see, the list of design ideas not only provides visually appealing slides but also provides icons or images that go well with the topic. If I choose the first one to keep the bottom graphic from my template (*Figure 5.9*), we can see icons that are relevant to the short sentences. I can also confirm that the colors chosen for the icons are chosen from the color palette of my template. The only thing

I would change from this design idea is the color of the third icon (**1**) because the contrast might be problematic when viewing on some devices or screens. That type of adjustment will be discussed in the last section of *Chapter 6, Adding and Modifying Visual Elements*.

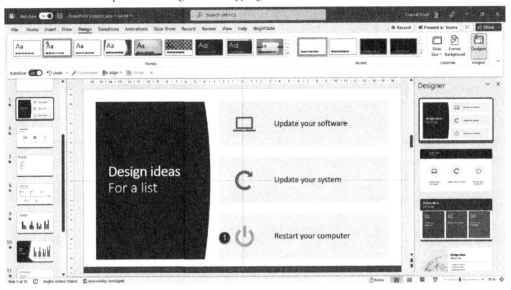

Figure 5.9 – Design idea with icons applied to a slide

If you are provided with a layout you like but an icon does not fit with your view of the topic, it can easily be changed (*Figure 5.10*). You simply need to right-click on the icon (**1**) and use the **Change icon** feature (**2**). You can then select another icon in the short list the system provides, or you can click on the **See all icons…** link (**3**) to access the whole library:

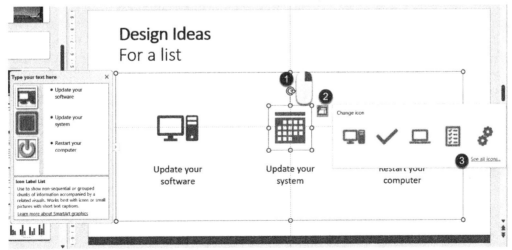

Figure 5.10 – Changing an icon provided in a design idea layout

> **Tip**
>
> Many times, Designer will automatically create a new **SmartArt** type that you will not necessarily see in the standard layouts you can choose from. If you are provided with one that you like, make sure to keep a resource file with a copy of the slide so you can easily reuse it in the future.

Here is one last example of how Designer will help improve the quality of your presentations. A while back, I started a slide with a title, a simple list of animals, and a task to care for them (*Figure 5.11*). The Designer feature provided design ideas with animal icons and text for the task below them. The only thing I had to do was change the last icon to a bird instead of *scissors*. That was a quick redesign.

Figure 5.11 – Design idea supplied according to the meaning of the text

Let's move on to design ideas that create a timeline.

Design ideas from dates

The Designer feature can also help you with the creation of project timelines. Starting with a list of dates, you will be provided with design ideas. In *Figure 5.12*, you can see examples of layouts I was provided with after entering a list of dates. I have found that the list of design ideas might look very different over time. The layout on the left (**1**) is the result of using Designer a long time ago when timeline creation started being supported. And the layout on the right (**2**) is one created while writing this book; most layouts provided had icons instead of a timeline:

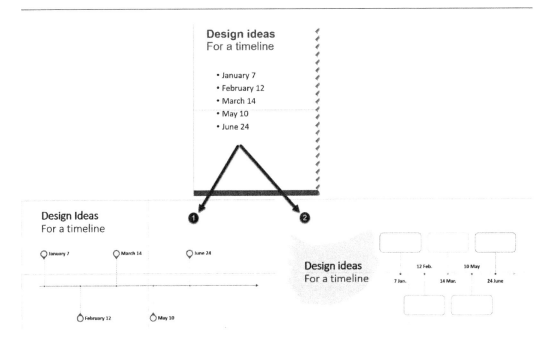

Figure 5.12 – Design ideas for timelines

If you are in a situation where you must comply with a rigid corporate template, I would not advise using the second layout. In other situations, I would definitely consider it, as it creates a visual difference that helps keep your audience engaged. If you ever choose a different design for one of your slides, be consistent and use it every time you have to display similar content. In this example, if I had to display more than one timeline in the same presentation, I would use the same layout for every timeline.

Because AI is learning daily when users try Designer, and the development teams at Microsoft keep improving the engine, we will keep being surprised by how efficient the feature will be in our presentation creation process.

In this section, we have seen how the Designer feature can provide ideas aligned with the template in use. But what if you don't have a template? Or you are creating a special one-time-deal presentation and don't have a template for it? That is the topic of the next section, where we will see how Designer can help you create a theme for your presentation.

Using Designer ideas to start a presentation theme from scratch

You have been asked to present on a special topic and have no template for it. And of course, people come to you when deadlines are short. No worries, you can speed up the creation process by starting with a blank presentation and letting Designer provide you with a template. I can already see people rolling their eyes at this one, especially in big corporations where they have teams to create corporate templates, or budgets to hire a design agency to do it. But for small organizations with no team and no budget, Designer theme ideas can be a lifesaver.

These are the steps for using Designer ideas for your presentation theme:

1. The way it works is quite simple. Start with a blank presentation and inspire yourself with the design ideas in the **Designer** pane (**1**) (*Figure 5.13*). You will get designed title slides that provide quality images, short videos, or animated content displayed on various layouts and using a variety of font pairs and color palettes. If you are not provided with any design ideas, go back to the first section in this chapter so you can adjust your PowerPoint options.

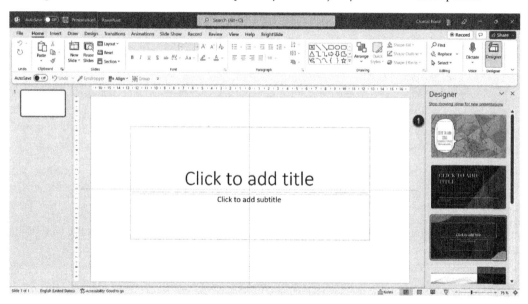

Figure 5.13 – Design ideas provided for a new, blank presentation

2. When you apply one of the designs and start adding slides, you will realize that layouts are also formatted and ready to use (*Figure 5.14*). And if you have read through *Chapter 3, Leveraging PowerPoint's Slide Master for Design*, you know how the Slide Master works and you can adapt the layouts, colors, and fonts if you want. The **Designer** pane will keep providing you with design ideas throughout your presentation if you want, and they will be aligned with the theme you have chosen.

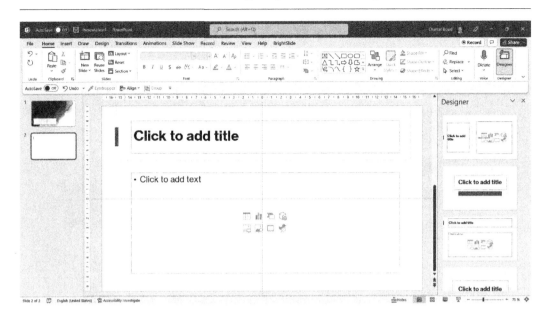

Figure 5.14 – Applying a Designer idea also gives formatted theme layouts

3. If you enter a title on your slide, Designer will not just supply random themes but also try to be relevant to your topic. As an example, I have entered the title Create impactful presentations (*Figure 5.15*) and I am provided with a list of design ideas:

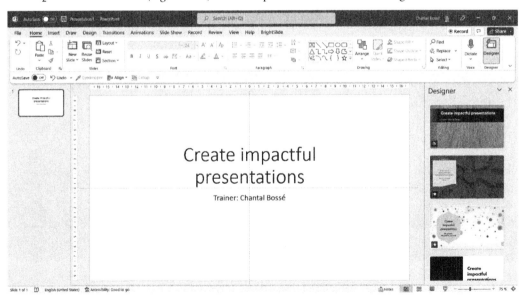

Figure 5.15 – Designer theme ideas from a title

4.   Make sure to scroll down the list and even use the button at the bottom to see more design ideas. When you see a theme you like, just apply it and start adding new slides and your content (*Figure 5.16*):

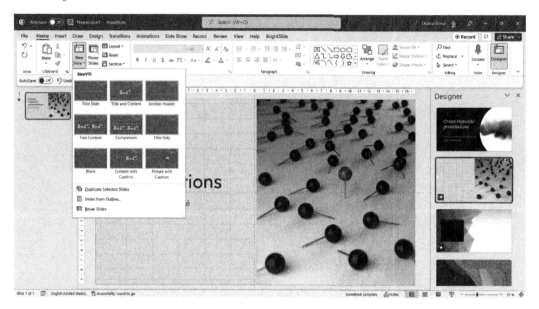

Figure 5.16 – Creating your presentation from a Designer theme idea

As you can see, it can be easy to start a new presentation theme with the help of Designer ideas. Just make sure you keep a critical eye for color contrast and font readability and adapt the provided layouts to your own needs.

In the next section, we'll see how the Microsoft Perspectives Engine can help you bring perspective to large numbers you might use on your slides.

Bringing perspective to your data with Designer

The human brain has a hard time figuring out what large numbers really mean. For example, the size of my country, Canada, is 9,985 million km^2 or 3,855 million square miles. That sure sounds big, but we could make it more relevant by comparing it to something else that might help make it more relatable. If I am presenting to a European audience, I could compare it to the size of France and add that Canada is 149 times the size of France. Finding relatable comparisons for large numbers can be time-consuming but we can again turn to Designer to help us, thanks to **Microsoft Research's Perspectives Engine**.

To see how it works, let's start with a simple example where I have added a title placeholder, Commercial planes fly at 30,000 feet (*Figure 5.17*). The Designer feature supplied a list of design ideas, and I applied the first one (**1**). First of all, it was great to have a nice-quality image supplied just because the word *planes* was recognized. But there is also a very subtle addition under the words *30,000 feet* (**2**) – a fine dotted line:

Figure 5.17 – Designer supplying layouts with images relevant to the word "planes"

We are familiar with underlined words for spell-checking, so the Perspectives Engine was made available in a similar way. When you right-click the underlined words (**1**) (*Figure 5.18*), the contextual window has a **Perspectives** category at the top (**2**). When you click on it, you get another window labeled **Consider a different perspective** (**3**) that lists ways to bring meaning to your large number. In our example, the list has comparison elements with a distance in another measuring unit, another with height, and the third one with a cruising speed:

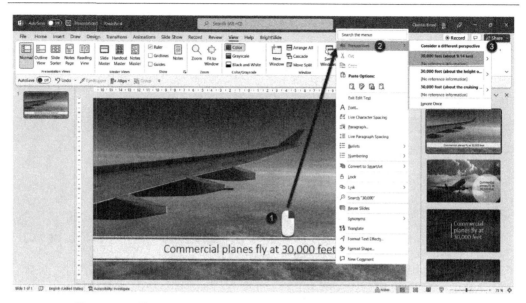

Figure 5.18 – The Perspectives Engine supplying a list of comparison elements

I chose the second item in the list, and it added the text information in my placeholder, now telling my audience that it is about the height of Mount Everest (*Figure 5.19*):

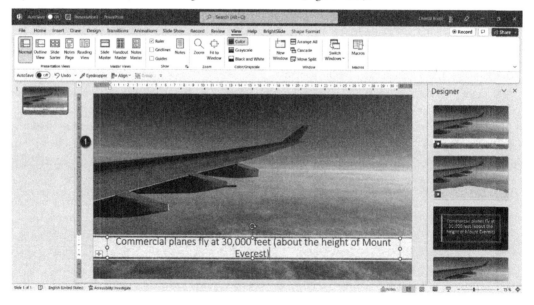

Figure 5.19 – Giving perspective to a large number with the help of Designer

Leveraging the Perspectives Engine might not be something you need a lot. But every time you must use large numbers on your slides, you should consider peeking at the list to see whether any of the suggestions make sense for your topic. In the upcoming months and years, we might be surprised by how valuable this feature becomes. You can read a Microsoft article on the Perspectives Engine in the *Further reading* section.

Summary

In this chapter, we discussed PowerPoint's Designer features, which can help you create more visually impactful slides quickly. You can now leverage the feature to create great layouts for slides that include many images, change bulleted lists to something more visually appealing, start a new presentation and leverage Designer theme ideas, and bring perspective to your large numbers.

Unless you don't already have a Microsoft 365 subscription, there is no reason to create boring slides with text only, or blank PowerPoint presentations with no design, because you feel like you are not creative, or are design-challenged. But I do need to warn you of one thing: if you skip all the planning steps and just add content that lacks structure, using any of Designer's design ideas will just make your slides look good, and not necessarily help have a clear message or make your presentation more impactful.

In the next chapter, we will be discussing how you can add and modify various visual elements in your presentations such as maps, SmartArt, and Microsoft's Stock Images library. You will also learn how to create new shapes with some tools available within the application.

Further reading

- Microsoft Designer support article (see the *Requirements* section): `https://support.microsoft.com/en-us/office/create-professional-slide-layouts-with-designer-53c77d7b-dc40-45c2-b684-81415eac0617`

- Microsoft article for Perspectives Engine: `https://www.microsoft.com/en-us/research/project/perspectives-engine/`

6

Adding and Modifying Visual Elements

Even if we discussed how AI can help us improve our presentations with more visual content, we need to constantly think about how we can make our content more visual. And PowerPoint has many features that can help you create more engaging presentations right from its interface.

If you have read through *Chapter 1, Analyzing Your Audience and Presentation Delivery Needs*, you probably remember I mentioned how important it was to start thinking about images or visuals that came to mind while planning content for your slides. Now is the time to start using some PowerPoint features to transform sentences and bullet points into relevant visuals that will grab people's attention and be remembered by your audience.

My goal is to help you discover some lesser-known tools, so I will not focus on adding simple shapes or inserting **stock images** without customizing them. In this chapter, we will discuss the following topics:

- Inserting and modifying a map
- Converting bullet points into SmartArt
- Creating new shapes with **Edit Points**
- Creating new shapes with the merging tools
- Using and customizing stock images and other graphics

Technical requirements

Most topics discussed in this chapter don't require having a **Microsoft 365 (M365) subscription**, the tools and features having been introduced in previous versions of PowerPoint. I will identify when a feature is in M365 only. Also, be aware that since the subscription version of PowerPoint is being updated on an ongoing basis, it is possible that some features will not look exactly the same in your version of the application.

Inserting and modifying a map

When I say you need to start thinking visually when creating presentations, it means to stop being on autopilot when creating your content. Any content you need to deliver needs to be examined to seek visual ways to create it. Let's look at an example of content that can be greatly improved with one of PowerPoint's features (**Office 365 (O365)** only): inserting a map. For the slide example in *Figure 6.1*, I created a table with data showing four Canadian provinces that should have more than 6 million people by 2043:

Canadian provinces with over 6 M people by 2043

Province	Millions of people
Ontario	18.265
Quebec	9.472
British Columbia	6.224
Alberta	6.619

Figure 6.1 – Table listing four Canadian provinces with their population by 2043

It is not a bad slide per se, but it does lack visual appeal. Instead, we can leverage PowerPoint's map feature so that we can make each province visible within Canada, as in *Figure 6.2*:

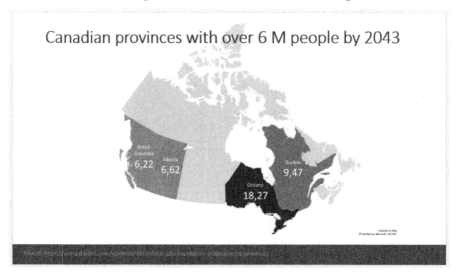

Figure 6.2 – Population information shown in a map of Canada

As you can see, it adds interest to the data by showing where the highest populations will be in the country by the year 2043, and we can even use varying shades to make it easy to see which province will have the biggest population. So, instead of simply listing data, you can use a visual that will help tell the story you want to put forward.

Since you cannot directly convert a table into a chart in PowerPoint, let's move on to the steps you need to go through to create your own map:

- Select the data in your table and copy it (*Ctrl + C*).

- Insert a new slide with the **Title and Content** layout and click on the **Chart** icon in the content placeholder (**1**). Then, select **Map** (**2**) in the **Insert Chart** window and click **OK** (**3**). See *Figure 6.3*:

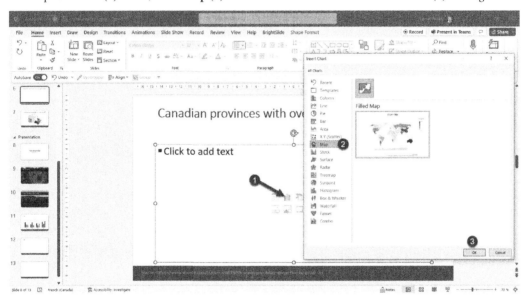

Figure 6.3 – Adding a chart from the content placeholder on a slide

- The placeholder will now include a world map (**1**) and an Excel window should appear, showing you a list of countries and data; select the data and delete it (**2**). If you don't see the Excel data, click on the **Edit Data** button in the ribbon (**3**). You can now paste your data in the first cell (*Ctrl + V*) (**4**) and click on the **Paste Options** icon (**5**) to make sure the data uses the destination formatting. This will remove the table formatting (*Figure 6.4*):

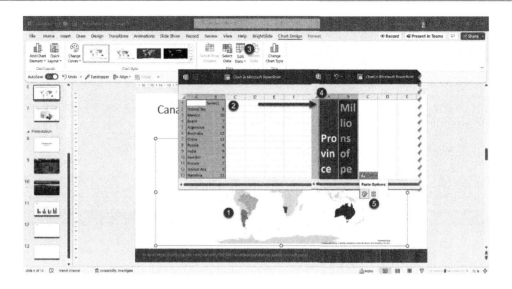

Figure 6.4 – Changing the default data for an inserted map

- You can now close the Excel data window and start working on formatting your new map. Ideally, we should remove at least the **Chart Title** (**1**) option since the title for the slide already gives enough information. To do so, you must click on the plus (**+**) sign on the right of the chart (**2**) and uncheck **Chart Title**. In my example, I also unchecked **Legend** since I wanted to show the name of the provinces on the map. If you are not satisfied with the colors of your map, you can click on the **Change Colors** button in the ribbon (**3**) to make the changes (*Figure 6.5*):

Figure 6.5 – Removing the chart title and legend for a map

- An easy way to quickly format all the information you want to show on your map is by opening the formatting pane. To do so, you need to change to the **Format** tab (**1**) and click on the **Dialog launcher** icon in the ribbon (**2**) to display the formatting pane. You can then use the **Chart Options** dropdown (**3**) to select the area of the chart you need to format (*Figure 6.6*):

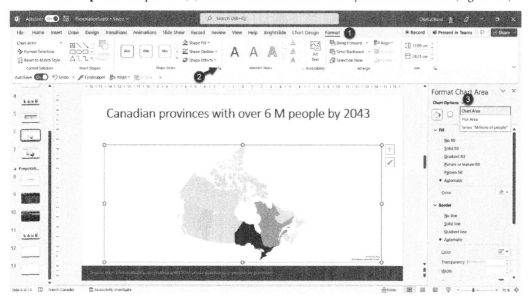

Figure 6.6 – Opening the formatting pane to quickly format chart areas

- When selecting **Series Options** from the **Chart Options** list, the formatting pane displays icons for three types of options you can customize: **Fill & Line** (**1**), **Effects** (**2**), and **Series Options** (**3**). Select **Series Options** to make any desired adjustments (*Figure 6.7*):

  - **Map projection** (**4**): This allows you to change the view of the map according to the various existing map projection styles. Using **Automatic** will probably fit most uses. Research the various styles if you have specific needs.

  - **Map area** (**5**): This allows you to select areas of the map you want to display. Test the options in the drop-down list to see what fits the message you want to convey the most. Also, always keep in mind which representation will make the most sense to your audience.

  - **Map labels** (**6**): This allows you to select displayed labels. In my example, I used **Show all** so that the name of the provinces would display on the map, helping whoever in an audience might not be familiar with the Canadian provinces. There is one caveat with this option, though: you won't be able to edit the size of the map labels. We will see another option later in this section.

  - **Series Color** (**7**): This allows you to choose between a two- or three-color gradient. In my example, I chose **Diverging (3-color)**, which allowed me to select a color for each of the data points:

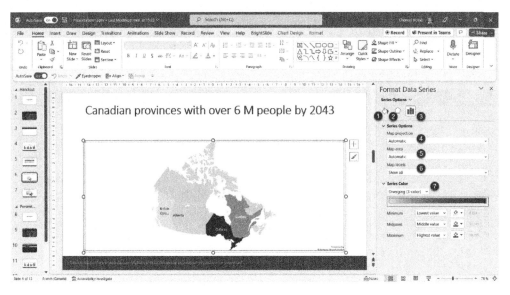

Figure 6.7 – Using the Series Options pane to adjust a map

- Now that we have our map customized with our colors and province labels, it is time to add the data. To do so, when the map is selected on the slide, click on the **Chart Design** contextual tab on the ribbon (**1**) so that you can access the **Add Chart Element** button (**2**). Next, choose **Data Labels** (**3**), then **Show** (**4**). Finally, click on **More Data Label Options…** (**5**) so that the **Format Data Labels** pane is ready for the next step (*Figure 6.8*). We now see the data displayed below the names of the provinces:

Figure 6.8 – Adding data labels on a map

Two things you might want to consider at this point are formatting the numbers to reduce the number of decimals and increasing the size of the map. This is what we accomplish in *Figure 6.9*:

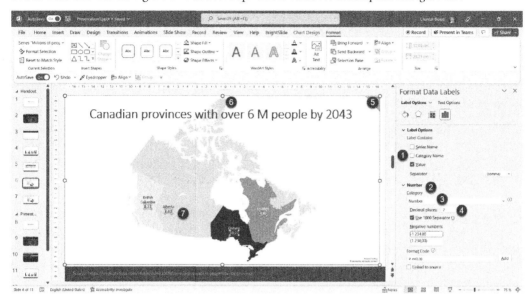

Figure 6.9 – Formatting data labels and increasing the size of a map

- If you want to add a **Category Name** (**1**) value to your labels so that you can format the font size and color, you need to check this checkbox. Keep in mind that you will probably have problems displaying the category and the data if the textbox is too small. If that is the case, don't add names and values with the chart options. Just use regular textboxes that you can easily modify or animate if needed.

- Open the **Number** category (**2**) so that you can change it to **Number** (**3**) and reduce the number of decimals to 2 (**4**). This will improve the readability of your data in your presentation. But we do need to make other changes to make it more readable, so continue reading!

- Increase the size of the map by selecting and dragging one of the corner handles (**5**) and make it as big as the slide can take. In my example, part of the Northern Territories was overlapping the title, so I used the **Send Backward | Send to Back** options (**6**) in the **Format** tab to make sure the title was still easily readable.

- We now must take care of the font size for the labels. Since we have worked on the label options, your data elements should be selected on your map (**7**). You can simply go back to the **Home** tab and change the font size; space allowing, I would suggest you use at least **24 points** to make the data easier to read.

> **Warning**
>
> When you change the font size of data labels in a chart, PowerPoint will unfortunately change the color to a default gray. To bypass this problem, you need to select the specific data for which this color causes contrast problems and choose another color.

As you can see, PowerPoint offers a nice way to put data related to regions or countries in context. If you are using an older, unconnected version of PowerPoint than the M365 subscription model, you will need to seek other alternatives for maps.

In the next section, we discuss another way to make your content more visual by converting your bullet points into SmartArt.

Converting bullet points into SmartArt

I am among the users that feel that the **SmartArt** feature would benefit from an upgrade. After all, it was introduced when Microsoft replaced the menus with the **Ribbon** in **Office 2007** and has not been worked on much since then. But I also feel anyone creating presentations should not have to work hard to produce their content, which is why using SmartArt can be a good starting point to reduce the number of bullet points you use.

Of course, if you are using the subscription model of PowerPoint with M365, you can leverage the **Designer** feature, as discussed in *Chapter 5, Using Artificial Intelligence to Improve Your Visuals*. But even so, there are times when design ideas might not fit with what you have in mind for your visuals. That is when using the **Convert to SmartArt Graphic** function might be helpful:

- When you are on a slide with bullet points, first select the content placeholder. Then, in the **Home** tab, in the **Paragraph** group, look for the **Convert to SmartArt Graphic** icon (**1**) (*Figure 6.10*). You can then select from the shortlist in the dropdown, which offers a live preview of your converted bulleted list, or click on **More SmartArt Graphics...** (**2**) to browse a complete list you can choose from:

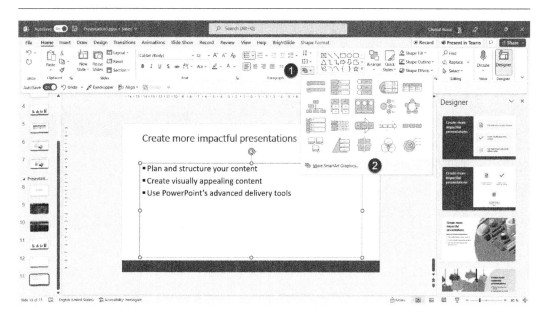

Figure 6.10 – Using the Convert to SmartArt Graphic function

- In the **Choose a SmartArt Graphic** window (*Figure 6.11*), you can browse a list of all the SmartArt layouts or browse by category. Don't just think about how the visual will look but also whether any of the layouts will make more sense to convey your message. In my example, I used a slide titled **Create more impactful presentations** and a bulleted list that I felt should be seen as a process. So, I can decide to use any of the **Process** category layouts to help make my list more visually appealing and click **OK** to apply it to my content:

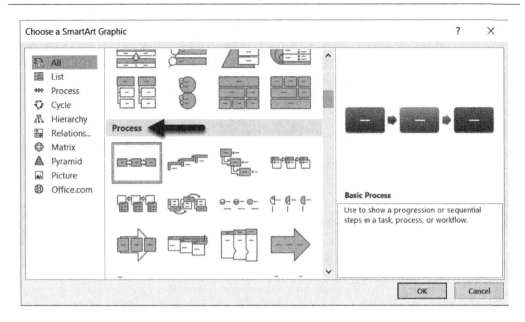

Figure 6.11 – Choosing a SmartArt layout

- Once a SmartArt layout has been applied, you get two new tabs to customize how it looks. In the **SmartArt Design** tab, you get access to many tools to help you create an overall look and include text in your shapes (*Figure 6.12*):

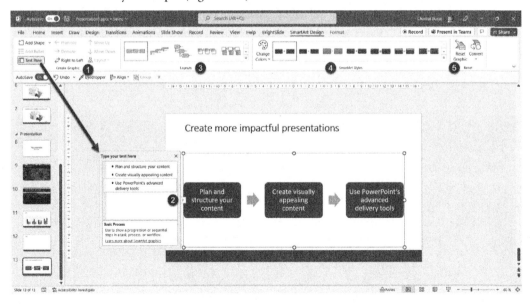

Figure 6.12 – Tools from the SmartArt Design tab

- In the **Create Graphic** group (**1**), you will find tools to help you add or remove shapes in your layout or promote or demote them to create subcategories. The active tools will depend on the layout you have chosen. And even though you can make the **Text Pane** box visible using the button in that group, it can also be opened from the small arrow on the left of the SmartArt layout (**2**). The **Text Pane** box can be used to enter new text and create new shapes at the same time, or you can edit the text in shapes. If you are using a hierarchy SmartArt, you can also promote and demote elements, meaning you are increasing or decreasing the level of the selected bullet or shape by using *Tab*, or *Shift + Tab* on your keyboard.

- The **Layouts** group (**3**) gives access to a gallery of layouts that have a live preview when hovering over any of them and gives you access to a whole list of layouts if you want to change the one you chose.

- Use the functions in the **SmartArt Styles** group (**4**) if you want to change the color scheme or the effects applied to the shapes in your SmartArt.

- In the **Reset** group (**5**), you can easily bring back your layout to its original look when you are not satisfied with all the changes you made. Just click on the **Reset Graphic** button. As for the **Convert** button, it allows you to go back to your bullet list or convert the SmartArt into separate shapes. An example of SmartArt-to-shape conversion will be shown later in this section.

You can now change to the SmartArt **Format** tab where you will see many of the formatting tools that can also be found in the **Home** and **Shape Format** tabs:

- The **Shapes** group (**1**) has some interesting tools when you want to customize your SmartArt even more. This is where you can change the shape of part of your layout (**2**) by choosing a new shape in the **Change Shape** gallery, or decide to change the size of one or more shapes in your layout by using the **Larger** or **Smaller** tools (*Figure 6.13*):

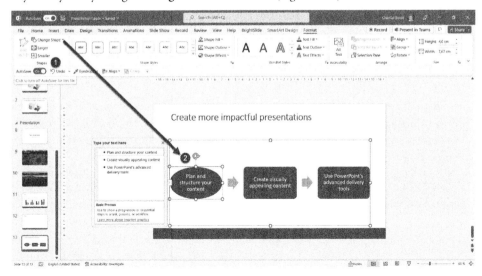

Figure 6.13 – Tools from the SmartArt Format tab

As you can see, SmartArt can be a nice way to help you reduce your design time while making your content more visual. Yes—there is still text, but having a visual layout instead of bullet points can help your audience grasp a concept or remember your content even more. I also refer you to Nolan Haims' *The Better Deck Deck* in the *Further reading* section so that you can get more inspiration on how to make your bullet points more visual, and maybe use a SmartArt graphic as a starting point afterward.

You can also use SmartArt graphics as a starting point for some of your content. Instead of creating a layout from scratch because you don't see a layout that fits your needs, I'll show you how to leverage the **Convert to Shapes** tool. The following example is from a slide I created for a conference I gave in French where I wanted to display the various challenges encountered with presentations in a structured layout of shapes (*Figure 6.14*):

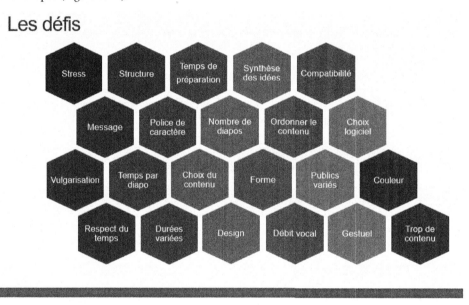

Figure 6.14 – Layout of structured hexagons

There is a SmartArt layout with hexagons, but it only allows you to add shapes vertically. But I used it anyway as a starting point to save some time. Here are the steps to recreate the layout used in my previous example, but do keep in mind that you can use any of the SmartArt layouts to do the same and save a lot of design time:

- Add the **Alternating Hexagons** SmartArt (**1**) and use the **Convert to Shapes** tool (**2**) in the **SmartArt Design** tab (**3**) (*Figure 6.15*):

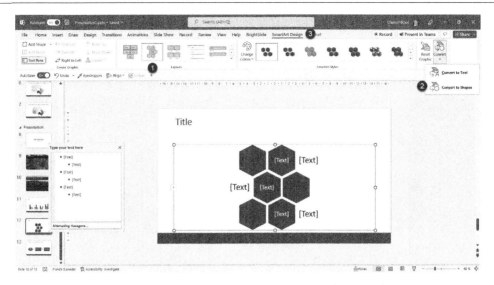

Figure 6.15 – Using the SmartArt Convert to Shapes tool

- After the conversion, we are left with one rectangle on the slide, and it needs to be ungrouped to see all the separate shapes. To do so, go to the **Shape Format** tab (**1**) and click on **Group | Ungroup** (**2**). You will now have all the separate shapes on the slide (**3**). For my needs, I deleted the empty rectangles before moving on (*Figure 6.16*):

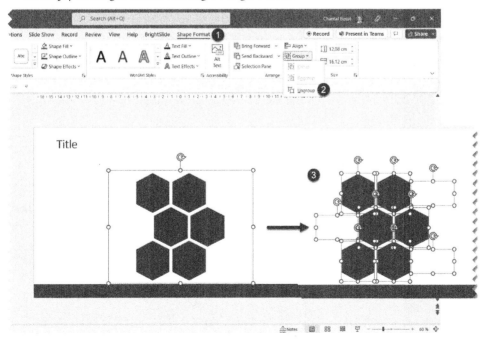

Figure 6.16 – Ungrouping shapes

- When you have all the shapes selected, you can use the *Ctrl + Shift* keys while using the left mouse button and dragging the shapes to the right (**1**). The *Ctrl* key is to duplicate, while the *Shift* key will help constrain the horizontal movement to a straight line while dragging the shapes. When you start seeing finely dotted lines (**2**), called **Smart Guides**, you will know where to stop when the guides show the same space between the two groups of shapes (*Figure 6.17*):

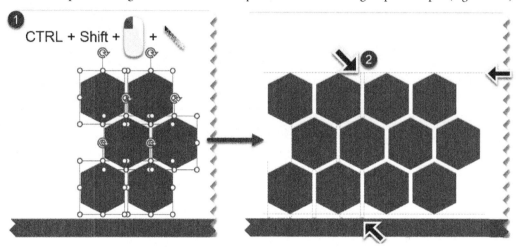

Figure 6.17 – Duplicating and aligning a group of shapes with keyboard keys and a mouse

You probably realize that I was able to save a lot of time because I did not have to create every hexagon and align them manually. So, even if I mentioned SmartArt could use a little modernization, as you can see, the layouts can still be useful as a starting point to create various visual elements.

Drawing shapes in PowerPoint has also been a way to make your content more visual for decades. But what if the default shapes are not helpful? There is a way to modify default shapes with the **Edit Points** tool, the topic of our next section.

Creating new shapes with Edit Points

There are many default shapes available in PowerPoint, but it does not mean they will always fit your needs. This is when the **Edit Points** tool can come to your rescue! Even though it has been available for over 20 years, many users are still unaware it exists. There are two ways of accessing **Edit Points**:

- The first way to access **Edit Points** is to select a shape (**1**), click on the **Shape Format** tab, and go to **Edit Shape | Edit Points** (*Figure 6.18*):

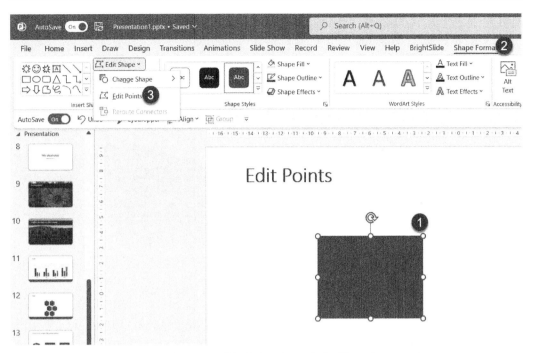

Figure 6.18 – Accessing Edit Points through the Shape Format tab

- The second way is by right-clicking on a shape and clicking on **Edit Points** (*Figure 6.19*):

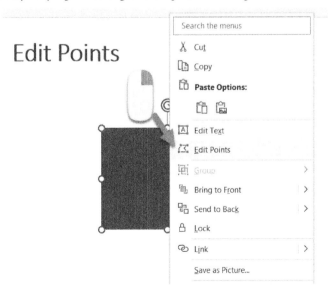

Figure 6.19 – Accessing Edit Points with a right-click on the shape

Whichever method you choose, your shape will now show black dots where two line segments meet or where a curve ends, depending on the shape you have on your slide. Those dots are called **vertexes**, and they can be dragged to change their position. The white squares are handles to help you add or change the curve of a segment. In the example I created for *Figure 6.20*, I used a rectangle and moved the vertex in the upper-right corner, and added a curve to it:

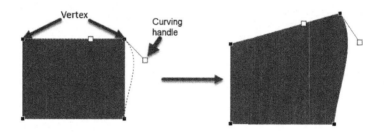

Figure 6.20 – Reshaping a rectangle with Edit Points

Repositioning vertexes and curving segments are not the only modifications you can make using **Edit Points**. If you right-click on a segment while in the **Edit Points** mode, you have access to a contextual menu that allows you to make more changes to your shape, such as adding a point or deleting a segment. Your mouse cursor's shape will change to a plus (+) sign with a rectangle, as seen in the oversized example (**1**) in *Figure 6.21*:

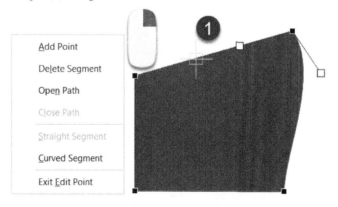

Figure 6.21 – Right-clicking the menu after clicking on a segment

Actions in the menu may be grayed out depending on the segment you clicked on, and if you right-click on a vertex point, you will get a list of actions specific to points. If you are a keyboard shortcut fan, I suggest that you have a look at the Microsoft article listed in the *Further reading* section. If you don't know about the **Freeform** shape tool, the article will also help you learn more about it.

I could continue adding static images to try and convey everything you can do with **Edit Points**, but the best way to learn more is by experimenting by yourself. If you have been following along with PowerPoint open, I suggest that you take a moment to try the basic actions I just showed you. It might give you a few ideas for your future presentations.

Edit points is not the only way to create new shapes in PowerPoint, and this is the topic of the following sections with the merging tools.

Creating new shapes with the merging tools

If you have read through the book chronologically, you might now be at a point where you have many creative ideas to make your presentations more visually appealing. At the same time, you might also be feeling stuck with the same old standard shapes list within PowerPoint, thinking you will have to reach out to a graphic designer to create what you have in mind.

Wait until you have read this section before reaching out for help! The **Merge Shapes** tool might be just what you need. I will show you how to use the tool with three specific examples that might be helpful for any business presentation.

But first, let's explore where you will find the **Merge Shapes** tool and which options are available to create new shapes. As the name implies, you need to select at least two shapes on your slide to activate the tool (*Figure 6.22*):

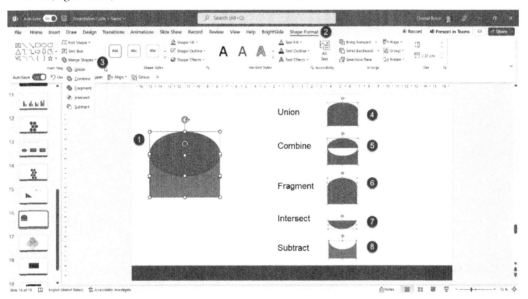

Figure 6.22 – Activating and finding the Merge Shapes tool

Select the shapes on your slide (**1**), then click on the **Shape Format** tab (**2**) to find the **Merge Shapes** tool (**3**). When you open the drop-down list, you will find the following options:

- **Union** (**4**)

- **Combine** (**5**)

- **Fragment** (**6**)

- **Intersect** (**7**)

- **Subtract** (**8**)

The results you get always depend on the order in which you selected your shapes. The **Union** shape (**4**) in *Figure 6.22* is the result of selecting the darker ellipse first, then the rectangle, and the **Subtract** shape (**8**) is the result of selecting the rectangle first, then the ellipse. When you hover over the list of options, you get a live preview of the result. If you realize the results are not what you expected, whether in terms of shape or final color, you can deselect the shapes and start selecting them in a different sequence.

Merge Shapes selection trick

Predicting the results you will get when using the **Merge Shapes** tool can be mind-boggling. But I will share with you what I think is the best analogy I have heard to help you understand the concept, from my friend Mike Parkinson at Billion Dollar Graphics. You need to think of your shapes as using dough and a cookie cutter. Decide which shape will be the dough—the first shape you will select—and which shape(s) will be the cookie cutter(s). Doing so will help you picture in your mind what will be removed or cut out.

Now that you know how to activate the tool, where to find it, and which options are available, let's move on to examples of uses in presentations.

Breaking apart a Venn diagram

Showing an intersecting relationship between various components has often been done by using a **Venn diagram**. The quickest way to create one that is perfectly aligned is using the Venn diagram layout in SmartArt. But what if you need to put emphasis on one or more intersecting parts, or even use a subtle animation to make intersections stand out in a specific sequence? We can try to draw the separate intersections by hand, but that is not the most efficient way to do it. Instead, use the **Convert to Shapes** and **Ungroup** tools on the Venn diagram SmartArt layout. If you have not read this chapter from the start, you can go back to *Figure 6.15* to review how to convert and ungroup a SmartArt layout.

In *Figure 6.23*, you can see the ungrouped Venn diagram (**1**) on the left. On the right (**2**), you can see the resulting shapes after applying the **Fragment** option of the **Merge Shapes** tool. *I did increase the spacing between the shapes to help you see they are all standalone pieces.* Now, you can apply various colors to the shapes to help you focus on specific data. You now have a much more flexible visual than simply using the original SmartArt layout without having to spend a lot of time creating it. You can use any SmartArt that has overlapping shapes to accomplish something similar:

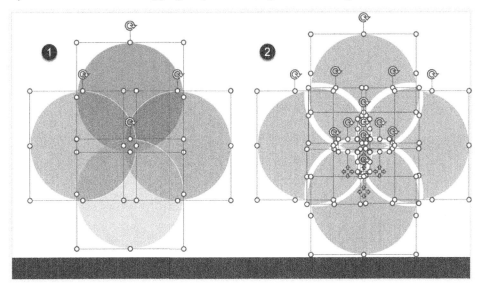

Figure 6.23 – Converting, ungrouping, and segmenting a SmartArt layout

Now, let's have a look at how you can create special text effects by using the **Merge Shapes** tool.

Creating special text

If you ever tried to create special movement effects with letters without knowing about the **Merge Shapes** tool, I'm quite sure that you had to spend a lot of time creating separate textboxes, and maybe feel stuck because some shape effects did not show on your letters.

Again, let's put the **Merge Shapes** tool to work so that you don't have to spend so much time creating beautiful effects. You can follow the steps shown in *Figure 6.24*:

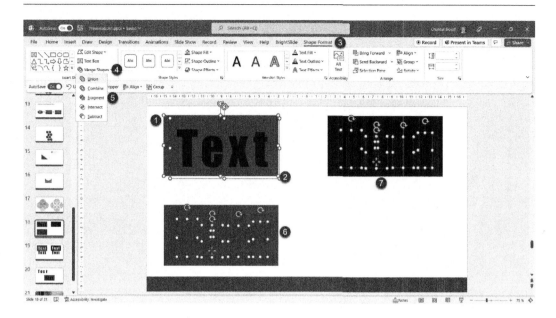

Figure 6.24 – Using Merge Shapes to create letter shapes

- Insert a shape into your slide and fill it with the color you want for your text, or any other color will do (**1**). Then, add a textbox and format the font, size, and color of the text (**2**).

- Select both shapes and go to the **Shape Format** tab (**3**), click on **Merge Shapes** (**4**), and select **Fragment** (**5**).

- If you selected your shape first and your textbox second, you will have segments of the color of the shape (**6**).

- If you selected your textbox first and the shape second, you will have segments of the color of the font in your original textbox (**7**).

In both cases, you only need to move the letter shapes away and use the shape formatting tools to create the desired effect. If you are not familiar with the shape formatting tools, you can find them in the **Shape Format** tab by clicking on the **Shape Effects** button on the ribbon. In *Figure 6.25*, you can see I applied a **Bevel** effect on the lighter text (**1**), and a **Reflection** effect on the darker text (**2**):

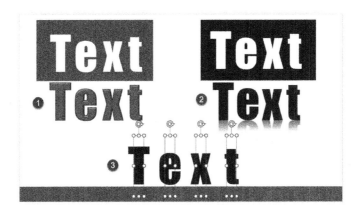

Figure 6.25 – Applying shape effects to letter segments

To help you understand the advantage of using this method, I also added separate textboxes that have the same letters, with the same font type and size (**3**). They have a reflection effect applied to them, but it does not show. You could create a few effects if you had used shapes to type in the separate letters, instead of textboxes, but it would still be less efficient than using the merging tools.

As seen in *Figure 6.25*, we have letter shapes but also a rectangle with the word cut out of it. Here is an example of how you can get creative with those rectangles. Add a full-slide image and a textbox with your text over it, use the same steps you have just learned, but make sure the first element you choose is the image so that the letters are the same color as the image. Apply a shape effect, and voilà! You now have a beautiful slide effect that took only a few minutes to create (*Figure 6.26*):

Figure 6.26 – Using the Fragment option to create text effects on images

I gave you examples of some specific effects with the **Fragment** option of the **Merge Shapes** tool so that you could easily use them in the future. But don't forget that you can create many creative shapes with the other options too. The best way to get more familiar with the tools is to try them.

In the last section of this chapter, we will discuss how we can use PowerPoint's **Stock Images** option as a starting point and how we can customize images and graphics to our needs.

Using and customizing stock images and other graphics

If you have been using PowerPoint for a long time, you might remember the **Clipart gallery**, a collection of graphic elements supplied by Microsoft in the Office suite for many years. It became out of date and most of the time was not considered professional in a business setting as design expectations evolved.

With the introduction of the M365 subscription model, Microsoft has brought back a whole new set of **stock images**, and I must say they look very good. They also add new elements to it on a regular basis. If you have an Office 2021 version, you will have access to stock images although you will not get the full selection, as this license does not get feature updates. And if you are a user of PowerPoint for the web, which connects to the site with a Microsoft account, but no M365 license, you will get a subset of stock images that do not include elements considered **Premium** content.

You might be wondering how you are allowed to use stock images and graphics. Here is the good news: as long as you have an M365 license and you use them within a Word document, an Excel workbook, a SharePoint site, or a PowerPoint presentation, whether delivered as a slideshow or exported as a .pdf file, you can use the **Stock Images** content, even for commercial use. The two things you are not allowed to do are the following:

- Copy and paste material into non-Microsoft applications (for example, websites)
- Save the creative material as an image or video file to be used elsewhere

If you want to see the Microsoft article on the topic, have a look at the link provided in the *Further reading* section.

To access **Stock Images**, you need to go to the **Insert** tab (**1**), then click on **Pictures** (**2**) and choose **Stock Images…** (**3**), or you can click on the **Stock Images** icon (**4**) in a content placeholder (*Figure 6.27*):

Figure 6.27 – Inserting stock images

You then get a new window that has seven categories of content to choose from. For each category, the creative content is sorted into various categories, and they are also searchable by keywords. Take note that the keywords need to be added in the language of your application. Let's have a look at a sample of each category (*Figure 6.28*):

Figure 6.28 – Seven categories of creative content in Stock Images

1. **Images**: These are high-quality photos.

2. **Icons**: These are modern-looking icons that are easily resized and recolored.

3. **Cutout People**: These are photos of people without backgrounds.

4. **Stickers**: These are cartoon-like like the ones on social media.

5. **Videos**: These are short video clips with varying levels of movement.

6. **Illustrations**: These are vector graphics that can easily be resized and recolored.

7. **Cartoon People**: These are cartoon representations of people with various parts.

Inserting creative content from **Stock Images** is easy, but your job is to make sure that the elements you include are aligned with your message and the overall look you want to give to your presentation.

That means you might have to customize or adapt them. We will start with the picture formatting tools you can use within PowerPoint.

Using Picture Format tools

When you insert a picture from **Stock Images**, you have access to many tools that can help you adapt it to your presentation needs. Let's start with a quick overview of all the tools before I give you a few examples (*Figure 6.29*):

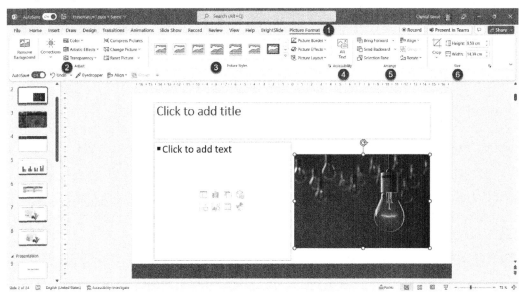

Figure 6.29 – Overview of the Picture Format tools

- When you have a picture selected, you will see the **Picture Format** tab (**1**).

- In the **Adjust** group of functions (**2**), you will find tools that will help you change the visual aspect of the picture. We will see some of them in upcoming examples.

- In the **Picture Styles** group (**3**), you have access to a library of predefined styles, and you can customize the border and apply various effects to your image.

- The **Accessibility** group (**4**) gives you access to a button allowing you to quickly add Alt Text to your images. This is a feature you should use in all your presentations to make sure your content is accessible to people using screen readers.

- The **Arrange** group (**5**) has tools that help you layer, align, and rotate all objects on your slides, and the **Selection Pane** helps you see a list of all the objects on your slides.

- And in the **Size** group (**6**), you can access tools that will help crop your image and shape its size.

You will see the **Picture Format** tab (**1**) when you insert images or cut out people from the **Stock Images** library. Many tools in this tab are easy to use; you just need to try them out on your own. The following are a few examples of how to use some of them in a creative way so that you can build more impactful presentations.

Removing the background of an image

If you have planned your content properly, as discussed in *Chapter 1, Analyzing Your Audience and Presentation Delivery Needs*, you should have ideas about the visuals you want to include in your presentation. Instead of wasting a lot of time searching for the perfect image, you can search for images that include the element you are looking for and use the **Remove Background** tool in PowerPoint to discard what is not required.

> Tip
> For the best results when using the **Remove Background** tool, you need a photo in which the element you want has a sharp contrast with the rest of the image. If your image is composed of too many elements, or the borders of the subject you want to extract are blurred by the rest of the content, you will have to work much harder, and the results might not be as good as you want.

In the following example (*Figure 6.30*), I inserted a photo of a bird available in **Stock Images** that has a blurred background (**1**). Then, I went to the **Picture Format** tab (**2**) and clicked on the **Remove Background** tool (**3**):

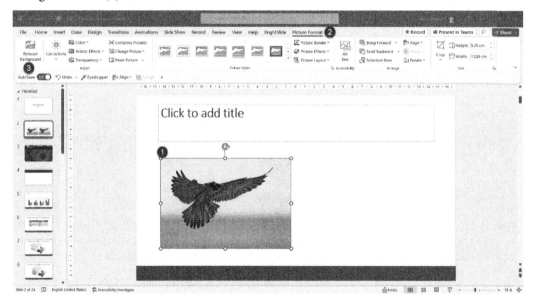

Figure 6.30 – Finding the Remove Background tool

In *Figure 6.31*, you now have a new tab named **Background Removal** (**1**), and the background determined by the tool takes a magenta or flashy pink color when on your computer. In my example, it looks like a grayed-out area in the image (**2**) showing what will be removed. You need to pay close attention to this step because you may have areas of your subject that are not included in what will be kept. In my example, there are five magenta wing-feather tips and missing white tail tips (**3**), meaning that if I don't make adjustments the bird won't look good.

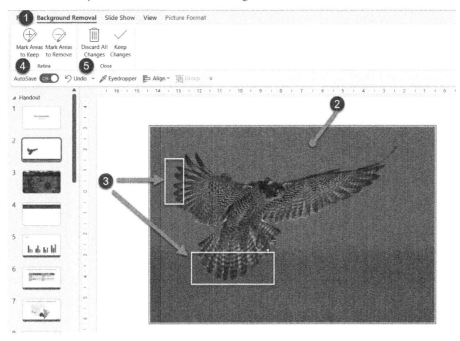

Figure 6.31 – Using the Background Removal tools

This is when you need to use the tools in the **Refine** group of the **Background Removal** tab (**4**):

- **Mark Areas to Keep**: If you click on this button, your mouse cursor takes on the shape of a pencil when you hover over your image. You need to left-click and draw over the parts you want to include—it will draw a green line that disappears when you release the left mouse button. You might see the border of your subject change during the process, including or excluding parts of it as the system tries to find pixel colors you just included elsewhere in your image. Therefore, you need to start with an image where your subject has a sharp contrast with the background and does not include too many details.

- **Mark Areas to Remove**: If there are areas you don't want to include, or that were included during the previous process, this tool allows you to mark them. It is the same process as keeping areas, except that the line you draw is red. You also need to keep an eye on any other selection changes made during this step.

In both cases, you don't need to precisely draw the whole area—you just need to draw a line over the colors that need to be included. In the **Close** group (**5**), you can choose **Discard All Changes** if you are not satisfied with the results or **Keep Changes** to confirm the removal of the background. Pressing the *Esc* key on your keyboard will also keep the changes you made.

Here is the result for the image used in my example (*Figure 6.32*):

Figure 6.32 – Image before and after using the Background Removal tool

Besides being able to use an image with no background in your presentation, using the **Background Removal** tool can also help you create special effects.

There are times when you probably don't need to remove the background of your image but still want a closer focus on a specific area. That is when the various cropping tools in the next section can come in handy.

Using various image-cropping tools

When you want to resize an image and change its focus, the cropping tool can be your best friend. When you have an image selected on your slide, it is found in the **Picture Format** tab (**1**) (*Figure 6.33*) as the **Crop** button (**2**). When you click on it, you will see black corner and side handles that allow you to decide which area of your image will be displayed (**3**). In my example, I removed the left and right portions of the image so that it would be the same size as the placeholder on the left:

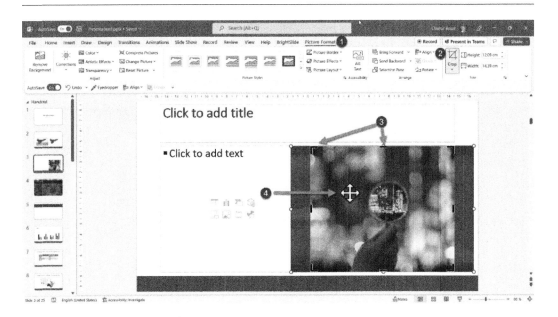

Figure 6.33 – Using the Crop tool on an image

When you hover over the image, your mouse cursor becomes a four-way arrow (**4**) allowing you to position it so that an element of focus is displayed properly. To confirm the changes, simply click on the **Crop** button again (**2**), hit the *Esc* key on your keyboard, or click outside of the selected image.

There are two other cropping options that might be useful when creating your content: **Crop to Shape** and **Aspect Ratio**. To access them, you first need to select at least one image on your slide and then click on the small arrow below the **Crop** button in the **Picture Format** tab (*Figure 6.34*):

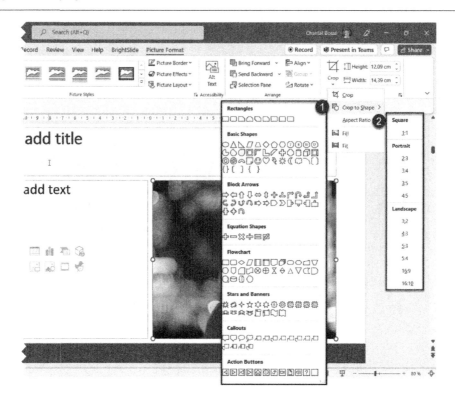

Figure 6.34 – Accessing the Crop to Shape and Aspect Ratio options

When you select the **Crop to Shape** option (**1**), you will see a gallery of all the basic shapes available in PowerPoint to choose from. When selecting a shape, it automatically crops your image and changes its shape. This can be convenient if you have decided all your images need to be displayed in a special shape. You can also apply this cropping option to an **image placeholder** on layouts in your **slide master** so that it automates your design choice. You can refer to *Chapter 3, Leveraging PowerPoint's Slide Master for Design*, if you need a refresher on layouts and placeholders. The **Aspect Ratio** option (**2**) gives you a list of common aspect ratios to choose from, allowing you to reduce manual cropping.

An example of when this option can be useful is if you need to build a layout of images that all have the same aspect ratio on a slide and have more images than the **Designer** feature can handle. You could make all images square with the 1:1 aspect ratio, then use the alignment tools to quickly display them on the slide.

Before we end this chapter, we'll see how we can customize icons and illustrations, two creative content elements available in **Stock Images**.

Customizing icons or illustrations

At the beginning of this section, we saw seven creative content types available in **Stock Images**. Now we will see how to customize **icons** and **illustrations** so that they integrate well with the overall look of your presentation.

In the following example, I inserted a computer that can be customized (*Figure 6.35*):

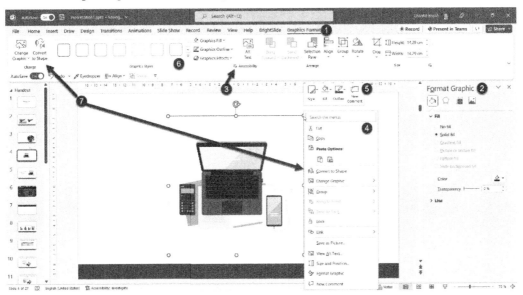

Figure 6.35 – Accessing the graphics formatting tools

You can access formatting tools from the **Graphics Format** tab (**1**), opening the **Format Graphic** pane (**2**) from the **Dialog launcher** icon (**3**) on the ribbon, and right-clicking on the illustration to access the options in the contextual menu (**4**). This last action also makes the floating formatting tools available (**5**).

Depending on the illustration you inserted, you will be able to change the fill color of some elements in the graphic, give a different look by choosing a contrasting outline color, and apply graphic effects (**6**). You just need to try changing a few options to see how the illustration you have inserted reacts. If doing so does not give you enough customization options for your needs, then you need to click on **Convert to Shape** (**7**). This action results in ungrouping the shapes so that they each become available to apply custom formatting to each one (*Figure 6.36*):

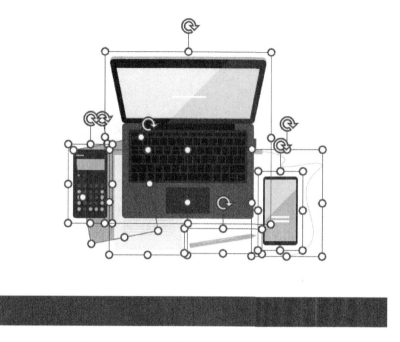

Figure 6.36 – Result of using Convert to Shape on an illustration

After ungrouping, you can either use the shape formatting tools on each one or even delete or move some of them. As you can see, browsing the creative content supplied in **Stock Images** can be a great starting point to help you save some design time. Just use the tools you have learned about in this section to customize and adapt them to your needs.

> **Tip**
>
> After ungrouping an illustration to get separate shapes, you can even go a step further and use the **Edit Points** and **Merge Shapes** tools we have discussed in previous sections of this chapter. The possibilities are endless if you start using the power of many tools!

The steps I just described can also be used with the icons supplied in **Stock Images** because they are like illustrations; both categories are considered vector objects that are easily resized and formatted. As an example, if you need a map but don't have to show any data, such as in the **Chart** maps we discussed at the beginning of this chapter, you could find a map of any of the world's continents in **Icons**. Afterward, you only need to resize it, convert it into shapes, and start customizing the colors or remove any areas not relevant to your message.

If you have not tried any of the tools described in this chapter, I strongly suggest that you put some time aside to do so. The only way to get more comfortable with features and tools you did not know about before is practice.

Summary

In this chapter, we discussed how to create more visually appealing elements on your slides by adding maps and using and customizing SmartArt. We also learned how to create our own shapes with **Edit Points** and **Merge Shapes**, and customize the creative content supplied by Microsoft in the **Stock Images** library.

You now have enough knowledge about the tools and features to start creating your own visual content or adapting any default elements supplied in PowerPoint. Yes—there will be times when you will feel overwhelmed by the possibilities. After all, our brains don't have a creative switch that we can flip on or off!

Just give yourself time to get more comfortable with the tools, and don't feel as though you need to change all your visuals at once. Here is a challenge for your next presentation: plan more design time before your event and set the goal of using one technique you learned in this chapter. As you get more familiar with the tools and features, you can implement more visual changes in your content.

In the next chapter, we will be discussing how to add and modify multimedia elements. You will learn how to include video and audio in your presentations, use some basic editing tools, and create videos with PowerPoint.

Further reading

- Get more information on *The Better Deck Deck*, by *Nolan Haims*: http:// thebetterdeckdeck.com/

- **Edit Points** keyboard shortcuts: https://support.microsoft.com/en-us/ office/draw-or-edit-a-freeform-shape-44d7bb9d-c05c-4e1c-a486- e35fc322299b

- Stock images terms of use and licensing, in plain language: https://support.microsoft. com/en-us/topic/what-am-i-allowed-to-use-premium-creative- content-for-0de69c76-ff2b-473e-b715-4d245e39e895

7
Adding and Modifying Multimedia Elements

In terms of visual content creation, so far, we have learned about some of PowerPoint's features that leverage AI and others that help us use graphical elements instead of text and bullet points. It is now time to level up your presentation game even more by learning how to include multimedia elements.

Adding multimedia elements will help make your presentations more impactful by providing content variety while making some topics easier to learn about via short videos rather than long text explanations.

In this chapter, we will discuss the following topics:

- Inserting and formatting videos
- Inserting and formatting audio
- Using the Cameo feature
- Inserting a screenshot or screen recording for a demo
- Creating a video file or GIF from a presentation

Technical requirements

Most topics discussed in this chapter don't require having a **Microsoft 365 (M365) subscription**, the tools and features having been introduced in previous versions of PowerPoint. I will identify when a feature is in M365 only. Also, be aware that since the subscription version of PowerPoint is being updated on an ongoing basis, it is possible that some features don't look exactly the same in your version of the application.

Inserting and formatting videos

Inserting videos into your presentations can sound like a daunting task, the main reason usually being that many users feel lost with all the formats available and compatibility issues with the PowerPoint version they are using. So, let's start by defining the supported file formats.

Supported video file formats

There used to be so many variables to choosing a video file format in PowerPoint! The supported file format was highly dependent on the Microsoft Office version installed, if we were using Windows or Mac, which version of the operating system was installed, and which device the presentation would be viewed on. The good news is that we can reduce the complexity of that list with modern versions of PowerPoint (**2016**, **2019**, **2021**) and **Office 365** (**O365**).

> **Warning**
>
> If you are still using **Office 2010**, this version stopped being supported in October 2020, opening up your computer to major security risks. And if you are still using **Office 2013**, you will be opening up your computer to security breaches as of April 2023. My best advice is to invest in an up-to-date version such as **Office 2021** (one-time purchase, supported until October 2026) or an **M365** subscription so that you are always using the latest version in terms of features and security. As for **Windows 7** users, support ended in January 2020. **Windows 8.1** will stop being supported in January 2023.

There are still quite a few video file formats circulating—see the *Further reading* section for a Microsoft article on the topic—but keep in mind that we want to make sure the videos included in your presentation will play on most devices and are supported by most operating systems. Here are two formats you can look for:

- The .mp4 format is supported on Windows, macOS, iOS, and Android
- The .avi format is supported on Windows and macOS

Some people might say that I am skipping many technical details here, and they would be right. I am just keeping my promise to all businesspeople that need to keep things simple. If you insert either of the preceding video file formats in your presentations, you will most likely avoid running into problems. And if you do have problems, have a look at other Microsoft resources listed in the *Further reading* section because you can find valuable information in case your hardware has problems supporting video playback in your presentations.

Now that you have a little more knowledge about video file formats, we can move on to inserting videos into presentations.

Inserting video files

Using videos in your presentation can be valuable either to help you tell a more powerful story or to demonstrate a manual process more quickly than a textual description. Either way, make sure you are selecting a video that is relevant and short. People's attention spans are becoming shorter because of our fast-paced world, so I would recommend keeping the length of your videos under 3 minutes. If you are showing a process that is longer, we will see how to use the formatting tools that will help you cut the file into shorter snippets in the following section.

Inserting videos in your presentation can be done from one of three PowerPoint placeholders or by using the **Insert** tab. We will see both methods.

Inserting from a placeholder

I have created a slide layout that includes the three types of placeholders from which you can insert a video file in your presentation (*Figure 7.1*):

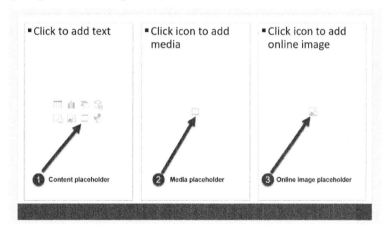

Figure 7.1 – Slide with content, media, and online image placeholders

- From the content placeholder (**1**), you need to click on the film strip icon to open a window to browse files from your computer. This means that if you synchronized cloud storage to your File Explorer, you could also access the files from the same window.

- From the media placeholder (**2**), there is only the film strip icon to click on, and it opens the same window as the previous placeholder to choose your file.

- From the online image placeholder (**3**), you have only the online image icon to click on and it opens the **Microsoft Stock Images** library, in which you have a **Videos** tab where you can browse available videos or search by keyword.

> **Important note**
>
> Media and Stock Images placeholders used for videos do not constrain the inserted video to the size of the placeholder, as we saw for image placeholders. You will need to work with the video formatting tools and do some manual work. The slide example in *Figure 7.1* would not be an efficient layout in real-life conditions.

If you need a refresher on placeholders, go back to *Chapter 3*, *Leveraging PowerPoint's Slide Master For Design*. And for inserting media from the Stock Images library, the next section will bring back a visual.

When you plan your slide layouts ahead of time, including videos in your presentation is only two clicks away: one to select the layout, and the other one to click on the appropriate icon. But if you are not using video often, you can simply use the **Insert** tab with any layout you have in your file.

Inserting video from your computer or stock images

You might not always have slide layouts planned for videos. If that is the case, just use any layout and click on the **Insert** tab (**1**), then the **Video** button on the ribbon (**2**) to get an **Insert Video From** list (*Figure 7.2*):

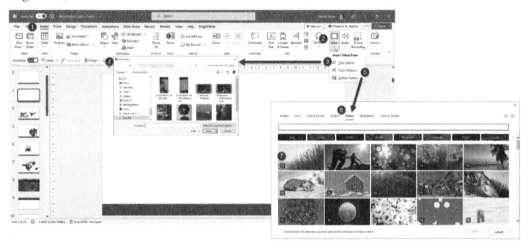

Figure 7.2 – Using the Insert tab to add video from your device or stock images

You can then choose **This Device…** (**3**) and choose a video file from the **Insert Video** window (**4**). Just browse locally or on any network server or synchronized cloud files.

When you choose **Stock Videos…** (**5**), it opens the **Stock Images library** in the **Videos** tab (**6**). Each thumbnail in the list has a small camera icon (**7**) showing they are video files.

It is important to mention that when you insert a video from a placeholder or with the **Insert | Video** options, the video file becomes part of your PowerPoint file. You can use your presentation file on any computer knowing it includes your video, although you will need to test the playback to make sure your presentation will run smoothly. But it does mean that the size of the video is added to the overall presentation file size, which can become huge if you select a large video file. We will discuss how to handle file size later in this chapter.

Linking to a video file

When inserting a video file from your device, the **Insert Video** window does have another hidden option (*Figure 7.3*):

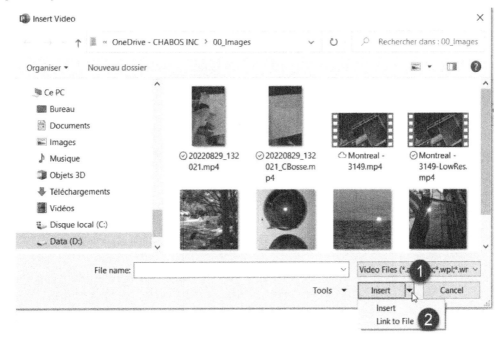

Figure 7.3 – Link to File in the Insert Video window

Instead of clicking on the **Insert** button, you need to click on the small arrow on its right (**1**) to open the drop-down list that includes the **Link to File** option (**2**). This option does exactly what it says, so it reduces your presentation file size. But there is a caveat: if your video file is moved from its original place or renamed, you will get an error message. The safest way to use the linking feature is to always have the video file in the same folder as your presentation file. And if you need to present on another computer, you need to make sure you are accessing the folder that includes the video file, whether you are using a USB portable device or your cloud storage.

Inserting online videos

There is one final video insertion feature I want to show you, also available from the **Insert** tab and by clicking on the **Video** button (**2**)—the **Online Videos…** (**3**) option (*Figure 7.4*):

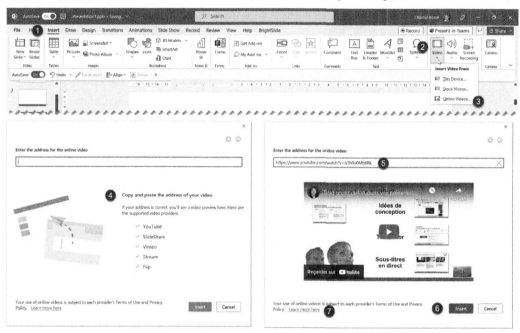

Figure 7.4 – Inserting an online video into your slide

Choosing **Online Videos…** opens a new window with a **Copy and paste the address of your video** prompt (**4**), giving you a list of compatible sites. As an example, I copied the address of one video I have on my **YouTube channel** (**5**) to show you what is displayed. When you click on the **Insert** button (**6**), the video is made available on the slide. You will have to resize it and the still image will look pixelated, but it will look perfect when shown in the slideshow view. These are two important things to consider if you decide to show an online video during your presentation:

- The video is not included in your file. It links to its address on the internet. If you are presenting in an environment where you don't have Wi-Fi or wired web access, it will not play.

- When linking to a video on the web, you need to make sure you have the right to show the video. When it is not your own content, make sure to read the **Terms of use** and **Privacy policy details** on the site. Have a look at the Microsoft support article on the topic in the *Further reading* section, or click on the **Learn more here** link in the window (**7**).

It is important to keep in mind that online videos cannot be edited or formatted using PowerPoint's video formatting features, which is the topic of our next section.

Formatting video files

After inserting a video file into your presentation, when you select it on the slide, you get access to many formatting features. Let's start with a quick overview of the tools in the **Video Format** tab (**1**) before I give you a few examples (*Figure 7.5*):

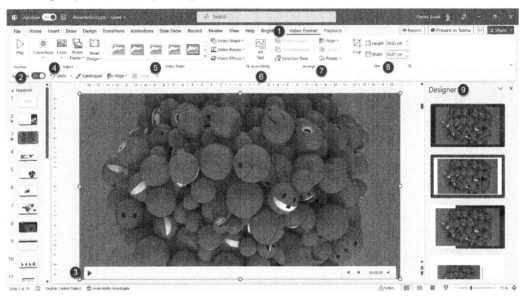

Figure 7.5 – Using the formatting features in the Video Format tab

- In the **Preview** group, you can use the **Play** button (**2**) to start and pause your video. You can also use the playback button available at the bottom of the video on the slide (**3**).

- In the **Adjust** group (**4**), you have access to tools that help you correct brightness and contrast and recolor your video too. We will discuss **Poster Frame** and **Reset Design** in upcoming examples.

- The **Video Styles** group (**5**) gives you access to a library of predefined styles, and you can customize the shape and the border and apply various effects to your video.

- The **Accessibility** group (**6**) gives you access to a button allowing you to quickly add Alt Text to your videos. This is a feature you should use in all your presentations to make sure your content is accessible to people using screen readers.

- For the **Arrange** group (**7**), you have the same tools that were available for pictures, as seen in the previous chapter. They help you layer, align, and rotate all objects on your slides. You can also open the **Selection Pane** from this group of functions.

- And in the **Size** group (**8**), you can access tools that will help crop and resize your video.

- Unless you have disabled **Designer** (**9**), you should also see design ideas after you have inserted a video.

Many tools in this tab are easy to use; you just need to try them out on your own. The following are a few examples of how to use some of them to help you modify a video to your needs.

Choosing a poster frame for your video

A poster frame is the still image we see before playing a video. Let's see the options that help you control what that still image will show (*Figure 7.6*):

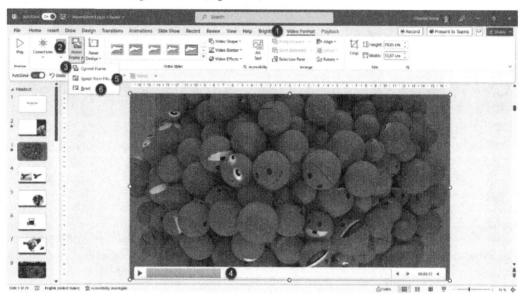

Figure 7.6 – Options to change the poster frame of a video

- Make sure your video is selected and open the **Video Format** tab (**1**).

- Click on the **Poster Frame** button (**2**).

- The **Current Frame** option (**3**) allows you to pause the video on a certain image (**4**) and use it as the still image. This option can be useful when you have someone with an unflattering facial expression as the poster frame.

- You can also choose **Image from File…** (**5**) and choose an image you have in a corporate library.

- The **Reset** option (**6**) simply erases the poster frame changes you made to bring back the video to its original display.

An example of when changing your poster frame can be useful is if you have a corporate video and would rather see a large logo or an image of your offices as the still image before playing it. If you don't like what you see before playing your video, change it! Let's move on to changing the shape and the focus point of a video.

Changing the shape and cropping a video

When using videos in a presentation, you are not stuck with a plain old rectangle. I created an example by first inserting three videos on a slide, which results in having the videos layered one on top of the other and covering the whole slide. To save some time, I applied a **design idea** that resized and positioned the videos on the slide in one click (**1**). In the **Selection** pane (**2**), we can see that we have three videos (**3**) and two straight connectors (**4**) added by **PowerPoint Designer** (*Figure 7.7*):

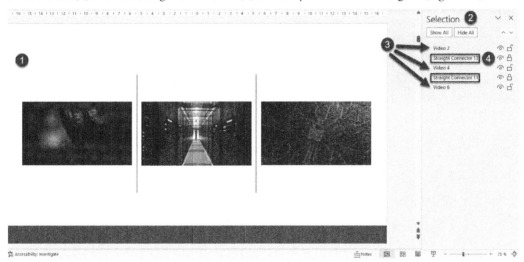

Figure 7.7 – Three videos on a slide layout created by applying a design idea

> **Tip**
> If you don't remember how to show the **Selection** Pane box, go back to *Chapter 3, Leveraging PowerPoint's Slide Master for Design*, in the *Using the lock feature for placeholders or objects* section.

When you have decorative items added by **Designer**, you can simply select them in the **Selection** Pane and hit the *Delete* key on your keyboard. By default, objects added by **Designer** are always locked, but you can easily unlock them in the **Selection** Pane using the lock icon. As a reminder, **Designer** and its design ideas are only available as connected services with an M365 license.

To change the shape of a video, you first need to make sure it is selected so that you can access the **Video Format** tab (**1**), click on the **Video Shape** button (**2**), and select any of the shapes in the gallery. My next example has been created with a **pentagon** (**3**) and two **chevron** shapes (**4**). And if you change your mind about a shape, you can always click on the **Reset Design** button (**5**) (*Figure 7.8*):

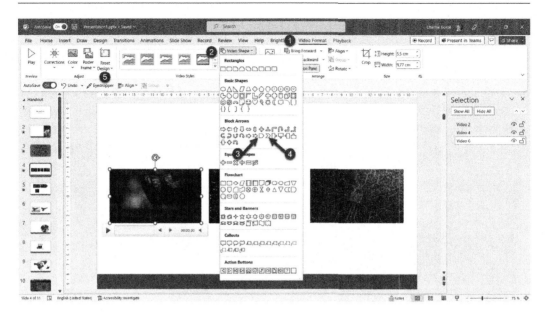

Figure 7.8 – Changing the shape of a video

If you choose your videos wisely and give each of them a shape that conveys a process, they could show each step of the process you are explaining. An example of this is shown in *Figure 7.9*:

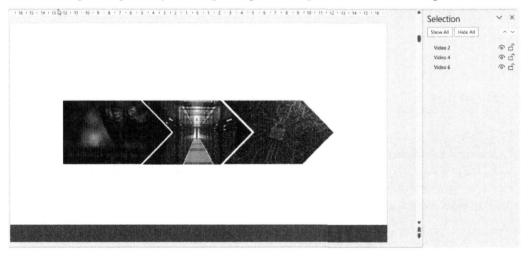

Figure 7.9 – Three videos shaped like a pentagon and two chevrons to show a process

Changing the shape of a video might not always suit your needs. What if you simply want to have a square instead of a rectangle? That is when the **Crop** tool can help you (*Figure 7.10*):

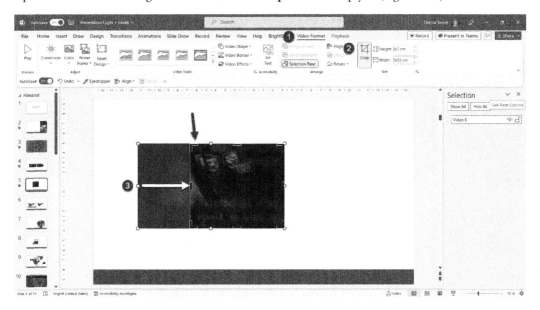

Figure 7.10 – Using the Crop tool on a video

- With the video selected, click on the **Video Format** tab (**1**) if it is not already displayed.

- Click on the **Crop** button (**2**). Use any of the black cropping handles on the border to hide parts of the video while it is playing.

- In the example, the handle on the left (**3**) was moved to the right so that the video would become a square.

It is important to note that if after cropping a video you change your mind, you need to go back to the **Crop** button and move the handles or slide other elements into the focus area. Using the **Reset Design** button has no effect on the crop. Now that we have seen some formatting options for videos, it's time to talk about the playback options.

Changing some video playback settings

When a video is selected (**1**), there is a second tab allowing us to make changes. Let's have a quick look at the **Playback** tab (**2**) ribbon (*Figure 7.11*):

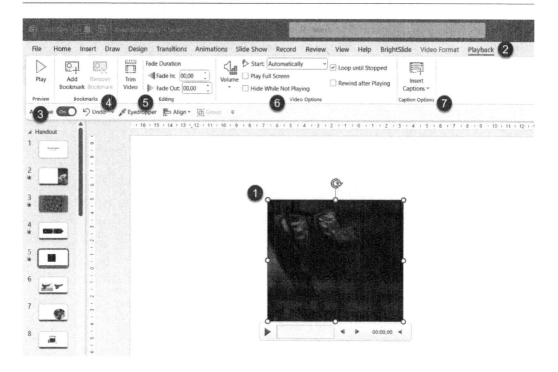

Figure 7.11 – Video playback tab options

- The **Preview** group (**3**) has a **Play** button allowing you to start or pause the video.

- The **Bookmarks** group (**4**) is used to add bookmarks that can be used in advanced animation sequences. An example will be given in *Chapter 8, Working with Transitions and Animations*.

- In the **Editing** group (**5**), you have tools to trim video and add a simple fade in and fade out.

- The **Video Options** group (**6**) allows you to make various changes to volume, when it starts, and how it plays.

- And the **Caption Options** group (**7**) allows you to upload a captions file in the .vtt format. This step should not be overlooked if you want to make your presentation more accessible. It allows people to read the words spoken during the video. This is different from subtitles, which can be used during your live presentation to show your spoken words to the audience.

From the various options listed previously, we will first have a closer look at the **Trim Video** feature. Just as its name implies, it helps you trim the beginning or the end of your video. It does not replace professional video editing software, but it can be used as a quick fix when you don't have other software than PowerPoint, or support from a creative team.

To access the trimming options, you need to first select a video and go to the **Playback** tab (**1**), then click on **Trim Video** (**2**) (*Figure 7.12*):

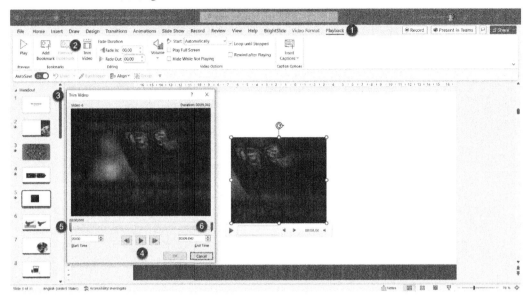

Figure 7.12 – Accessing and using the Trim Video feature

- Right below the **Trim Video** dialog box's (**3**) title bar, you will find the name of the video and its duration. In our example, we see **Video 6** and **Duration: 00:09,042**.

- You can use the playback arrow or the previous or next frame arrows (**4**) to help you find where you want to start and end your video.

- A quicker way is to click and drag the start marker on the left (**5**), colored green in the interface, and watch the preview window to stop moving it where you want to start. You can do the same with the end marker on the right (**6**), colored red in the interface, to choose where you want to stop the video.

After moving both markers, you will see the new clip **Duration** (**1**), and the precise **Start Time** (**2**) and **End Time** (**3**) details. The only action left to do is to click on the **OK** button (**4**) to confirm the changes (*Figure 7.13*):

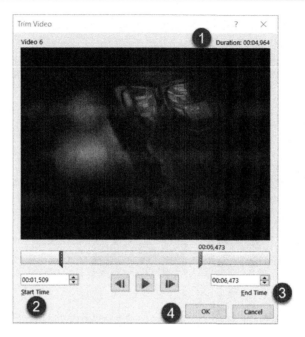

Figure 7.13 – Trimming the start and end time of a video

Finally, let's have a closer look at **Video Options** available in the **Playback** tab so that you have a better understanding of what you can change and why (*Figure 7.14*):

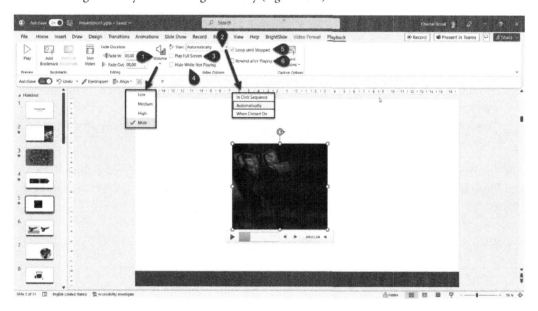

Figure 7.14 – Overview of Video Options in the Playback tab

- The **Volume** button (**1**) allows you to choose a level for your clip. Using the **High** setting is probably best in most cases, giving you—or the audience when presenting virtually—the chance to adjust your speaker's volume. Our example shows a check mark beside the **Mute** setting because the clip does not have sound.

- The **Start** option (**2**) is usually set to **Automatically**, meaning that your video starts automatically when you reach that slide during the slideshow. Clicking on the arrow brings up a list allowing you to choose another setting. **In Click Sequence** means you can start the video within your animation sequence, making it easy to use a presentation remote. The **When Clicked On** option requires you to click on the video or the player to start it. We will see an example of video animation settings in the next chapter.

- The **Play Full Screen** option (**3**), when checked, makes sure the video will read fullscreen when in slideshow mode. If you want to display many videos on a slide, like a menu, you can use this option to make sure you focus on one fullscreen video at a time.

- The **Hide While Not Playing** option (**4**) allows you to keep a video hidden until you play it. Be careful! If you have chosen this option and the **When Clicked On** start option, you will never be able to click on the video.

- The **Loop until Stopped** option (**5**) is nice if you want to make sure a short clip will keep playing until you click on it to pause or change to another slide.

- The **Rewind after Playing** option (**6**) can be used if you want to make sure the video brings back the first frame or the poster frame once it finishes playing.

Now that we have seen the basics of inserting and formatting videos in a presentation, let's move on to inserting and formatting audio clips.

Inserting and formatting audio

Using audio in your presentation can be very useful in some circumstances, but I often hear users feel lost with all the formats and compatibility issues, as we discussed for videos previously. Again, let's start by defining the supported file formats.

Supported audio file formats

Since versions and compatibility issues are very similar between audio and video, I won't repeat the introduction I did in the video section. I will again refer you to the Microsoft article discussing video and audio formats in the *Further reading* section. If you want to make sure audio files included in your presentation will play on most devices and are supported by most operating systems, here are three formats you can look for:

- The .mp3 format is supported on Windows, macOS, iOS, and Android

- The .mp4 format is supported on Windows, macOS, and iOS

- The .wav format is supported on Windows, macOS, and Android

Again, I am skipping many technical details. But as Microsoft mentions in its own support article, knowing the names of files will be enough to look for the right files or use a file converter if need be. If you insert one of the preceding audio file formats into your presentations, you will most likely avoid running into problems. And if you run into any problems, the Microsoft resources listed in the *Further reading* section will help you.

Now that you have a little more knowledge about audio file formats, we can move on to inserting audio in presentations.

Inserting audio files

Using audio in your presentation can be valuable either to help you tell a more powerful story or help your audience understand better by hearing than by explaining. There are also instances where audio is required to add narration when a presentation will be viewed without a presenter. Just as we mentioned for videos, audio should be relevant and short.

When using audio during a presentation you are delivering, I recommend keeping audio clips shorter than videos since you are only soliciting hearing—less than 90 seconds would be a good target. If you are using PowerPoint to create training, use the same rule of thumb in terms of the length of audio files so that people don't spend a long time on each slide.

Inserting audio into your presentation cannot be done from a placeholder. We need to use the **Insert** tab (**1**) (*Figure 7.15*):

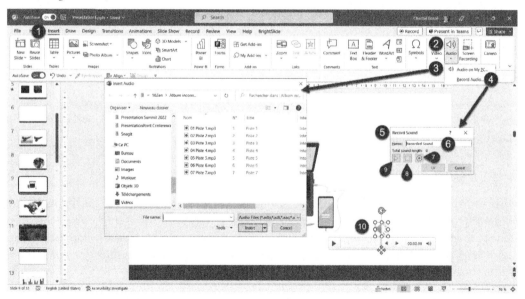

Figure 7.15 – Inserting audio into a presentation

- When you click on the **Audio** button (**2**), you open a list of two options.

- Clicking on the **Audio on My PC…** (**3**) option opens a window to browse your computer for a file.

- Clicking on the **Record Audio…** (**4**) option opens the **Record Sound** dialog box (**5**) where you can give your recording a name (**6**). When ready, use the **Recording** button (**7**) to launch it, the **Stop** button (**8**) when you are done, and the **Play** button (**9**) to listen to your recording before inserting it into your slide. *Please note*: make sure you have a microphone connected to your computer if you want to record audio.

- After inserting an audio file from your computer or recording a clip, you will see an audio icon on your slide (**10**) with the player underneath for playback options.

When your audio file has been inserted and it is selected on your slide (**1**), you have access to two new tabs: **Audio Format** (**2**) and **Playback** (**3**) (*Figure 7.16*):

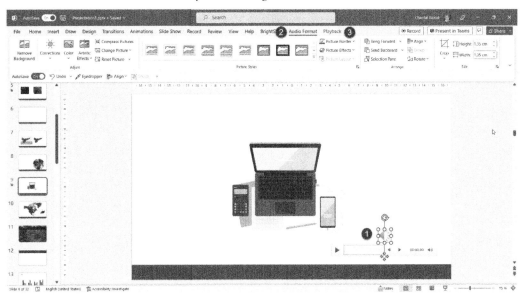

Figure 7.16 – A selected audio file gives you access to Audio Format and Playback tabs

Let's see which elements can be useful in the **Audio Format** tab.

Formatting audio files

In the **Audio Format** tab, you see groups of functions such as the ones we saw in the previous chapter while discussing picture formatting. This is mainly because the icon for your audio file is considered a picture object. Since the icon is usually hidden during a presentation, you probably don't have to spend any time in this tab. But there is one nice trick I will show you that might be interesting for some presentations.

If your topic requires that you play a few audio clips from a slide, you could replace the icon by using the **Change Picture** button (**1**) and replace the audio icon with an image (**2**) or an icon (**3**). Doing so would give you a nice visual clue to choose the audio you want to play (*Figure 7.17*):

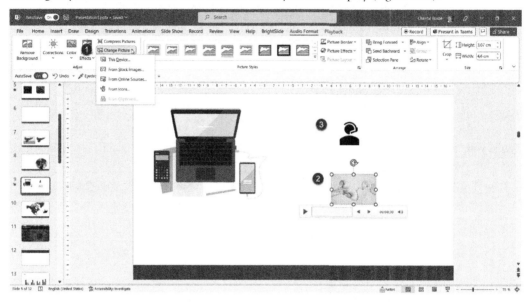

Figure 7.17 – Replacing the audio clip icon with a picture or icon

Be aware that after replacing the original icon you will not be able to reset it back. But you can go back to the Microsoft icons library and search the content for an icon similar to the original one; using the audio keyword will give you nice results.

Most of the time, you will not need to change anything in the **Audio Format** tab and simply open the **Playback** tab, the topic of the following section.

Changing some audio playback settings

When an audio clip is selected (**1**), there is a second tab allowing us to make changes. Let's have a quick look at the **Playback** tab (**2**) ribbon (*Figure 7.18*):

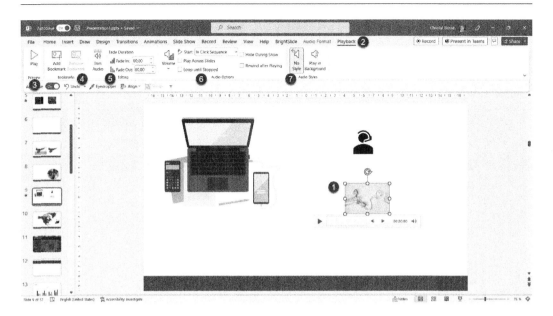

Figure 7.18 – Audio playback tab options

- The **Preview** group (**3**) has a **Play** button allowing you to start or pause the audio.

- The **Bookmarks** group (**4**) is used to add bookmarks that can be used in advanced animation sequences.

- In the **Editing** group (**5**), you have tools to trim audio and add a simple fade in and fade out.

- The **Audio Options** group (**6**) allows you to make various changes to the audio volume, when it starts, and how it plays. Only two options are different from the ones we discussed in the previous *Formatting video files* section:

  - **Play Across Slides** is an option that allows sounds to be played in the background.

  - **Hide During Show** is the option to use if you want to make sure the audio icon is not visible during your presentation. The icon can also be dragged outside the slide while in normal view, but doing so might make it more difficult to see while you are editing the slides, depending on which zoom factor you are using.

- In the **Audio Styles** group (**7**), you have two buttons:

  - **No Style** helps you reset audio options back to their default in one click

  - **Play in Background** helps you set the audio to play across all your slides, such as background music, in one click

Currently, there is no way to add captions to audio files to improve accessibility.

Using the Trim Audio tool

The **Trim Audio** tool works mostly like the **Trim Video** tool we discussed previously. The same comment that it does not replace professional audio editing software applies, but it can be used as a quick fix when you don't have other software than PowerPoint, or support from a creative team.

To access the trimming options, you need to first select an audio file and go to the **Playback** tab (**1**), then click on **Trim Audio** (**2**) (*Figure 7.19*):

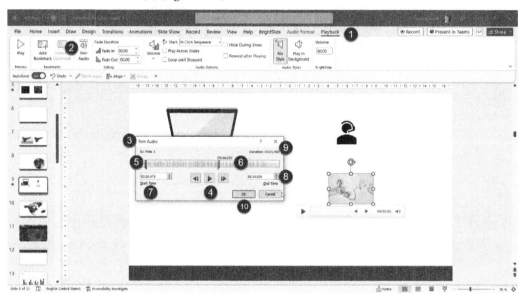

Figure 7.19 – Accessing and using the Trim Audio feature

- Right below the **Trim Audio** dialog box's (**3**) title bar, you will find the name of the audio and its duration.

- You can use the playback arrow or the previous or next frame arrows (**4**) to help you find where you want to start and end your audio. Obviously, make sure you have a headset or that your speakers are on to hear the audio.

- To trim the beginning of your clip, you need to click and drag the start marker on the left (**5**), colored green in the interface. Since you don't have a visual preview for an audio track, you will need to use the playback buttons to check whether it starts when you need it to.

- You can do the same with the end marker on the right (**6**), colored red in the interface, to choose where you want to stop the audio. Again, this is a trial-and-error process, especially if your audio clip is longer. You have no possibility to zoom in on the audio waves on the track.

- In this case, you might want to make micro-adjustments to the **Start Time** (**7**) and **End Time** (**8**) settings by using the arrows or even entering the time manually into the fields.

- After moving both markers, you will see the new clip duration (**9**). You just need to confirm your changes by clicking on the **OK** button (**10**).

Trimming audio might be more labor-intensive within PowerPoint if your file is longer, but it is still worth it if you don't have any other software or creative team to help you. Keep in mind that it does not change your file per se—it only changes the start and end times for playback.

Microsoft introduced a new way to increase engagement in presentations by allowing presenters to insert a live camera feed into their slides. This will be the topic of our next section.

Using the Cameo feature

We must keep finding new ways to engage our audiences, and using the **Cameo** feature could be interesting in some situations. At the time this book was written, it was available in the **desktop version of PowerPoint** with an M365 license, and in the preview version of **PowerPoint Live in Teams**. In short, Cameo allows you to embed a live camera feed into your slides. I see the value of adding presenter proximity when presenting virtually, or in a large venue where some people in the audience might not see you clearly. It could also be used to focus a camera on a sign language interpreter, which is a great way to be more accessible and inclusive.

To access the feature, you need to click on the **Insert** tab (**1**) and go to the far right of the ribbon to click on the **Cameo** button (**2**). It automatically adds a camera object (**3**) in the lower-right corner of the slide and might also open the **Designer** pane (**4**) to suggest design ideas that include a camera feed (*Figure 7.20*):

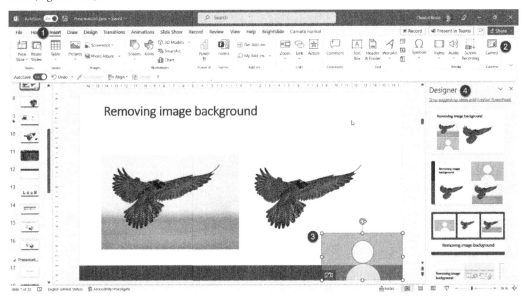

Figure 7.20 – Accessing Cameo and inserting a camera object

Since it is a camera object on the slide, this means that you also get formatting features for it. When **Cameo** is selected on your slide (**1**), you get a **Camera Format** tab (**2**). Let's review the tools you can use to format the camera object (*Figure 7.21*):

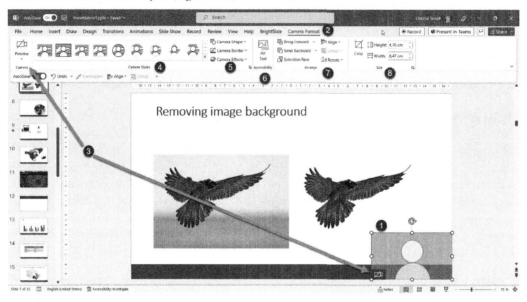

Figure 7.21 – Using the Cameo formatting tools

- You can get a preview of your camera if you click on the **Preview** button in the **Camera** group or the camera icon in the bottom-left corner on Cameo (**3**).

- In the **Camera Styles** group (**4**), you can access some styles that can be applied to your Cameo object. Hovering over each one with your mouse cursor gives a live preview of what it will look like. Simply click on the one you want to apply to your camera object. You can also use **Camera Shape**, **Camera Border**, and **Camera Effects** (**5**) to change the visual aspect of Cameo. Try some options to see what they look like but remember that it will be your live camera feed, so there is no need to overdo it on effects.

- There is also an **Alt Text** option (**6**) since the object is considered very similar to videos. Make sure people using screen readers will know that it is the live feed of your camera.

- The **Arrange** (**7**) and **Size** (**8**) groups have the same types of features available when formatting pictures, shapes, or videos.

When you have formatted your Cameo object on one slide, it can be copied and pasted onto other slides so that you don't need to redo the formatting every time. It is also possible to get creative by using some slide transitions and animations that will move Cameo just where you want it on every slide. As you can see, in some instances, adding Cameo will help improve audience engagement.

If there have been times where you have wished you could easily use a screen capture or a short screen demo in your presentation, the next section is exactly what can help you do it right within PowerPoint.

Inserting a screenshot or screen recording for a demo

Sometimes it is much easier to show an image of an application or website than try to explain everything with words. That is when you should be going to the **Insert** tab (**1**) to use the **Screenshot** feature (**2**) (*Figure 7.22*):

Figure 7.22 – Using the Screenshot feature in PowerPoint

- After clicking on the **Screenshot** button, the **Available Windows** section (**3**) shows you a list of all the active windows on your computer. If you take the time to open the exact application, document, or website you want to grab a capture from before you use the feature, inserting the capture is as simple as clicking on the preview you want to include on your slide.

- The **Screen Clipping** option (**4**) will allow you to grab a specific area with your mouse cursor. Here are the steps:

  - Open the window from where you want to grab a specific portion to include in PowerPoint and place the PowerPoint window on top of it.

  - When you click on **Screen Clipping**, it reduces the PowerPoint window to show the next window behind it. Your mouse cursor becomes a plus sign (+) and the screen takes a semi-transparent white shade.

- Click and drag your mouse cursor over the area you want to select and let go.

- The screen clipping is inserted on your slide.

Whether you inserted a whole window or a clipping, it then becomes easy to annotate elements over them and even use animations to help direct the audience's eyes toward the important elements of your picture. The **Screenshot** feature might be lightweight compared to some screen capture applications such as TechSmith's **Snagit**, but it can be a huge time saver if you only need to capture a few images.

And when a still image is not enough, PowerPoint can offer you a screen recording feature too. When in the **Insert** tab (**1**), look for the **Screen Recording** button (**2**) on the far right of the ribbon (*Figure 7.23*):

Figure 7.23 – Finding the Screen Recording feature

To prepare for your screen recording, you need to make sure the window you want to demo is right behind the PowerPoint window. As soon as you click on the **Screen Recording** button, the PowerPoint window is minimized, and a recording toolbar shows in the middle of the top portion of your screen (**1**). In the example I created, you see a partial Microsoft Teams window that could be used to demonstrate how to use channels (*Figure 7.24*):

Figure 7.24 – Using the Screen Recording feature

- The first thing you need to do is decide whether you want to use **Record Pointer** (**2**) and **Audio** (**3**). Those buttons are shaded/active by default, but you can click on either one to avoid recording sound or pointers.

- Next, you need to click the **Select Area** button (**4**) so that your mouse cursor becomes a plus sign (**+**), allowing you to click and drag over the area you want to capture. The recording area will have a dashed red outline (**5**).

- Finally, you click on the **Record** button (**6**) to start recording. You will see a big countdown square with an important keyboard shortcut on it: *Windows key + Shift + Q*. This combination will allow you to stop the recording without having to try to make the recording toolbar visible again by moving your mouse cursor to the top middle of your screen. There is a small pin icon (**7**) that keeps the toolbar visible for you to see the **Stop** button (**8**), but that means you will see the toolbar on your recording too; not a good option if you want to avoid having to do video editing.

- The **Record** button becomes a **Pause** button during the recording, but since it disappears when you have started recording, you would need to make it reappear, and have the full toolbar in your recording too. Instead, if you want to pause the recording, use this keyboard shortcut: *Windows key + Shift + R*.

- As soon as you stop the recording, the video clip is inserted into your slide. It looks exactly like any video file with its playback options. It can also be formatted with the same tools discussed for video formatting.

Try it yourself

The best way to get familiar with the **Screenshot** and **Screen Recording** tools is to try them out yourself, especially since showing manipulations in a book is not as complete as seeing a recorded demo. If you have not tried this while reading the steps, I suggest that you do so right now. It will make the steps clearer and easier to remember when you eventually need to use the features.

Now that you have learned how to insert a video into your presentation and create a quickly recorded demo from within PowerPoint, let's move on to creating videos and GIFs in the next section.

Creating a video file or GIF from a presentation

After creating your presentation, it might be a good idea to reuse it in a video format that is easy to view on many platforms while making it more difficult to reuse parts of your content. It could also be done so that you have a video clip to insert back into a presentation. As you can see, the possibilities are endless, and it is easy to create.

Exporting a presentation as a video

When you are done creating your presentation, or the small set of slides that you need to have a video for, you need to click on the **File** tab to view what is called the **Backstage** view (*Figure 7.25*):

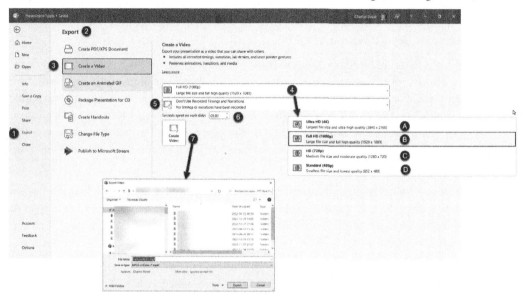

Figure 7.25 – PowerPoint's Backstage view to create videos

- First, click on the **Export** menu (**1**) on the left so that you have access to the **Export** pane (**2**).

- Then, click on **Create a Video** (**3**) to access the settings. The export process will keep everything you have included in your presentations. If you are not familiar with animations and transitions, *Chapter 8*, *Working with Transitions and Animations*, will be helpful.

- Choose the video resolution (**4**), or in simple language the quality of the video you want to produce. In the drop-down list, you will see the following:

  - **Ultra HD (4K)** (**A**): This is the highest quality and the largest file size. Unless you plan on playing the video on a 4K device, you don't need to export with this setting.

  - **Full HD** (**B**): This is a high-quality and large file size. This option meets the needs of most situations.

  - **HD** (**C**): This is of moderate quality and has a medium file size. It is the best setting if you want to add a video to a website. Using higher quality might impact the viewing experience on the web.

  - **Standard** (**D**): This is the lowest quality and smallest file size. It should not be used unless file size is a major issue.

- If you do not have automatic transitions or narrations, the system will show the **Don't Use Recorded Timings and Narrations** setting (**5**). And if you do, it will be set to **Use Recorded Timings and Narrations** automatically.

- The number of **Seconds spent on each slide** (**6**) will be applied when you don't have any recorded timings or narrations; the default is 5 seconds per slide. The time spent on a slide also depends on the number of animations you have on a slide, so if animations take longer than 5 seconds, the export will respect timing for animations in spite of this setting. When there is no animation, then this setting is applied.

- When everything is set, click on the **Create Video** button (**7**) so that you have access to the **Export Video** window allowing you to change the name and folder where the `.mp4` file will be saved.

After the export is complete, you have a video file to share or insert back into your presentation. If your need is to have a shorter media file, then you could create a GIF file from PowerPoint, the topic of our following section.

Creating an animated GIF

Having short, looping video clips has become common practice in the content shared on social media. You could repurpose a few animated slides on your social media accounts, or as marketing material, if you export them as GIF files. To access this feature, you first need to click on the **File** tab to access the **Backstage** view (*Figure 7.26*):

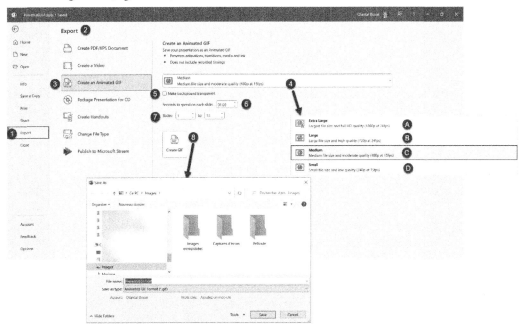

Figure 7.26 – PowerPoint's Backstage view to create GIFs

- First, click on the **Export** menu (**1**) on the left so that you have access to the **Export** pane (**2**).

- Then, click on **Create an Animated GIF** (**3**) to access the settings. The export process preserves animations, transitions, and any media included in the slides you choose.

- Choose the quality of the GIF file (**4**). The default setting is **Medium**, which suits the needs of many users, especially since animated GIFs are considered in the heavyweight category of animated files. In the drop-down list, you will see the following:

  - **Extra Large** (**A**): This is the highest quality and the largest file size. If you absolutely need this level of quality, make sure you are creating the file with very few slides to avoid huge export times.

  - **Large** (**B**): This is a high-quality and large file size.

  - **Medium** (**C**): This is of moderate quality and medium file size. It is the best setting if you want to easily use the files on most platforms.

  - **Small** (**D**): This is the lowest quality and smallest file size. It should not be used unless file size is a major issue.

- You have a **Make background transparent** setting (**5**), which is valuable if you want only the slide content.

- The number of **Seconds spent on each slide** (**6**) allows you to decide how fast the animation will go.

- Select the number of consecutive slides you want to include in the file by entering their number in the first and second fields (**7**). Remember that the more slides you have, the larger the file will be. Keep in mind that GIF files are usually only a few seconds long, so there is no need to use many.

- The last thing to do is to click on the **Create GIF** button (**8**) so that you have access to the **Export Video** window allowing you to change the name and folder where the `.gif` file will be saved.

After the export is complete, you have an animated GIF file to share or insert back into your presentation. This can be a great way to share short snippets of your content for more visibility.

Summary

In this chapter, we discussed how to add and modify multimedia elements such as videos, audio files, screenshots, and screen recordings, and export a file as a video or GIF that can then be inserted back into your presentation file.

You now have enough knowledge about the tools and features to start using more media elements in your presentations. When you have the feeling it will take a long time to create graphic elements to show a process or explain your idea clearly, stop and think about using other types of media that will help the audience understand your concept more quickly.

We have added one more building block for more engaging and impactful presentations. And remember that even though there is a lot of creative content available in Microsoft's Stock Images library, you can always create your own with your own smartphone. But if your need is for a big marketing campaign, then it might be wiser to hire professionals to create relevant videos.

In the next chapter, we will be discussing how to use transitions and animations efficiently. You will learn how to create interesting visual effects that serve your message and how to use more advanced animation techniques.

Further reading

- *Microsoft article on supported video and audio file formats*: https://support.microsoft.com/en-us/office/video-and-audio-file-formats-supported-in-powerpoint-d8b12450-26db-4c7b-a5c1-593d3418fb59

- *Tips for improving audio and video playback and compatibility in PowerPoint*: https://support.microsoft.com/en-us/office/tips-for-improving-audio-and-video-playback-and-compatibility-in-powerpoint-a3458b91-684a-4104-9a3f-697967a34755

- *Are you having video or audio playback issues?*: https://support.microsoft.com/en-us/office/are-you-having-video-or-audio-playback-issues-e0a94444-8ea7-4a00-974b-6ad0d6edc4b1#codecs

- *Support article on inserting a video from a website*: https://support.microsoft.com/en-us/office/insert-a-video-from-youtube-or-another-site-8340ec69-4cee-4fe1-ab96-4849154bc6db?ui=en-us&rs=en-us&ad=us#OfficeVersion=Newer_versions

8

Working with Transitions and Animations

By now, you should have a better idea of the visuals you can create and multimedia elements you can use to create better presentations. If you started creating a new presentation or modifying an existing one while reading through the previous chapters, now is the time to learn how to create a better visual flow during delivery. Using transitions and animations will make complex topics easier to comprehend.

I should add that you will learn to create movement with purpose, not just make your content move around and fly all over the screen just because you learned how to use new features! It is all about helping you tell a better story and make your content easier for the audience to remember.

In this chapter, we will discuss the following topics:

- Using slide transitions wisely
- Leveraging the Morph transition
- Using advanced animation sequences
- Using triggers for on-demand animations

Technical requirements

Most of the topics discussed in this chapter don't require having a **Microsoft 365 (M365) subscription**, as the tools and features have been introduced in previous versions of PowerPoint. I will identify when a feature is in M365 or newer versions only. Also, be aware that since the subscription version of PowerPoint is updated on an ongoing basis, it is possible that some features don't appear exactly the same in your version of the application.

Using slide transitions wisely

Using slide transitions in a meaningful way can help you create a movement that helps the audience follow along. The important thing to remember is to avoid using a transition just because you can, and to use it because it adds value to your content. In regular business settings, you can use just a few of the available transitions and your presentations will always look professional. Let's start by discussing how transitions work in the next section.

Understanding transition basics

To access the transitions gallery, you simply need to click on the **Transitions** tab (**1**). In the **Transition to This Slide** group (**2**), click on the **More** button (**3**) to open the transitions gallery (**4**) (*Figure 8.1*):

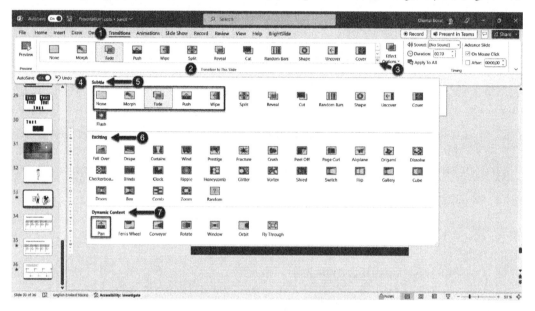

Figure 8.1 – PowerPoint's slide transition gallery

You have many transitions available, and they are sorted into three categories: **Subtle**, **Exciting**, and **Dynamic Content**. Whether you feel overwhelmed or excited about all the choices, let me start by saying that you could create all your presentations with no transition or a simple Fade for the rest of your business life and no one would complain. Here is a list of transitions that can be useful and when to use them:

- In the **Subtle** (**5**) category, I have picked out the ones I feel are most suited for business presentations:

  - **None**: As mentioned previously, having no transition won't be distracting. It is the default when you create a new presentation file.

- **Morph**: This transition can be so useful that it will be covered all by itself later in this chapter. If you are using a PowerPoint version older than **2019**, you won't have access to this transition.

- **Fade**: A transition that softly changes to the new content, giving a cue that the content is changing. This one is my personal favorite for all my slides.

- **Push**: Depending on the direction we give it and how the slide is created, it can help you create the illusion of moving forward.

- **Wipe**: Also dependent on the direction and the way we create the content, it can help you create the illusion that the new content is wiping over the actual one.

- In the **Exciting** (**6**) category, here are two personal comments:

  - I would avoid this category in most regular business contexts because those these transitions can be very distracting.

  - Have I ever used any of these transitions before? Yes. In self-running presentations for trade shows where viewers need something that will catch the eye. For example, I could use a specific one every time the content moves to a new section. The idea is not to create the expectation of which new cool transition will be seen but rather, letting the viewer know we are changing to a new topic.

- In the **Dynamic Content** (**7**) category, let's define what it does, and which one is the most useful:

  - Let's first define what dynamic content means. When using one of the transitions in this category, anything in the background of the slide will not move during the transition. This is applicable if you have filled the background of your slides with a picture, or any graphic element that is added to the slide master.

  - **Pan**: This is the only dynamic transition I have used in a regular business setting, helping me create a forward movement for a timeline before the **Morph** transition was available. All of the others are more distracting than the added value of using dynamic content.

If you have not used slide transitions much, the important thing to remember is that the effect is applied when we move to that slide during a slideshow.

Viewing slide transitions

There are tools within **Normal view** to help you preview the transition and adjust various options, such as effects and timings (*Figure 8.2*):

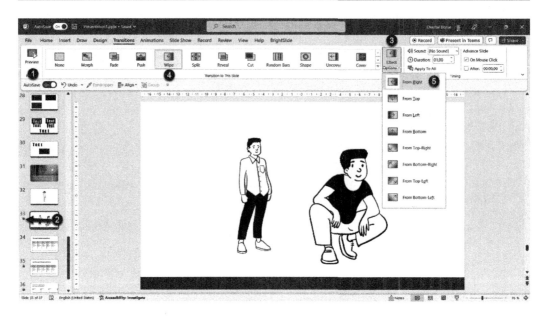

Figure 8.2 – Slide transition options and timings

- You can preview a slide transition you just applied either by clicking on the **Preview** button in the ribbon (**1**) or the *star icon* beside the slide thumbnail (**2**), **33** in the previous example.

- Depending on the slide transition you have selected, you will have access to various **Effect Options** (**3**). In the previous example, the **Wipe** transition (**4**) has an effect called **From Right** (**5**).

Try it yourself

The best way to get familiar with effect options is to apply different transitions to a slide and view the list to test each option. If you have not used transitions much in the past, you should take some time now to try them. You can either use an existing presentation or just create a few slides in a new file, then add different transitions to each slide. Finally, explore the **Effect Options** list available for each transition you select.

Adjusting the Timing options

Still in the **Transitions** tab, the **Timing** group (**1**) has a few settings that can be changed (*Figure 8.3*):

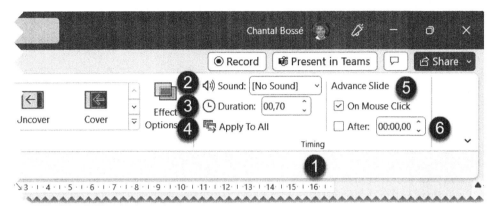

Figure 8.3 – In the Transitions tab, the Timing group settings can be adjusted

- It is possible to add **Sound** (**2**) during a transition. Since we are discussing how to make business presentations more impactful, you should avoid this option to stay professional.

- The **Duration** setting (**3**) is the number of seconds the slide transition takes to change the slide. Usually, the default is good for most presentations, but you can experiment with longer or shorter durations if you want to create a specific mood. In our example, a fade transition was applied, and it has a duration of 0.70 seconds.

- The **Apply To All** setting (**4**) allows you to apply the selected transition to all your slides in one click. As an example, you could select a simple fade transition, adjust any other option in the **Timing** group, and then apply it to all the slides in your presentation.

- There is a subgroup in the **Timing** group named **Advance Slide** (**5**). By default, the check box for **On Mouse Click** is checked, meaning that during a slideshow, you advance slides by clicking the mouse or using certain keyboard navigation keys. If you are not familiar with which keyboard keys can be used during presentation delivery, they will be discussed in *Chapter 11, Practicing Your Presentation Delivery*.

- If you uncheck the **On Mouse Click** check box, it will allow you to remove the possibility to navigate with the mouse or keyboard when the presentation is in slideshow mode. The only way to navigate the slides then requires built-in navigation elements with hyperlinks. If you are not familiar with hyperlinks in PowerPoint, they will be discussed in *Chapter 9, Building Flexibility and Interactivity in to Your Presentation*.

- The last setting in the **Advance Slide** subgroup is the **After** checkbox (**6**). Checking this option allows you to select a duration for the display of a slide before PowerPoint automatically transitions to the next one. The format is `minutes: seconds, tenths of seconds`

(**00:00,00**). This option can be used when you want to create a self-running presentation, or simply because you want a slide displayed for a short period of time and not to have to click to get to the next one.

Now that you have a better understanding of how slide transitions work, let's have a closer look at the Morph transition in the next section.

Leveraging the Morph transition

When Microsoft introduced the **Morph transition**, it was an amazing game-changer for presentation creators! It was finally possible to create real movement **during a transition** to another slide without having to spend hours tweaking animation effects or using automatic transitions. In short, Morph allows you to smoothly move objects from one slide to the other.

Let's see the steps to help you create your first Morph transition with the help of *Figure 8.4*:

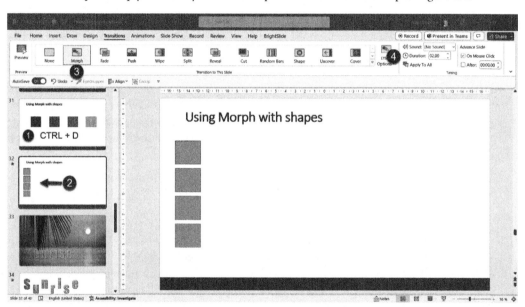

Figure 8.4 – Creating a movement effect with the Morph transition

1. Create a slide similar to slide **31** in the previous example, using four squares of different colors. Then duplicate the slide – using *Ctrl + D* (**1**) on your keyboard. This step is essential to make the transition work because PowerPoint needs to have the same object names to calculate where the shapes start and where they finish. You can also copy and paste objects from one slide to the other, but duplicating the slide has the advantage of not having to select all the objects to copy and paste them.

2. On the newly duplicated slide (slide **32**), move the squares, make them smaller, and change their color (**2**) to a color different from the ones you chose previously.

3. Apply the **Morph** transition to the second slide (**3**) and use the **Preview** button to see what it looks like.

4. The default duration for Morph is 2 seconds (**4**). This allows the four shapes to smoothly move to their new position while being reduced and having their color changed.

I can only applaud the great engineering wizardry responsible for the calculations and rendering of this transition! The previous example was done with basic shapes, but Morph has quite a few more tricks in reserve. First, let's see how to use Morph **Effect Options** in the next section.

Using Morph Effect Options

We saw how easy it was to apply the Morph transition for a duplicated slide. What we have not seen is that this transition also has **Effect Options** (**1**) that can be changed depending on the results we want to achieve (*Figure 8.5*):

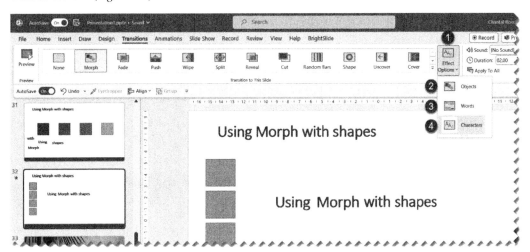

Figure 8.5 – Using Effect Options for Morph

- By default, the option is on **Objects** (**2**) when you first apply the Morph transition to a slide. This means that any object on the slide can be moved, resized, or recolored. When using a textbox or a shape with text, the whole object is moved with no effect on the text itself.

- When using the **Words** option (**3**), any changes you make to text from the initial slide to the duplicated slide will rearrange the words themselves. As an example, you could have a sentence from which you remove and add words. The Morph transition will show the words disappearing, moving, and appearing in their final place.

- The **Characters** option (**4**) works in a similar way to the previous one, except that letters will move to recreate the final state. Microsoft refers to it as *creating an anagram effect*, which is a great name to trigger the creative use of words on your slides.

Once again, you can adjust the duration of the transition to create the effect you want. Just keep in mind that if you make the duration very short, the movement might be too intense, even creating dizziness for some people. Let's move on to how you can leverage the Morph transition to help you move on a timeline.

Creating a moving timeline with Morph

For years, I wished I could make timelines bigger and easily move forward seamlessly from one slide to the next. It was not impossible, but we had to think it through and sometimes use dynamic content transitions to help. With the Morph transition, things are much simpler.

I have created a timeline example to show you how to do it (*Figure 8.6*):

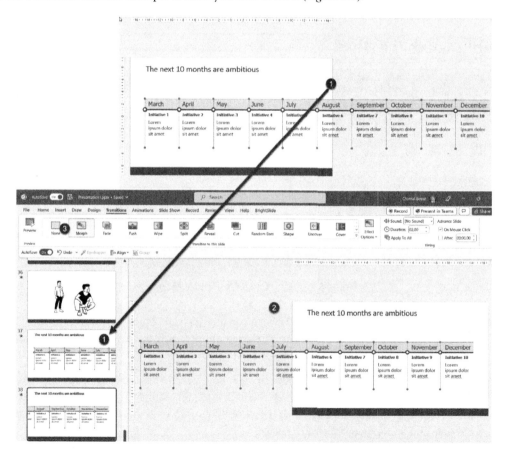

Figure 8.6 – Creating a moving timeline with Morph

1. First, you need to create the whole timeline on a slide (**1**). Make it as big as needed to make sure your text is easy to read, letting it extend out of the canvas in to the gray area. Duplicate your slide with *Ctrl + D*.

2. Move your timeline to the left so you get the remaining content on the second slide in its final position (**2**).

3. Apply the Morph transition to the slide (**3**).

Next time you need a timeline, there is no reason to try to fit everything on one slide. Make it as big as possible and use Morph. When you keep the same title, your audience will only see the seamless movement of the timeline. It can be used more than once if your timeline or process is very long. Just start the process again from the last slide and move your objects a second time. I have also used this trick to show a very long web page, giving my audience the illusion that I was scrolling from top to bottom.

Morph can also be very useful to create a zooming effect, which is the topic of the next section.

Creating movement and a zooming effect with Morph

Since the steps to get to the Morph transition were already described in previous sections, here we will focus on the canvas and slide thumbnails to show you how to create a zooming effect with an image. I suggest that you try the steps in PowerPoint as you are reading.

The example I chose to create includes an image of a road and three road signs. The Morph transition will be used to create the illusion that we are driving on the road and see three signs as we move forward. The creative content was found in **Stock Images**.

Creating the first slide

Start by inserting your image into a slide, making sure it is the same size as the slide. If **Designer** gives you a design idea of an image filling the slide, use it. In *Figure 8.7*, you have the various components required to create the zooming effect:

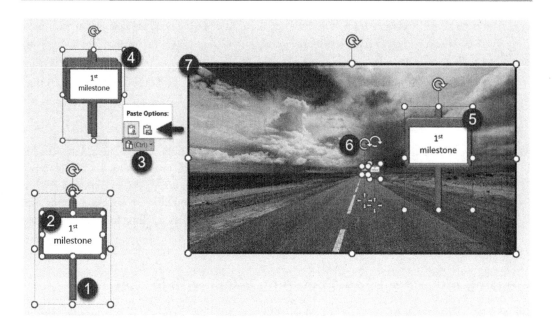

Figure 8.7 – Creating the first slide for a Morph zooming effect with an image

- Search icons in Stock Images for a road sign like the one used in the example (**1**). Instead of keeping the original black color, you can change it to a light gray and use a bevel effect, so it looks similar to real road sign structures. I added a white rectangle (**2**) so the text would be visible over the image.

- Using shapes with text when we have to resize objects for perspective has one big disadvantage: the text will not resize. Therefore, the best thing to do is to copy and paste the road sign and rectangle (*Ctrl* + *C*, and *Ctrl* + *V*) and use **Paste Options** (**3**) to convert the objects into one picture (**4**).

- After repeating the previous step to create three road signs with their own text, it becomes easier to place the images over the road picture (**5**) and resize them (**6**) to create the perspective we need.

- Make sure to add a rectangle with no fill (**7**) so you can easily see the border of the slide in the next step.

Now that the first slide has been created, we can move on to the creation of the zooming effect with Morph.

Creating the zooming effect with the second and third slides

After creating the first slide, we can start creating the movement and zooming effect with the Morph transition. As seen previously, the quickest way is to duplicate the slide with *Ctrl* + *D* (**1**) (*Figure 8.8*):

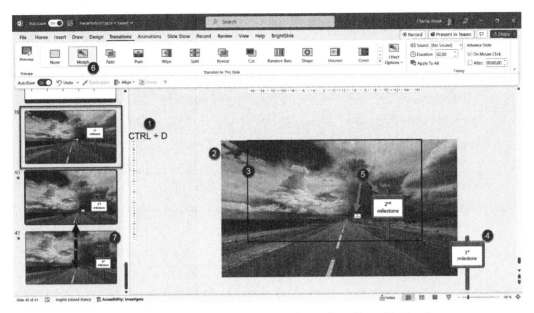

Figure 8.8 – Creating the movement and zooming effect with Morph

- On your second slide, you now need to increase the size of your picture (**2**) so it overflows the slide area. Even if you can see the borders of the slide when resizing the picture, having a rectangle with no fill (**3**) becomes a great guide to help you move and resize your objects.

- You can move your first road sign diagonally out of the slide area (**4**) to create the illusion of driving past it. Move and resize the two other signs (**5**) so they seem to be growing as you move toward them. Apply the **Morph** transition to the slide (**6**).

- Repeat the previous step to create the third slide (**7**), making sure that when you look at the slide thumbnail, your road is still aligned with the previous slide. You might have to move your road picture upward to make the movement more realistic.

Preview your work and make any changes that would improve the movement or zooming effect. When you are satisfied, make sure to remove the rectangle with no fill so you don't see a slide border while in slideshow mode.

You can adapt this example for many business scenarios, such as showing a big plan that you move through while zooming in and out. The only limit is your creativity. Next time you have a hard time fitting all your information on one slide, and you need to show some sort of navigation between the elements while taking a closer look, consider trying this Morph transition trick.

I cannot write about Morph without discussing the exciting feature it has of allowing us to morph one object into another – the topic of our next section.

Morphing an object into another using the !! naming scheme

Microsoft has built in the ability for Morph to force various objects to morph into other ones. At the time this book was written, here are the types of objects that can be transformed:

- Forcing a shape to change in to another one, such as a square becoming a circle.

- Forcing the same shape that includes different text from one slide to the other to morph.

- Morphing two different images.

- Morphing between any two similar objects, such as one table in to another table, or a SmartArt object in to another SmartArt object. It does not work for charts.

- To take control over how your objects can morph, a **!! naming scheme** was introduced. Since we are talking about the name of slide objects, you might recall that we discussed the **Selection Pane** feature in *Chapter 3, Leveraging PowerPoint's Slide Master for Design*. We will use it now to bring the Morph transition to a whole new level.

We will create a simple slide with a rectangle and an oval that will respectively morph into a smaller triangle and larger pentagon (*Figure 8.9*):

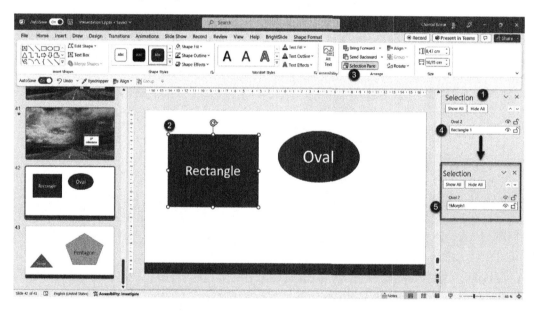

Figure 8.9 – Using the naming scheme to morph shapes

- After creating the two slides, open the **Selection** pane (**1**). The easiest way is by selecting a shape (**2**) and clicking on the **Selection Pane** button (**3**) of the **Shape Format** tab.

- Click on the name field of a shape (**4**), start by typing two exclamation points (! !), and then give it a name such as `Morph1` (**5**). Whatever name you use, keep it short and relevant because we need to use it again on the next slide. Change the name of all the objects you want to transform across slides.

On the next slide, we need to rename objects with the same naming scheme as the previous slide, so the Morph transition does its magic (*Figure 8.10*):

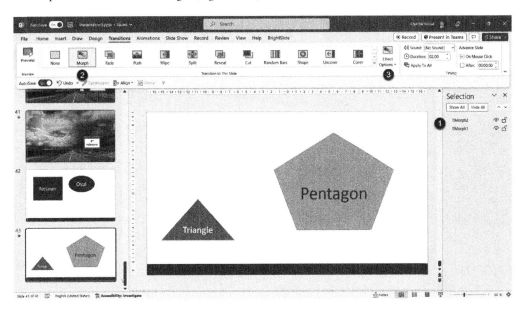

Figure 8.10 – Using the naming scheme on the second slide to morph objects

- In my example, the triangle was renamed ! !`Morph1` so it transforms from the rectangle shape, and the pentagon was renamed ! !`Morph2` so it transforms from the oval (**1**).

- When you are done, apply the **Morph** transition (**2**) to the slide, and feel free to use one of the effect options (**3**) to create the effect you want. Preview your work.

The only way to make the feature work is to make sure you start the name of an object with ! ! and make sure the name is the same for the two objects you want to morph. Also, make sure your naming scheme is unique on a slide. For example, you cannot have two objects named ! !`Shape` on the same slide – this is why I usually name objects `Morph1`, `Morph2`, and so on, making it easy to see which objects are used with Morph directly in the **Selection** pane.

There are other elements to consider when working with custom shapes, or with versions of PowerPoint that support the ! ! naming scheme. You should have a look at Microsoft's support article mentioned in *Further reading* for more details.

As exciting as the Morph transition can be, it might not be suited to every animation need you might have in a presentation. This is when learning about advanced animation sequences might be helpful, which is the topic of our next section.

Using advanced animation sequences

Even though the goal of this section is to discuss more advanced animations, let's start with a short review of the **Animations** tab (**1**) (*Figure 8.11*):

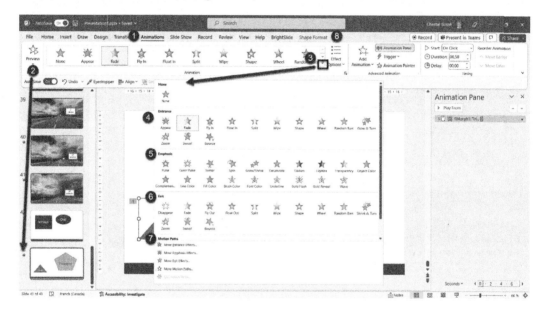

Figure 8.11 – Review of the Animations tab

Just as we have seen for **Transitions** in the first section of this chapter, you can preview animations on a slide by using the **Preview** button (**2**) on the ribbon or by clicking on the *star icon* beside a slide thumbnail. Clicking on the **More** arrow (**3**) opens the animation gallery where you will find four categories of animations:

- **Entrance** (**4**): This applies an effect when an object appears on the slide
- **Emphasis** (**5**): This applies an effect to an object already on the slide
- **Exit** (**6**): This applies an effect to an object we want to make disappear from the slide
- **Motion Paths** (**7**): This moves an object already on the slide

At the bottom of the list, you have access to the complete list of effects and paths when you click on one of the links. After you have applied an animation to an object, you can also configure how the effect will play by changing it from the **Effect Options** button (**8**); the effects available will depend on the animation you have chosen, just like what we have seen for the slide transitions.

I have one big word of caution regarding animations: it is not because you see a long list of effects that you should be using them all, randomly, on all the objects on your slide. Any animation should bring value in terms of understanding your content or helping you describe a complex process, one step at a time, while you are talking. You should always animate with intention.

To that end, you could probably create all your business presentations with no animation or simple fades and wipes for the rest of your career. And no one will complain if you have done a good job at creating content that conveys one idea per slide.

That being said, there are times when using animations is a wise choice to help our audience understand our concepts and ideas better. Let's see how we can combine animations and use the **Animation Pane** option in the next section.

Reviewing animations basics with the Animation Pane option

To introduce more complex animations and how to work with the **Animation Pane** (**1**), let's start with a simple **SmartArt** object (**2**) to which a **Fade** entrance animation (**3**) was added (*Figure 8.12*):

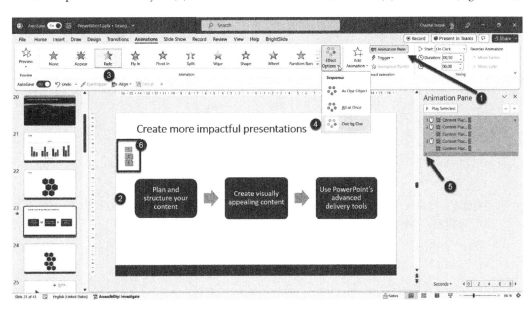

Figure 8.12 – SmartArt animated with a Fade entrance in Animation Pane

The effect option selected is **One by One** (**4**), and the small **Click to expand/hide contents** arrow (**5**) has been clicked to expand the list of animations applied to the SmartArt object. Using the **One by One** effect created a three-step animation sequence, as listed in **Animation Pane** and shown by the three rectangles beside the SmartArt object (**6**).

Before making changes to the animation sequence, let's briefly review the **Timing** options we have available (*Figure 8.13*):

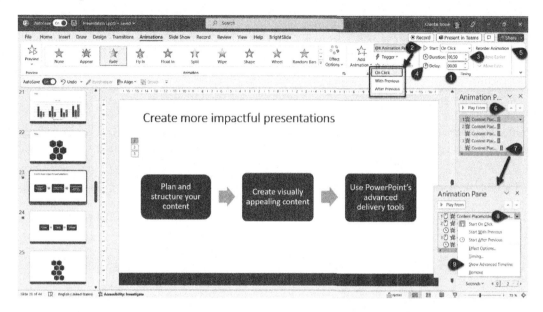

Figure 8.13 – Animation Start options definitions

In the **Timing** group (**1**), the first option we have is how to start the animation (**2**), for which you have three choices:

- **On Click**: This option means that when you click, the animation of the object will start (entrance, emphasis, exit, or path)

- **With Previous**: This option means that the animation of the object starts with the previous one, without having to click

- **After Previous**: This option means that the animation of the object starts after the previous one, without having to click

The **Duration** option (**3**) works the same as discussed for slide transitions, meaning you can make it shorter or longer depending on the effect you want to achieve. The **Delay** option (**4**) allows you to add a delay before the animation starts. I would recommend not using it with the **On Click** start because it will make you think your click is not working during your presentation. But it can be useful to create sequential movement with the other two options.

The **Reorder Animation** subgroup (**5**) can help you change the sequence of the animations, having the same effect as the *small arrows* (**6**) in **Animation Pane**. Since the object in our example is a SmartArt object, reordering animations is not available. The duration of animations is also shown in the **Animation Pane** with the **Advanced Timeline** markers (**7**); each rectangle shows the start and end times. If you don't see the timeline, either right-click on one of the animations or click the arrow on its right (**8**) and select **Show Advanced Timeline** (**9**).

Now that we have reviewed some important functions, let's move on to modifying and adding animations to our SmartArt example.

Modifying existing animations and creating an advanced sequence

When we applied a **Fade** animation to the SmartArt object, PowerPoint applied the same animation effect to all its components. In our example, it would be better to create a movement effect toward the right for arrows, helping guide your audience's eyes in the process. To make the movement even more natural, making sure that arrows appear after each rectangle would be even better.

Many people might be tempted to just have an **On Click** animation for all objects on their slide. It would work, but I have seen many presenters forget how many clicks they used to animate a slide and get distracted from their content delivery. Let's see a better way to create the sequence while reducing the number of clicks (*Figure 8.14*):

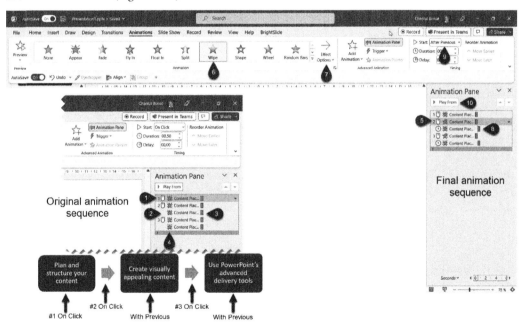

Figure 8.14 – Creating an advanced animation sequence

In the original animation sequence, we see **On Click** animations, represented by the *mouse icon* (**1**), and **With Previous** animations (**2**); the only visual clue confirming this option in the **Animation Pane** is the *timing marker* (**3**) on the right showing the same start time as the previous object. The *star icon*

(**4**) represents the animation effect applied to each object. You can also hover over each animation to get a tooltip with complete information.

To modify animations effects and the way they start, here is what you need to do:

- Click on the second animation (**5**), which is applied to the first arrow, and change it to a **Wipe** effect (**6**) by clicking in the gallery. In **Effect Options** (**7**), choose **From Left**.

- Click on the third animation (**8**), which is applied to the second rectangle, and change the **Start** option to **After Previous** (**9**) – this will add a *clock icon* on the left.

- Repeat the previous steps so the second arrow and third rectangle get the same final animations.

- To test your animation sequence, select the first animation in the list and click the **Play From** button (**10**).

Everything you have learned about in this SmartArt example can be applied to any object you want to animate on your slides. It will take practice before you feel comfortable creating sequences that feel natural and look professional. My advice is to first imagine what your animation sequence should look like, and even write it down. Just as planning our presentations away from PowerPoint can help make our presentations more impactful, planning your animations can save you a lot of time.

Let's now see how we can add some emphasis animation to our SmartArt example so each component is grayed-out when new objects appear on the slide.

Adding new animations to objects already animated

We can create nice effects when using multiple animations on slide objects, but it can be tricky if we are not well organized. If you decide to create a more complex animation sequence, the first thing you should do is rename your slide objects in the **Selection** pane, as we have seen earlier in this chapter. Unfortunately, when using SmartArt, as in our example, you can only rename a whole object, not its components. If you are using the SmartArt example for the next steps, I suggest you rename the object to something short such as SA, the initials for *SmartArt*.

When the SmartArt animation has been customized for each shape composing it, selecting the whole SmartArt object on the slide will show it has **Multiple** animations (**1**). To add animations, we need to click on the **Add Animation** button (**2**). Choosing an **Emphasis** animation such as **Desaturate** (**3**) will help us create a faded look as soon as we move to the second shape (*Figure 8.15*):

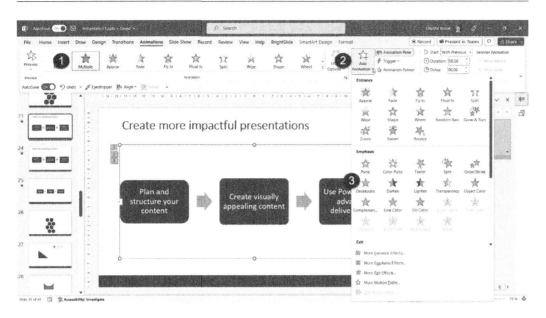

Figure 8.15 – Adding new animations to an animated SmartArt object

After applying the new animation, it is added in the **Animation Pane** (**1**), and we need to click on the **Click to expand contents** arrow (**2**) to see every added animation (*Figure 8.16*):

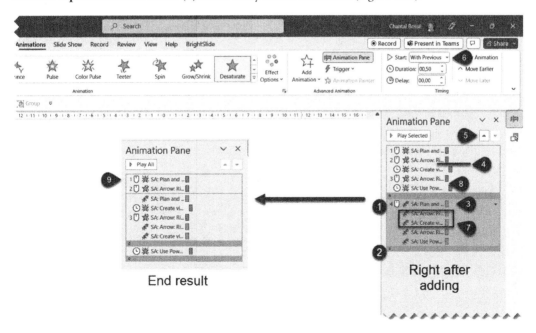

Figure 8.16 – Sequencing the new animations in the timeline

As we can see, an **Emphasis** animation was added to all the components of the SmartArt object. If we were to leave them in the actual sequence, the color change would happen after the first sequence, making all the shapes a gray shade. What we want is to start the emphasis right after we click for the second animation. Here is how we will accomplish this:

- Click on the first emphasis animation (**3**). The name, **SA: Plan and…,** is the same as the first animation at the top. This is how we can figure out more easily where it will be moved.

- Knowing we want the first rounded rectangle to fade when we click to make the first arrow and the second rectangle appear on the slide, we can click and drag the animation right under the second one (**4**), or we can select it and use the small arrows to make it move upward (**5**). When it is done, you need to change the start of the animation to **With Previous** (**6**) so the first rectangle fades as the arrow and the second rectangle appear.

- On the third click, we want to fade the first arrow and the second rectangle, so we need to move the second and third emphasis animations (**7**) right under the third animation at the top of the **Animation Pane** (**8**). You don't need to change the start of those animations because they are already set to **With Previous**.

- There are two emphasis animations left. You can simply select and delete them.

- You can validate your timeline with the visual of the end result (**9**) on the left in the previous figure, and preview your animation sequence.

It is possible that you feel overwhelmed with all the steps, and this is normal! I knew using a SmartArt object would be quite a challenge for any of you that had not tried animations before. But I also felt it was a great complex example that would help you go through any simpler animation needs with other types of objects. The best thing to do is make sure you plan your animations and complex sequences first, then try creating them with simple shapes to help you practice.

Of course, there are many more animation combinations you can do. If you are wondering why I have not discussed motion paths, it's simply because M365, Office 2021, and Office 2019 users have a much simpler way to create motion with the Morph transition, as we have discussed in a previous section. If you are using an older version, you should have a look at the Microsoft support article on motion paths in the *Further reading* section.

Now that we have discussed how animations work, you might be wondering whether there is a way to show content on demand, when you choose to show it and not include it in an animation sequence. This is exactly what we will discuss in our next section on triggers.

Using triggers for on-demand animations

Using triggers in your presentations allows you to have full control over what you show, and when you show it. As an example, I am using triggers to discuss the meaning of colors in one of my presentations where I can show the meanings one at a time, in no particular order. I simply need to click on one of the shapes while in slideshow mode to either display or hide a definition (*Figure 8.17*):

Figure 8.17 – Example of how triggers can be used to show a list of color meanings

Since discussing colors in a black-and-white book would not be convenient, we will be creating a simple example with shapes in the following section.

Using triggers with shapes and images

To help you follow along with this technique, you should create a slide that has three shapes labeled **Event 1**, **Event 2**, and **Event 3** (**1**), and add three images that will be used to depict each of the events (**2**). Then, make sure you open the **Selection** pane (**3**) (*Figure 8.18*):

Figure 8.18 – Create a slide with three event buttons and three images with the Selection pane open

The first thing you need to do to make your use of triggers simpler is to rename all objects so you can easily identify the buttons and the pictures for **Event 1**, **Event 2**, and **Event 3** (**4**). Trust me, you will thank me later.

When you have renamed them, you can proceed to animate the pictures by using triggers. You can quickly add a **Fade** entrance animation to the three pictures at the same time by selecting them all before adding the animation. This will create the first animation, **On Click** (**1**), followed by the two others starting **With Previous** (**2**). Use the **Add Animation** button (**3**) to add **Exit Fade** to all three pictures too, so you have a second set of animations in the **Selection** pane (**4**) (*Figure 8.19*):

Figure 8.19 – Using an Entrance and Exit Fade animation on pictures before using triggers

The result we want is to be able to click on the **Event 1** button to fade in the first picture and hide it when we click again on the same button. The way to configure this is by selecting the entrance and exit animations for the first picture in the **Animation Pane** (**1**) – the star for the entrance animation is green, and it is red for the exit animation (*Figure 8.20*):

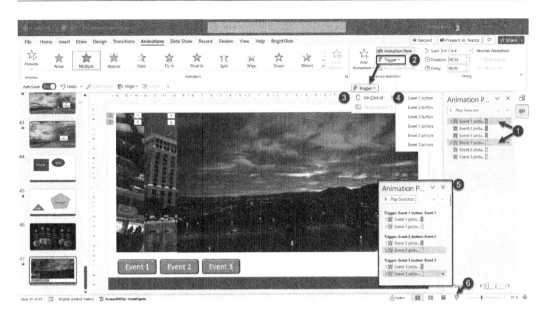

Figure 8.20 – Configuring the trigger animations

- Click on the **Trigger** button (**2**), then **On Click of** (**3**), and since we want the first picture to animate in and out when we click on the **Event 1** button (**4**), that is what we need to choose in the list. This is the reason why renaming your objects is a time-saver. You don't have to remember which generic name to choose from.

- Repeat the same process for the second and third pictures. And make sure you align the pictures in the same position.

- When you are done, your **Animation Pane** will now have three groups of triggered animations (**5**). They are identified as *Trigger: name of object on which we click: name of object that is animated.* Just make sure they are all **On Click**.

- Test your work by using the **Slide Show** button in the status bar (**6**). Press *Esc* on your keyboard to exit the slideshow.

You have now configured your first trigger animations. They can be useful in many ways in business presentations, such as having a hidden graphic you can show on demand or being able to show only one part of the slide at a time on demand. Triggers can also be used with video bookmarks, which will be the last topic of this chapter in the following section.

Using triggers with a video bookmark

In *Chapter 7, Adding and Modifying Multimedia Elements*, we mentioned that we could add bookmarks to the videos. Now is the time to see how we can use them to animate objects on a slide at a specific moment in a video.

In *Figure 8.21*, we see an inserted video (**1**) and a callout (**2**) with an **Entrance Fade** animation (**3**). The **Trigger:Video 5** (**4**) animation is there because of the option to pause the video and is automatically added when the video is inserted:

Figure 8.21 – Adding a trigger animation to a callout, set on a video bookmark

- A bookmark (**5**), represented by the circle on the playback tool, was added to the video from the **Video Playback** tab (**6**). When you hover your mouse cursor over the bookmark, you will see a tooltip (**7**) with the name of the bookmark.

- To animate the callout at the bookmark when the video is played, you need to select the callout, then click on the **Trigger** (**8**) | **On Bookmark** (**9**) | **Bookmark 1** (**10**) buttons.

- After you are done, your **Animation Pane** will have an extra trigger to animate the callout when the video reaches the bookmark (**11**).

You can get very creative with this feature in a business setting. For example, you could have a video of a specific operation in your organization to which you add in and fade out callouts at different moments. You only need to plan how to put the bookmarks in the right positions before using them as triggers.

Summary

In this chapter, we have seen how to use slide transitions wisely, discussed how to leverage the Morph transition to create various types of movements between slides, and learned how to use the advanced animation timeline to create complex animation sequences or use triggers to control our animations.

Using animations can be extremely time-consuming if you don't plan what you want to achieve before trying to create complex sequences. Just like most of the topics we have covered so far in this book, it will take more time the first few times you decide to create animations, unless you are only creating simple ones. Remember that there is nothing wrong with using simple animations, or no animations at all if you don't need them.

I hope that the topics in this chapter will open up new possibilities for your next presentations, helping you decide whether they can help tell your story more efficiently while helping your audience remember your content for longer. Just remember that just because there are many animation effects available, you don't have to use them all!

In the next chapter, we will discuss how to build more flexibility and interactivity in to your presentations so you can engage your audience even more. Being able to let them choose or showing them you can easily navigate your whole content is very impactful.

Further reading

* Microsoft Support article on using the Morph transition: `https://support.microsoft.com/en-us/office/use-the-morph-transition-in-powerpoint-8dd1c7b2-b935-44f5-a74c-741d8d9244ea`

* Microsoft Support article on tips and tricks for Morph: `https://support.microsoft.com/en-us/office/morph-transition-tips-and-tricks-bc7f48ff-f152-4ee8-9081-d3121788024f`

* Microsoft Support article on motion paths: `https://support.microsoft.com/en-us/office/add-a-motion-path-animation-effect-f3174300-0d24-4671-a1c2-e286b41efba6`

9

Building Flexibility and Interactivity into Your Presentations

Creating well-planned visuals is a great thing but being able to build flexible content that helps you interact with your audience is even better, for you and your audience! Yes—it does take some more planning, but the rewards can be huge. It can help you feel more confident, knowing that you always have the right visual to pull up to answer questions, and it helps keep your audience engaged because they realize they can ask you to go back to a topic.

Building bigger presentations that contain flexible elements might even allow you to reuse more content instead of recreating new presentations all the time. You will be the judge after reading through the topics of this chapter, where we will discuss the following:

- Using navigation elements in a presentation
- Creating custom shows
- Using the Zoom feature to navigate your content
- Creating triggered menus

Technical requirements

Most topics discussed in this chapter don't require having a **Microsoft 365 (M365) subscription**, the tools and features having been introduced in previous versions of PowerPoint. Only the Zoom feature requires Office 2019, Office 2021, or M365.

Be aware that since the subscription version of PowerPoint is being updated on an ongoing basis, it is possible that some features don't appear exactly the same in your version of the application.

Using navigation elements in a presentation

Navigating in a presentation means that we click on an object, or move the mouse cursor over it, to access other content. It requires being comfortable with having to click on those slide objects during your presentation, whether using your mouse or a remote allowing mouse cursor control. You also need to plan your navigation ahead of time to make sure that if you access other content, you have the possibility to come back to the slide you were showing.

This section will help you create your navigation even if you don't have a recent version of PowerPoint (Office 2019, Office 2021, or Office for M365). Later in this chapter, we will discuss the Zoom feature, which allows creating navigation in an easier way, but it's only available and compatible with recent versions of PowerPoint. Let's start with our first section on the use of action buttons.

Navigating with action buttons

If you don't know where to find **action buttons** in PowerPoint, you can access them from the **Home** tab (**1**) and click on the **More** arrow (**2**), or you can use the **Insert** tab (**3**) and click on the **Shapes** button (**4**). Both will open the shapes gallery where **Action Buttons** (**5**) will appear as the last section (*Figure 9.1*):

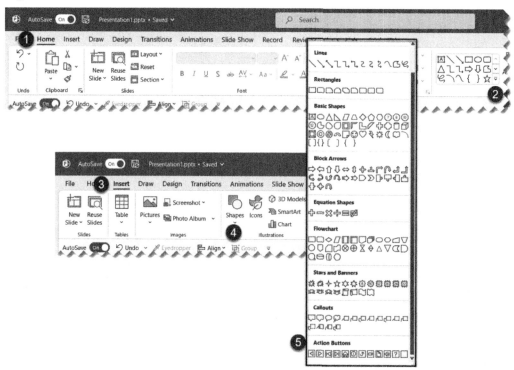

Figure 9.1 – Accessing action buttons from the Home or Insert tab

When you choose any of the buttons, you can draw the object on your slide just as any other shape in the gallery. But it gives you access to special settings—the topic of our next section.

Creating your navigation buttons

There are 12 preset action buttons available in the shapes gallery (*Figure 9.2*):

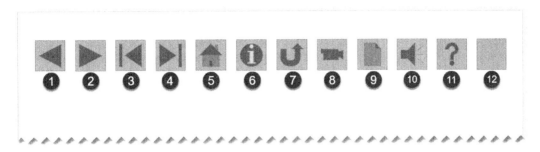

Figure 9.2 – 12 preset action buttons are available

Let's start by describing what they are before we discuss the settings they have:

- **Previous Slide** (**1**): A button that has a hyperlink to the previous slide. Unless you are creating a presentation for a kiosk, I don't recommend using it as it adds visual clutter without adding much value.

- **Next Slide** (**2**): A button that has a hyperlink to the next slide. The same comment as for the previous button applies.

- **First Slide** (**3**): A button that has a hyperlink to the first slide of your presentation. It can be valuable if you have created a special interactive menu on your first slide.

- **Last Slide** (**4**): A button that has a hyperlink to the last slide of your presentation. It can be valuable if you want quick access to your closing remarks because you're running out of time.

- **Go Home** (**5**): A button that has a hyperlink to the first slide of your presentation. It is the same type of hyperlink as #3, so you can choose the one with the visual you prefer.

- **Get Information** (**6**): A button allowing you to configure access to extra information. You choose the type of action in the settings window.

- **Return** (**7**): A button that has a hyperlink to the last slide viewed. This button can be very valuable if you have built extensive navigation within your presentation and need to return to a slide that is not the previous or next one. PowerPoint remembers the slide number you were on before and brings you back to it when you click on the button.

- **Video (8)**, **Document (9)**, **Sound (10)**, and **Help (11)**: Buttons that trigger the opening of the settings window but don't have anything configured yet. They are useful if their icons suit your needs and you want easy access to the settings.

- **Blank (12)**: This button can be described the same way as the previous ones, except that you can format it with the various shape formatting tools to customize it to your needs.

After drawing any of the buttons described previously, you will get the **Action Settings** window (**1**) where you will find two tabs: **Mouse Click** and **Mouse Over** (**2**). The settings are the same for both tabs. **Mouse Click** is used when you want to click on an object to produce an action, while **Mouse Over** configures the action for when your mouse cursor goes over the linked object, without needing to click (*Figure 9.3*):

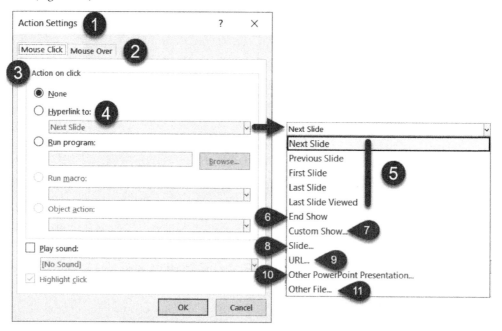

Figure 9.3 – Options in the Action Settings window

Even though there are five setting options in the **Action on click** (**3**) section in the **Action Settings** window, we will focus on the **Hyperlink to:** (**4**) option since the topic discussed is creating navigation and interactivity in our presentations. The first five options (**5**) have some preset action buttons for them. As for the other six options, they can be used for action buttons that don't have presets or to customize the ones that do. Let's see what each of them does:

- **End Show** (**6**): This allows you to configure an object that ends your presentation.

- **Custom Show…** (**7**): This allows you to link to a specific set of predetermined slides. Custom shows will be the second main topic of this chapter.

- **Slide...** (**8**): This allows you to link to a specific slide in your presentation. As an example, you could have a hidden slide that you can access with this setting. To go back to where you were, you then need to plan on using an object with the **Last Slide Viewed** setting.

- **URL...** (**9**): This allows you to open a web browser page on a specific page. When you don't need the page anymore, you can simply close it to get back to your slideshow.

- **Other PowerPoint Presentation...** (**10**): This allows you to open another presentation in slideshow mode, over the one you are presenting. Ending that second presentation brings you back to your first slideshow.

- **Other File...** (**11**): This allows you to open another type of file, such as a Word document, an Excel spreadsheet, or a PDF. As long as you have the software to open a file, it will open on top of your presentation.

To test your action buttons, you need to be in slideshow mode.

Try it yourself

The best way to understand action buttons is to try using them right away. Here is a quick exercise you can try:

- Create a few slides that either have a distinctive title or a different shape on each.

- Insert these action buttons: **Go Home** and **Return**. You can copy and paste them on every slide, or you can add them to your slide master so that they are present on all the layouts you add to your presentation.

- Add a hidden slide and add an action button that links to it from the first slide in your presentation.

- Start the slideshow and try navigating between the slides.

Action buttons are a nice starting point to quickly implement a simple navigation system in your presentation. But you can also create hyperlinks on any other types of objects—we will show a few examples of this in the following section.

Using other slide objects for navigation

Creating a navigation system in your presentation does not require that you use action buttons; any clickable object on your slide can be used. You can even use shapes added on the slide master, which then becomes a clickable navigation system on all the slides.

Let's start with an example of a slide on which you have four pictures of people on your team that are speaking during a corporate event and for which you would like easy access to their slides. Four slides have been added to represent the speakers' content. There is also the need to plan a **Return** button to the speakers' slide, but you were asked not to use visible action buttons (*Figure 9.4*):

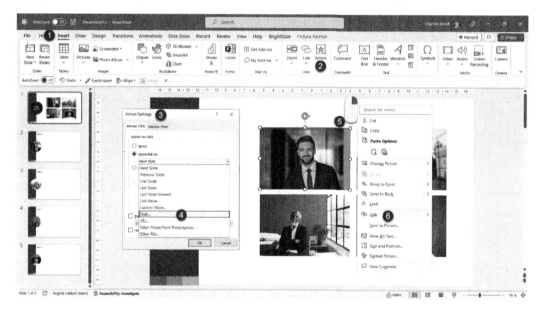

Figure 9.4 – Adding a hyperlink to a picture from the Insert tab or contextual menu

To insert a hyperlink on a selected object (in our example, it is the picture of the first speaker), you can go to the **Insert** tab (**1**), click on the **Action** button (**2**), and in the **Action Settings** window (**3**) choose **Slide…** (**4**) in the **Hyperlink to:** drop-down list. You can also *right-click* the picture (**5**) and select **Link** (**6**) in the contextual menu.

A new window opens in both cases, allowing you to choose the slide number. If you used the **Action Settings** method, the new **Hyperlink to Slide** window (**1**) is straightforward: you choose the slide number corresponding to the first speaker's content (**2**)—the list shows you the content of the title placeholder on each slide, confirming the importance of using different titles for each slide. Confirm it is the right one in **Preview** (**3**), and click the **OK** button to confirm (**4**) (*Figure 9.5*):

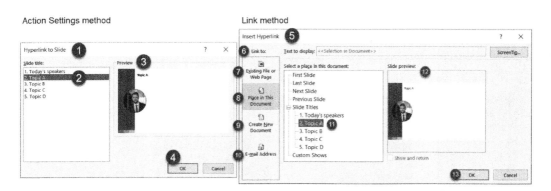

Figure 9.5 – Choosing a specific slide to create a hyperlink

The link method window is labeled **Insert Hyperlink** (**5**), and the **Link to:** pane on the left (**6**) allows you to create a hyperlink with the **Existing File or Web Page** (**7**), or **Place in This Document** (**8**) option—which is the option needed for our example—and gives you the **Create New Document** (**9**) or set up a link that allows setting up an **E-mail Address** (**10**) that starts a new email when the object is clicked. Continuing with our example, we need to choose a slide (**11**), check **Slide preview** (**12**), and click **OK** (**13**) to confirm the hyperlink.

If you have followed these steps, you now have the first picture from your menu slide linking to the second slide. Make sure you repeat the previous steps to link the remaining pictures to their respective slides. Now, let's create our invisible **Return** button so that we have an easy way to always go back to the first slide.

In my example, you might have noticed the small rectangles used as a design element in the bottom-left corner of the slides (**1**) (*Figure 9.6*):

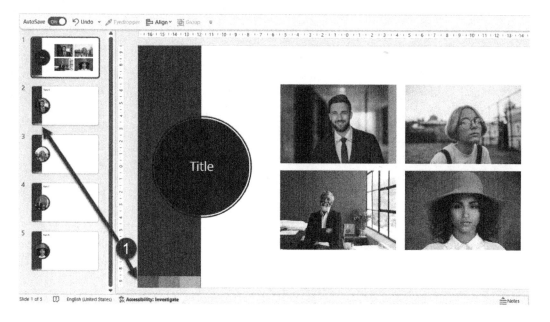

Figure 9.6 – Using design elements as clickable buttons

These rectangles can become subtle navigation elements. If you decide to use this technique for yourself, it's a great way to plan for extra content without letting your audience know, as long as you practice enough beforehand. If you want to deploy this technique for another person using the file, you need to let them know how it works well ahead of time so that they can practice too.

The best way to make sure the navigation buttons are available on all the slides, without having to do a lot of copy and paste steps, is to add them on the slide master or a specific layout in **Slide Master** view. In my example, I chose a specific layout in **Slide Master** view and did the following (*Figure 9.7*):

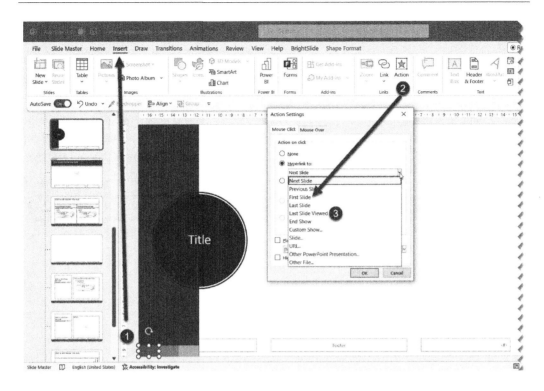

Figure 9.7 – Adding hyperlinks to slide elements in Slide Master view

1. First, *right-click* one of the shapes and go to the **Insert** tab.

2. Click on **Action** and open the **Hyperlink to:** list to choose **First Slide**. Confirm your choice by clicking **OK**. Every time I have this slide layout, I know that clicking on the first shape on the left brings me back to my menu slide.

3. Through the years, I've also made it a habit to use a second shape and use the **Last Slide Viewed** hyperlink to make sure that if I had to show something else, such as a hidden slide, I could easily come back and resume my presentation. Add this type of link to the second rectangle from the left and close the **Slide Master** view.

You can plan as many hidden links as you want, but remember that the more complicated your linking scheme is, the more practice it requires to use it seamlessly. Just as with the action buttons, the best way to understand hyperlinks in your presentations is to try them yourself. If you have created the previous linking scheme, put your presentation in slideshow mode and try the links. Start by clicking on one of the presenter pictures and practice going back to the menu slide with the hidden link.

The previous example made sense as an example in a learning environment such as this book but would not be realistic in the real world. Let's say your four presenters have many slides each—it would be much more efficient to leverage the custom shows that we will discuss in the following section.

Creating custom shows

Custom shows are a way to create and present a subset of a larger presentation file. In the past, I have used them to create a complex marketing dashboard for salespeople or even a training dashboard allowing me to choose content according to a specific topic or duration.

Let's continue with the same example used previously, except that now the presentation file has more slides for each presenter. We will want to create one custom show per presenter, and then change the hyperlink on our menu slide. Sections were created to make it easier to see the number of slides per speaker in the screenshot (*Figure 9.8*):

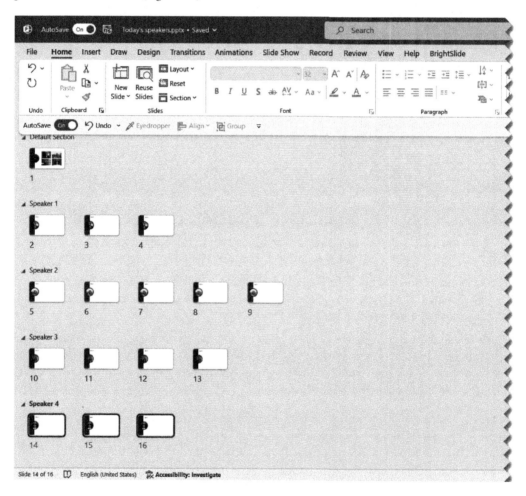

Figure 9.8 – Presentation in Slide Sorter view with four sections of speaker slides

To create custom shows, you need to go to the **Slide Show** tab (**1**) and click on the **Custom Slide Show** button (**2**) to access the **Custom Shows…** feature (**3**) (*Figure 9.9*):

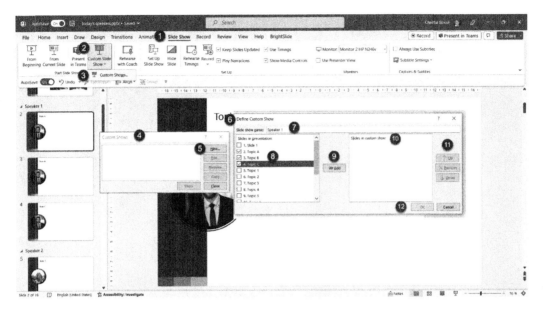

Figure 9.9 – Accessing Custom Shows… from the Slide Show tab

From the **Custom Shows** window (**4**), create a custom show by clicking on the **New…** button (**5**) to get to the **Define Custom Show** window (**6**). Here are the elements you need to set to create a custom show:

- Give the custom show a name in the **Slide show name:** field (**7**).

- Click on the *checkboxes* of the slides you want in it (**8**)—this step will be difficult if you have simple section names in the title placeholders and have not noted the slide numbers to include in each custom show.

- Click on the **Add** button (**9**) to include the slides in the **Slides in custom show:** field (**10**). You can select any slide included in this field to activate the **Up**, **Down**, and **Remove** buttons (**11**) to adapt the slide set and sequence. Click on **OK** (**12**) to confirm your custom show.

Repeat the steps to create the four custom shows needed for this example. After you are done, your **Custom Shows** window (**1**) should look like this one (*Figure 9.10*):

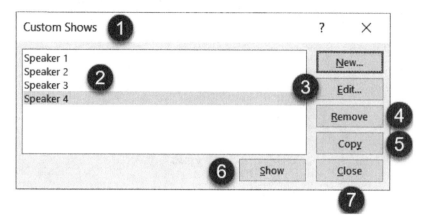

Figure 9.10 – Custom Shows window options

You will see your list of custom shows (**2**), and whenever you have one selected, you can use any of the following buttons to make some changes:

- The **Edit…** button (**3**) is used to make changes to the slides included in a custom show or their order.

- The **Remove** button (**4**) is used to delete a custom show you don't need anymore.

- The **Copy** button (**5**) allows you to make a copy of an existing custom show and then use **Edit…** (**3**) to rename and change the content or its sequence. It can be very useful when you need to create long custom shows that have only a few changes between them.

- The **Show** button (**6**) starts the selected custom show in slideshow mode so that you can view it.

- When you are done with making changes and don't want to view any of the custom shows, just click on the **Close** button (**7**).

It's now time to go back to our first slide of the presentation file and make some changes to the links we previously added. The first step is to *right-click* a speaker picture (**1**), then on **Edit Link** (**2**) (*Figure 9.11*):

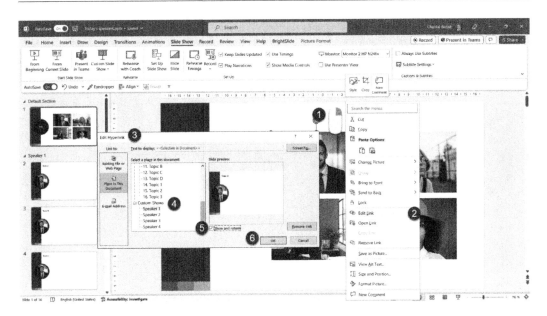

Figure 9.11 – Editing an existing hyperlink to point to a custom show

From the **Edit Hyperlink** window (**3**), you need to do the following:

- Scroll down the list of slides to view your newly created **Custom Shows** (**4**) list. Select the one corresponding to your picture.

- Click on the **Show and return** checkbox (**5**). This is a very important step to make your linking process efficient. Doing so means that when you reach the last slide of the custom show, the slideshow comes back to your first slide. No other **Back** button or linked slide object is required.

- Click on **OK** (**6**) to confirm the hyperlink change.

Repeat the same process for the remaining pictures, giving you an efficient selection board while reducing the number of navigation elements you have to create. We used a multi-speaker event example, but this concept can be applied to many types of presentations, such as training content.

If you have a very large file containing all the slides available for your topic, you can create custom shows simply to avoid having to create separate files every time you present. You can simply start a custom show from the **Slide Show** tab (**1**), click on the **Custom Slide Show** button (**2**), and select any existing custom show from the list to start your presentation (**3**) (*Figure 9.12*):

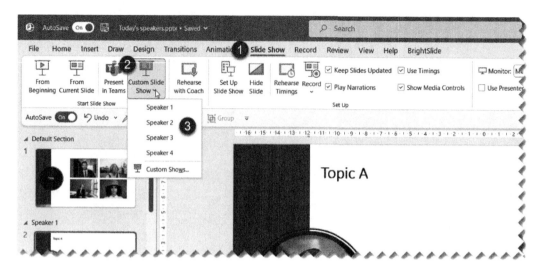

Figure 9.12 – Starting a custom show in slideshow mode

As you can see, building interactivity into your presentations can be done with features that have been available within PowerPoint for ages! If you are an Office 2019, Office 2021, or M365 user, you should consider using Zoom—a newer feature—discussed in our next section.

Using the Zoom feature to navigate your content

Microsoft describes its Zoom feature as a way to make your presentations more dynamic and exciting. I call it hyperlinking on steroids because you might not have to use the features described in the previous sections ever again.

> **Tip**
>
> The word *zoom* has been used a lot in the PowerPoint interface. The Zoom *feature* refers to hyperlinks created to other slides or sections, not to be confused with the Zoom *animation* (applied to slide objects), the Zoom *transition* (applied on a slide), and the tool used to magnify your slide view, also called *Zoom*.

Since the Zoom feature was introduced, I must say I have saved a lot of design time while still creating interactive content. There are three types of zooms in PowerPoint:

- **Summary Zoom** allows you to quickly create your navigation page in just a few clicks. It adds a new slide with the Zoom objects on it, linking to the selected sections.

- **Section Zoom** allows you to create a navigation page from the existing sections in your presentation file. It adds a Zoom object to an existing slide.

- **Slide Zoom** allows you to quickly create a link to a specific slide in your presentation. It adds a Zoom object to an existing slide.

Let's start with an example of how to create a summary zoom in the following section.

Creating a summary zoom

I suggest that you open a file that already has a few slides to follow along with the explanation of this feature, or you can simply choose one of the templates or theme files provided by Microsoft. The following example was created with the **Modern conference presentation** template.

To insert a summary zoom, simply go to the **Insert** tab (**1**), then click on the **Zoom** button (**2**) and select **Summary Zoom** (**3**) (*Figure 9.13*):

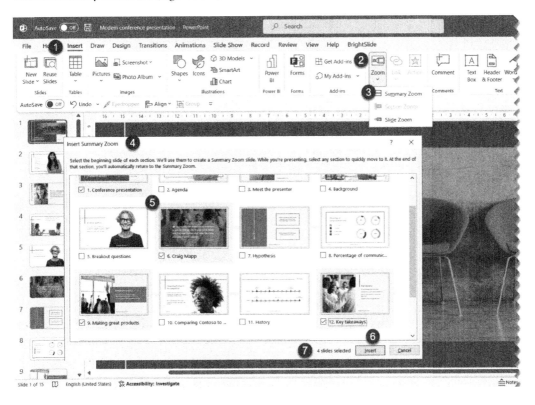

Figure 9.13 – Inserting a summary zoom

In the **Insert Summary Zoom** window (**4**), select the checkbox for all the slides you want to use to start a section you want to navigate to (**5**), then click the **Insert** button (**6**). In my example, four slides (**7**) were selected to create the summary.

PowerPoint automatically inserts a *new summary slide* (**1**) with the four thumbnails of the slides you selected as part of a *Zoom slide object* (**2**) that can be resized when selected. As you can see, *sections* are also automatically created (**3**) (*Figure 9.14*):

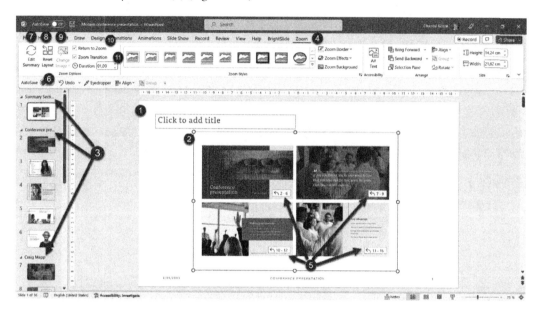

Figure 9.14 – Summary zoom slide inserted and sections created

With the *Zoom slide object* selected (**2**), open the **Zoom** tab (**4**) to access options and formatting tools. A small tooltip identifies the slide numbers included in each section (**5**). Since the formatting options in this tab are similar to many others discussed in previous chapters (for example, shapes, images, and so on), we will only discuss the **Zoom Options** types (**6**):

- **Edit Summary** (**7**): You can edit your summary slide by removing sections, or adding a new one you just created, without having to start the process over.

- **Reset Layout** (**8**): You can move, resize, and edit each section thumbnail individually. If you want to go back to the original layout provided by PowerPoint, this is the button to click.

- **Change Image** (**9**): This button will be available if you have selected one of the thumbnails in the summary. It allows you to change its image if you don't want to use the image of the first slide of the section.

- **Return to Zoom** (**10**): This checkbox is selected by default and acts exactly as the **Show and return** feature when linking to custom shows, as discussed in the previous section. If you uncheck it, it means that you are not going back to your summary slide when you finish a section.

- **Zoom Transition** and **Duration** (**11**): These options give the zooming-in effect after clicking on a thumbnail to reach a section and its duration; unchecking the **Zoom Transition** box removes the effect. I suggest that the only change you consider for the duration is increasing it, never reducing it. A very short duration increases the possibility of creating a motion-sickness effect for some people.

Without making any changes to the options, you would be ready to use your zoom. If you followed along, simply go into slideshow mode and try it. **Summary Zoom** is an excellent choice when you have a presentation file that contains many slides, even if you have not created any sections in it yet. And when you do have sections already, PowerPoint recognizes them and automatically selects the first slide of each section when you insert a summary zoom.

If you don't need a summary slide but would like to have easy access to a section already created in your presentation, that is when you need to use a section zoom, the topic of the next section.

Inserting a section zoom

Let's say you have a hidden resource section at the end of your presentation, just in case you need extra content to answer a question or support your idea. The easy way to access that content is to use **Section Zoom**. It requires that you plan where it would make sense to include it. If you have studied the topics described in *Chapter 1*, *Analyzing Your Audience and Presentation Delivery Needs*, you should have a good idea already.

Let's use the following example to insert a section zoom on slide **12** (**1**) where we might need our resources (*Figure 9.15*):

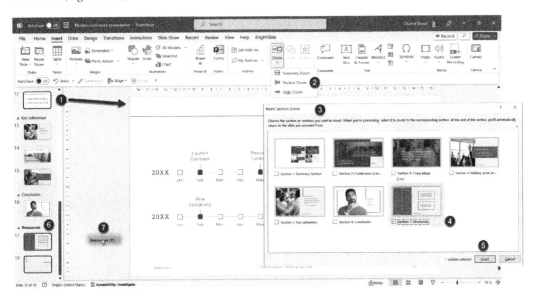

Figure 9.15 – Inserting a section zoom on a specific slide

You need to click on the **Zoom** button in the **Insert** tab and select **Section Zoom** (**2**) to get access to the **Insert Section Zoom** window (**3**). Select the **Resources** section (**4**) and click the **Insert** button (**5**). You can also click on the *section name* in the slide pane (**6**) and keep your finger on the left mouse button to drag the section onto the slide (**7**).

As shown in the next screenshot, you then get a **Section Zoom** slide object (**1**) that can be moved and resized. It shows which slide numbers are included in the section (**2**), and the **Zoom** tab (**3**) contains the same options and formatting tools as **Summary Zoom**. By default, you will return to your slide after showing the section (**4**) (*Figure 9.16*):

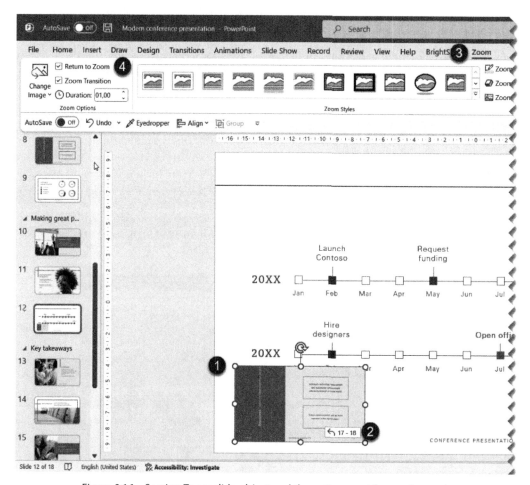

Figure 9.16 – Section Zoom slide object and the options and formatting tools

A section zoom is easy to insert and use, so now that you know how to do it, do not hesitate to plan more content that can be used to answer questions or show extra information because you have more time than you expected.

When you only need to access one slide, you don't need to create a separate section for it. You can simply use a slide zoom, which is the topic of our next section.

Inserting a slide zoom

If you have several unrelated slides to be used as extra content or resources, you can use **Slide Zoom**. It works exactly the same as **Section Zoom**, which we just talked about, except that the link points to only one slide.

You can again go to **Insert | Zoom**, but this time select **Slide Zoom** to access a window allowing you to choose the slide number you want to insert. Or, the method I prefer: click and drag the slide thumbnail from the slide pane onto the slide. The result is a **Slide Zoom** slide object (**1**) and a tooltip showing the *slide number* (**2**) where we will navigate. There is one important difference in **Zoom Options** (**3**), though: the **Return to Zoom** option is not selected! If your intention is to easily come back to your previous slide, make sure to check that box (*Figure 9.17*):

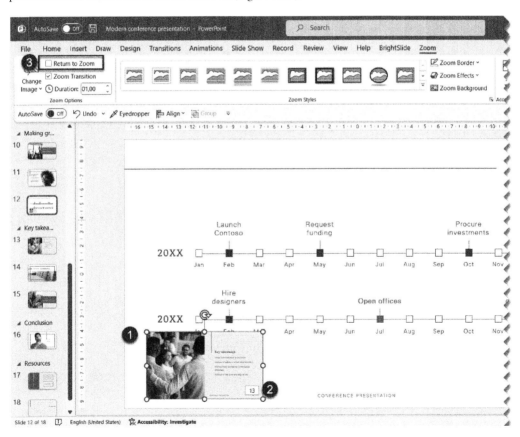

Figure 9.17 – Inserting a slide zoom

You now know the basics to quickly create a navigation system in your presentation with the help of the three Zoom features. Delivering this type of presentation can be as simple as clicking your remote or using your keyboard. But if you have included section or slide zooms on your slides, keep in mind that you will need to click on them to access their content. If that is how you want to evolve in terms of presentation interactions, I would suggest you start practicing with a remote that has a mouse control.

Your Zoom slide objects can be resized as much as you want, but maybe your goal is to have a completely hidden menu you can access only when you need it. That is what we will see in the last section of this chapter.

Creating triggered menus

Now that you have seen many features that can help you create more interactive presentations, let's create an advanced interactive menu with the help of slide zooms and a trigger animation. The result of this technique will be that when clicking on an invisible shape on my slide (**1**), a *menu with two slide zooms* (**2**) will move in from the left of the slide (**3**) to allow accessing either of the slides (*Figure 9.18*):

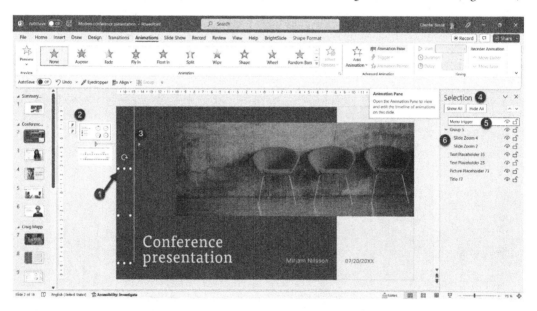

Figure 9.18 – Using a hidden Slide Zoom menu

As you can see in the **Selection** pane (**4**), the invisible shape has been renamed **Menu trigger** (**5**) and the *slide zooms* are part of **Group 5** (**6**).

Since we have discussed all the components included in the creation of this example in previous sections and chapters, I want to challenge you a little more to recreate it. What follows are all the steps to create a hidden menu that can be made visible with a trigger. Try it, then have a look in the *Further reading* section for a link to a tutorial video. Here are the steps:

1. Select a slide where you want to access your hidden menu.

2. Insert two slide zooms, resize them, and move them outside of the canvas in the gray area, on the left of the slide. Make sure the **Return to Zoom** option is selected.

3. Group the two slide-zoom objects together.

4. Insert a shape to be used as a clicking element. If you want to make it invisible, remove its outline and make the fill 99% transparent. Do not use 100% transparency as it has been known to make hyperlinks stop working, and it is not always predictable whether it will happen or not. You can also decide to leave it visible but include it in your design.

5. Open the **Selection** pane and rename the shape to find it easily when animating the objects.

6. Add a motion path to the slide zoom group, making it move to the right so that it ends on the slide area. Click on **Trigger** to select the shape that will be clicked on to start the animation.

7. Add an exit **Fade** animation to the slide zoom group. Click on **Trigger** again and select the same shape as the previous step.

8. Test your animation.

This advanced animation tip using triggers and zooms can be a very creative way to access extra content you have planned but want to access on-demand only. If you start using a few topics discussed in this chapter for your presentations, you will increase audience engagement tremendously.

Summary

In this chapter, we have seen how to create and use various navigation elements in our presentations and create custom shows so that we can easily access a subset of our slides without creating a new file. We have also discussed the use of the various Zoom features to quickly create more interactive content, and how to create a hidden Zoom menu with the use of triggers.

Becoming a more flexible and interactive presenter is something you should consider. Having the possibility to move away from a strictly linear delivery style is much more engaging for audiences. I have been including flexibility and interactivity in my presentations for many years now, even when I had to plan and create everything with hyperlinks, triggers, and custom shows. Even though it was very time-consuming, I was always rewarded by audiences asking me whether I could go back to a previous section or slide because they realized I was not stuck in a linear slideshow.

Now that PowerPoint offers us more features to speed up the process, not having enough time to consider flexible and interactive content is not a good excuse anymore, especially if you want to stand out in your industry and be perceived as an expert. It does require that you plan and practice more, but you will be rewarded with increased audience satisfaction, which might have a big impact on your presentation.

In the next chapter—the last one in the content creation part of this book—we will be discussing PowerPoint third-party add-ins that can help you improve your workflow or add features not included in the application natively.

Further reading

- *Microsoft Support* article on action settings: `https://support.microsoft.com/en-us/office/add-commands-to-your-presentation-with-action-buttons-7db2c0f8-5424-4780-93cb-8ac2b6b5f6ce`

- Link to a video tutorial on triggered menus: `https://youtu.be/f48e-dmYkSY`

10

Using PowerPoint Third-Party Add-Ins

By now, you probably realize that PowerPoint has become a very powerful creative application. It has functions and tools that will fit most creators' needs, but if your use of PowerPoint becomes intensive, you might find that some workflows could be improved to make your days more efficient. This is when you can consider using third-party add-ins. If you are part of a larger organization, make sure to check whether you can install any add-ins with your IT department. Some IT settings will block third-party installations.

There are a lot of PowerPoint add-ins available on the market – some of them are free and others need to be purchased. When I was reflecting on which add-ins I should include in this chapter, I decided to use trust and security as my criteria. If I was going to suggest some add-ins, I wanted to make sure I know the developers and that their add-ins are safe for your computers.

Therefore, all the add-ins suggested in this chapter are from people I know personally – I have even met them in real life! They did not pay me to talk about their products, but they did give me a license or shared some visuals with me for paid products that I did not already use. I know that their products are hugely popular in the presentation design industry. The add-in creators I have chosen to feature in this chapter are as follows:

- BrightCarbon
- Neuxpower
- Billion Dollar Graphics
- PPTools

Technical requirements

The add-ins featured in this chapter are known to be compatible with many desktop versions of PowerPoint on Windows and macOS. I suggest that you visit the developers' websites for more details on compatibility (see *Further reading*). Be aware that since the subscription version of PowerPoint is updated on an ongoing basis, it is possible that the screenshots shown in this chapter will differ from your version of the application.

BrightCarbon

BrightCarbon is a presentation and e-learning agency that was founded in the United Kingdom, with offices in Manchester, Bristol, and London in the UK, and Boston in the US. I have met Richard Goring, its director, and Jamie Garroch, its principal technical consultant, at The Presentation Summit many times – we are all trying to make a difference in our community as Microsoft MVPs specializing in PowerPoint and other M365 applications.

They have two products that help individuals, teams, and companies, which will be discussed in the following sections:

- BrightSlide is a free add-in that helps you be more productive
- BrandIn is a paid add-in that helps organizations create brand-compliant content

Using BrightSlide (for free)

This add-in was first created to help BrightCarbon designers make their design workflow more efficient, adding shortcuts and functionality users needed but that were not available in PowerPoint. With their first core value being "*Share our knowledge and our time*," it was not long before they decided to share their valuable add-in with the rest of the world. Needless to say, our industry experts were quick to spread the word to all presentation creators and designers. You can find BrightSlide on their products page via the link supplied in *Further reading*.

The BrightSlide add-in would probably be voted the most complete tool available for free in our industry. It has nine tool categories, each containing many features. At the time of writing this book, the add-in has over 50 different features for improving your workflow and productivity. This might be different by the time you try BrightSlide because Jamie and the BrightCarbon product team add features regularly as their designers or add-in users voice their needs.

To use BrightSlide, first, you need to download the Windows or macOS installer from the product page (see *Further reading*) and install it on your computer. When you open your PowerPoint application, you will see a new **BrightSlide** (**1**) tab (see *Figure 10.1*):

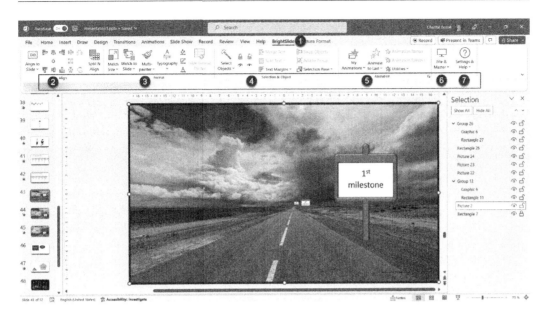

Figure 10.1 – The BrightSlide add-in tab in PowerPoint

Let's explore the main categories of features you will find in your new tab:

- **Align** (**2**): This category has tools that give you more control and options to align your slide objects beyond the standard alignment tools found in PowerPoint. For example, you can create a grid in shapes with only a few clicks. You can even choose to align objects to the first or last selected object.

- **Format** (**3**): The tools in this category will help you edit multiple objects at once or copy complex formatting. This category can help you copy the size, position, format, adjustments, and animations from an object to any other object.

- **Selection & Object** (**4**): This category is here to make your life easier. Selecting objects according to a specific characteristic, such as a fill or outline color, hiding or showing slide objects without scrolling down your **Selection** pane, and swapping objects are only a few of the gems in this group. Are you excited yet?

- **Animation** (**5**): The tools in this category will save you a lot of time when trying to recreate complex animations. You can use some of BrightSlide's starting sequences or add your own to the library.

- **File & Master** (**6**): This category has many tools to help you set up your templates, such as setting up guides, editing your theme colors, setting custom colors, assigning layouts in bulk, comparing multiple presentations, and many more. The features take care of most repetitive tasks.

- **Settings & Help** (**7**): This is where you can find add-in customization options for the ribbon and shortcuts. You also have access to two subcategories of features:

  - **Contextual Tools**: Those tools become available when you right-click on slide objects such as tables or lines and allow you to move sections within your presentation easily.

  - **Passive Features**: These are features that don't appear in the ribbon and modify default PowerPoint behaviors, which you can choose to turn off or on. As an example, you can copy and paste objects from one slide to other slides you have selected, duplicate comments when duplicating slides, or resize multiple lines in one go.

If you want the complete details, there is a **Help** section on their website that lists the features with a description of what they do, but I will share some of the tools I know that even part-time presentation designers should use to save some time. To help you find them, I will refer to the names of the groups on the ribbon in the following subsections.

The Align group

This group has so many alignments features that it's almost impossible to choose between them. I finally set my choice on three that I find particularly interesting to help you quickly overlay many objects one on top of the other, distribute them on a grid, or create a new grid.

The first feature helps us overlay all selected objects on top of each other and is named **Align Objects Centre and Middle** (**1**) (see *Figure 10.2*):

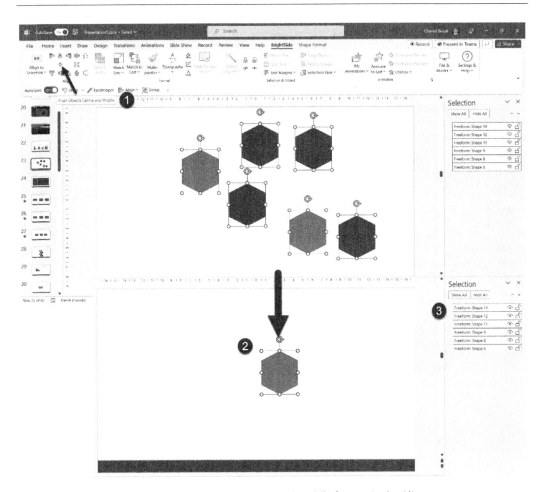

Figure 10.2 – The Align Objects Centre and Middle feature in the Align group

With several objects selected, hexagons in our example, just click on the feature in the ribbon to overlay all of them with one click (**2**). As you can see in the **Selection** pane (**3**), all the shapes are present on the slide. You can use this type of alignment for animations that reveal one shape after the other, always in the same position.

If I use the same starting point as the previous example, with six hexagons spread out with no specific alignment on the slide, and use the **Distribute to Grid** tool (**1**) this time, BrightSlide aligns and distributes them (**2**) and opens the **Distribute to Grid** dialog box (**3**), in which you can adapt the grid (*Figure 10.3*):

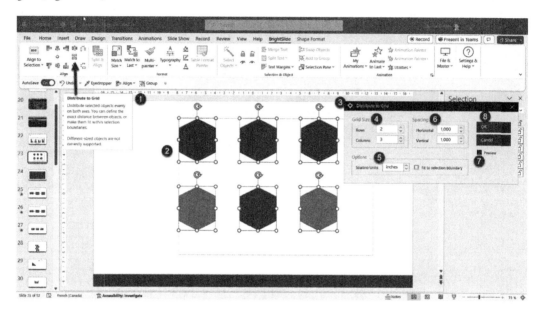

Figure 10.3 – The Distribute to Grid feature in the Align group

You can then adjust the number of **Rows** and **Columns** (**4**), set **Spacing Units** (**5**) as inches, centimeters, or pixels, and adapt the **Horizontal** and **Vertical** spacing (**6**) between your slide objects. The **Preview** checkbox (**7**) is checked by default and is very helpful for viewing what your grid will look like before clicking on the **OK** button (**8**) to confirm your choices.

Even though PowerPoint's **Smart Guides** have helped me align and distribute shapes on a grid for a long time, this BrightSlide feature saves many clicks in a day, making it much more efficient.

The third feature I want to show you from the **Align** group requires you to start from a single object or a group of objects on your slide (**1**) and use the **Split & Align** feature (**2**) (see *Figure 10.4*):

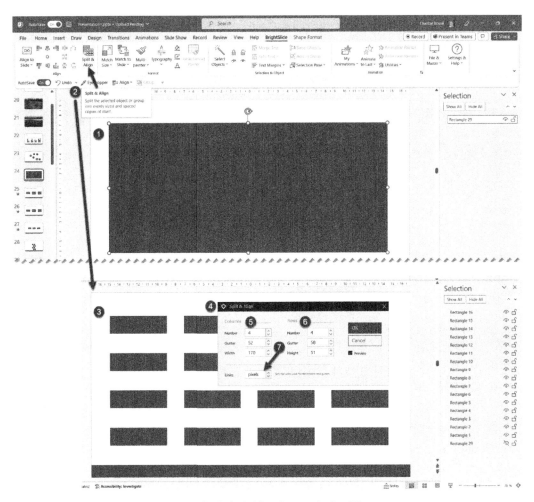

Figure 10.4 – The Split & Align feature in the Align group

As the tooltip suggests (**2**), this feature creates a grid of evenly sized and spaced copies of a group or the selected object. In my example, it created a grid of evenly sized and spaced rectangles (**3**) while opening the **Split & Align** dialog box (**4**). You can adjust the settings as needed for **Columns** (**5**) and **Rows** (**6**). The numbers you see for **Gutter** (spacing between the objects) and **Width** and **Height** (**7**) are impacted by the setting you choose for **Units**. When testing the feature, I realized that using inches or centimeters was not as flexible as using pixels, which are much smaller units. My best advice is to do a few tests the first time you try it. It will be time well invested because BrightSlide will remember your previous settings and use them the next time you use the **Split & Align** feature.

Many more features are available in the **Align** group. The best way to know which ones would be useful for your type of presentation work is to try them out, or at least review BrightSlide's **Help** section on the website.

The Format group

This category also has a great list of features to work with, but since I have limited space, I'll just point out the **Match Size** feature (**1**), which allows you to quickly make both **Width** and **Height** universal for objects on a slide (or either one of the two) with a single click (**2**) (see *Figure 10.5*):

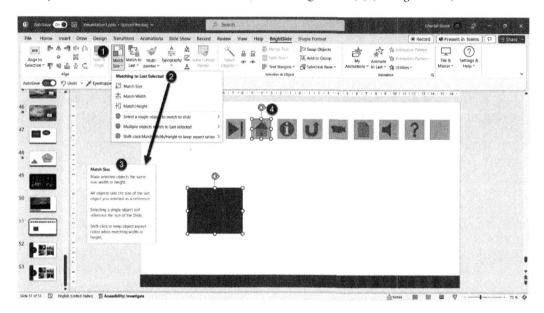

Figure 10.5 – The Match Size feature in the Format group

To make sure you get the desired result, pay attention to the tooltip when you hover over the feature button (**3**). By default, the last object selected becomes the size reference for any objects created afterward. In my example, if the **Home** action button (**4**) is selected last, then the **Match Size** feature will make the new rectangle I add a perfect square, the same size as the action button.

The BrightSlide add-in is a treasure trove for anyone creating visuals with PowerPoint. I could go on for many more pages, showing you features that can help you select objects according to characteristics such as shape, fill, or outline color, or others that help you review or export your file more flexibly than with the native PowerPoint features. My best advice is to download the add-in and give it a try. You don't have anything to lose – it is free! – but you have so much to gain in terms of efficiency and productivity. If you are wondering why BrightCarbon made this free to all users, it's because of their company culture, which believes in sharing with the community.

Let's now see an overview of their BrandIn add-in, helping users in organizations to stay on brand.

Using BrandIn (paid)

Many organizations struggle with keeping on brand. Most of the time, they have invested in creating a branded PowerPoint template that uses their corporate colors, provides graphic elements in sample slides, and was planned with a set of standard layouts – but users often don't have the PowerPoint proficiency required to navigate the whole template properly, or the time to read dozens of pages of a brand guide.

That is why BrandIn was created. It helps organizations offer easy access to a library of assets while helping users stay on brand with its brand-checking capabilities, all within PowerPoint. The add-in fixes many of the most annoying presentation creation problems in organizations:

- Users select the wrong fonts, colors, or shapes
- Users add online images instead of those from the brand library
- There are problems related to slides copied from other presentations, bloated templates, and masters
- Users waste hours struggling to make slides brand-compliant

When BrandIn is installed, it creates a new **BrandIn** tab (**1**) in PowerPoint (see *Figure 10.6*):

Figure 10.6 – The BrandIn tab in PowerPoint

It gives users access to six groups of features essential to help them stay on brand:

- **Brand Slides** (**2**): This group of features helps users access everything they need in terms of slides, such as layouts and a slide library.
- **Brand Font** (**3**): This group limits the font choices to the ones your organization has picked out.
- **Brand Images** (**4**): This group gives your users access to approved brand pictures while still being able to use other sources if required.
- **Brand Illustrations** (**5**): This is where users can access brand illustrations while still having access to other PowerPoint illustration features.
- **Brand Colours** (**6**): This group gives users access to brand colors easily, with no more guesswork.
- **Brand Check** (**7**): This feature is where the magic happens. It allows users to easily check their presentation for anything that could be off-brand. BrightCarbon also mentions on its website that it can make it work for multiple brands and sub-brands.

Let's have a closer look at the **Slide Library** button (**1**), which can be a huge time-saver for users (see *Figure 10.7*):

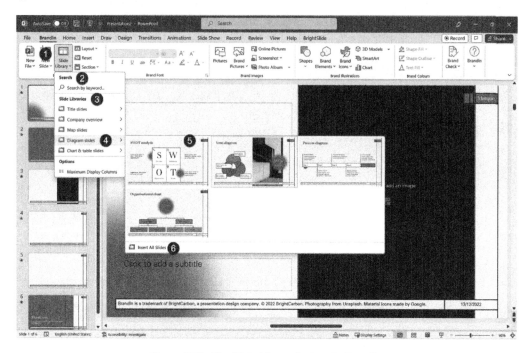

Figure 10.7 – The Slide Library feature in BrandIn

It has a **Search** feature (**2**), which allows users to use keywords to find slide models. They can use any of the **Slide Libraries** categories (**3**) and browse what the organization has made available. In the example, you can see the **Diagram slides** category (**4**) offers four different slides to choose from. Clicking on one of the slide thumbnails (**5**) inserts it into the presentation while the **Insert All Slides** feature (**6**) inserts all the model slides at once.

Similarly, users can access the **Brand Pictures** (**1**) and **Brand Icons** (**2**) buttons to either search for what they are looking for by keyword (**3**), or use the **Picture Libraries** (**4**) or **Icon Libraries** (**5**) categories (see *Figure 10.8*):

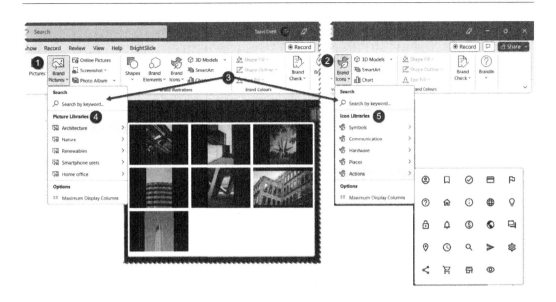

Figure 10.8 – Brand pictures and icons in BrandIn

Finally, let's have a look at what I would call the magic button in the BrandIn add-in, **Check Brand** (**1**) (see *Figure 10.9*):

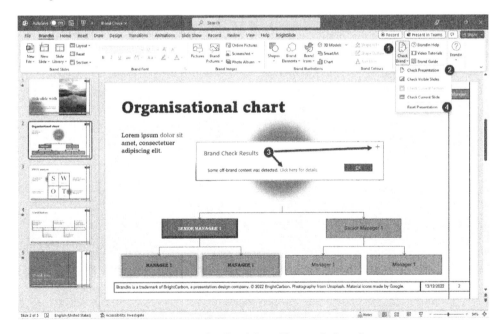

Figure 10.9 – The Check Brand button in BrandIn

Users can easily check the whole presentation with **Check Presentation** (**2**) or some parts of it with any of the other options. The add-in goes through the presentation contents and shows the user a **Brand Check Results** window (**3**), in which they can follow a link to check the details of the off-brand elements – or they can use the + sign to expand the details. The rules used to check the presentation are set by the client and can either be fixed automatically without exceptions (for example, the wrong font has been used for the title placeholder) or users can receive advisory information on elements that are off-brand and they can decide whether to ignore or fix them. If they have ignored certain changes and later decide they want to make their content fully compliant, they just need to go back to the **Check Brand** button and select **Reset Presentation** (**4**) in the list so they can run **Check Brand** again and pick up the non-compliant elements again.

The best way to assess what BrandIn can do for your organization is to read the product page on the BrightCarbon website. At the bottom of the page, you will also see pricing information. If you see this add-in as an unnecessary cost, it's because you have no idea how valuable the time of your whole team is and how much time you waste during a year struggling to make your presentations on brand. If you see it as an investment that will help you spend more time on other high-value tasks in your organization, I strongly suggest arranging a demo with the BrightCarbon team. They will be able to run through the features live, helping you decide whether it suits your needs.

BrightCarbon also added a brand new add-in as I was writing this book. Have a look at their site to learn about ShowMaker. Let's now move on to two other add-ins from Neuxpower in the next section.

Neuxpower

The **Neuxpower** team has been building software for over 20 years now – and I have had the pleasure of knowing Mike Power, the owner, for over 16 years! His passion and specialty are helping small business owners use technology to support and enable their growth. Neuxpower has amazingly efficient file compression applications and a PowerPoint productivity add-in that we will introduce in the following sections.

Using Neuxpower's compression tools

I remember when the biggest struggle I had with presentations, or any other Microsoft Office file for that matter, was the huge file size. The first time I used Neuxpower's compression tool, probably 16 years ago, I was blown away by how efficient it was at reducing the file size while making sure images remained high quality enough that the audience could not see the difference.

Since then, the product has evolved into five distinct products, which you can see on the products page on their website (see *Further reading*). In this section, I will introduce you to **WeCompress** (free) and **NXPowerLite** (paid). Even though this chapter is about PowerPoint add-ins, I feel any user who creates content should know about their compression tools.

If you don't have great needs in terms of file compression and your files have a maximum size of 50 MB, you can then head to the `wecompress.com` website (**1**), or click on the product name on the Neuxpower products page (see *Figure 10.10*):

Figure 10.10 – The WeCompress online file compression tool from Neuxpower

As you can see, you can compress the most common types of files used in organizations these days: **PDF**, **PowerPoint**, **Word**, **Excel**, **JPEG**, **PNG**, and **TIFF** files (**2**). You only need to click on the + sign (**3**) to browse your files and add one, or you can click and drag a file directly into the browser page. When the online application has finished processing your file, you will receive a **File ready** message (**4**). In our example, the initial **9.62 MB** file size was brought down to **716 KB** (**5**). The only thing left to do is click on the **Download** button (**6**) to move your compressed file into the `Downloads` folder on your computer.

The file I tested in the previous example showed the same photo quality as in my original file on all the slides. The only elements that seemed to be affected by the process were the small images created by the Zoom feature for my interactive menus. As you can see, it is very easy to use and has no cost at all.

If you have more frequent needs or your files are over 50 MB most of the time, I suggest that you invest in the NXPowerLite desktop version. You have much more control over specific compression settings, such as the level of **JPEG quality** (**1**) you want in your presentation files, or the creation of various custom settings for **PDF** files (**2**), **Word** files (**3**), **Excel** files (**4**), and **JPEG** files (**5**) (see *Figure 10.11*):

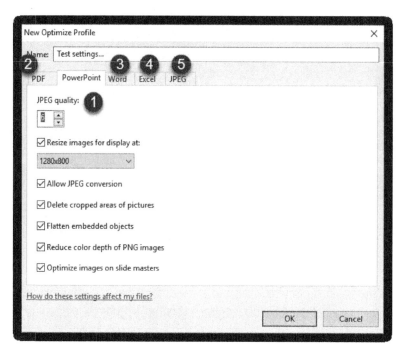

Figure 10.11 – Custom settings available in the NXPowerLite desktop compression application

NXPowerLite also integrates with your File Explorer on Windows, with Finder on Mac, with Outlook, and much more. The license is a one-time affordable purchase per user, and there is a 14-day trial available on their website. The desktop version installs an NXPowerLite group in the **Home** tab of your Office applications to help you optimize your files while you are creating them.

Even if the file compression tools are not PowerPoint add-ins per se, I'm sure you will find them useful when dealing with large presentations. In the next section, the Neuxpower product I want to discuss is an add-in that helps you manage key resources in a presentation file while flagging and fixing potential problems.

Using Slidewise (paid)

There are many pain points in presentation files. Users have been complaining for many years that it is difficult to check for fonts in a file and replace them, and trying to figure out which layouts are used in which slides can take forever if you have a presentation that contains many slides. These elements are some of the pain points addressed by Slidewise.

After installing Slidewise, you will see a new **Slidewise** button (**1**) in your **Home** tab (**2**) (see *Figure 10.12*):

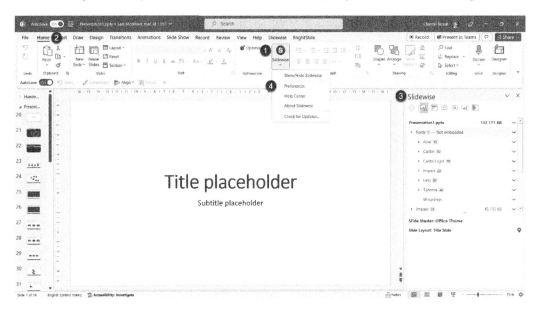

Figure 10.12 – The Slidewise add-in available on the Home tab

When you click on the **Slidewise** button (**1**) it will **Show** or **Hide** the **Slidewise** task pane (**3**) automatically. If you click on the bottom arrow of the button to open the features list (**4**), you can set your **Preferences** for the add-in, open the **Help Center** web page, find the **About Slidewise** window, where you will find your license information too, and **Check for Updates**.

Instead of showing a before and after result for only a few select features in Slidewise, I will show you various views of the task pane so you have a better understanding of everything the add-in can do. Let's start with the description of each view available in the task pane (see *Figure 10.13*):

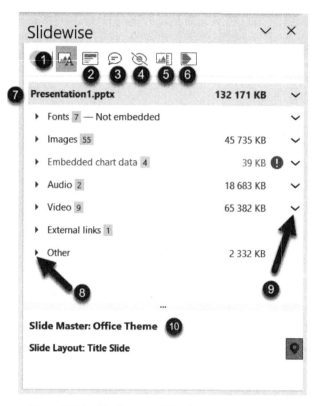

Figure 10.13 – The Fonts and Media view in Slidewise

- **Fonts and Media (1)**: This view allows you to manage various elements found in your presentation file, such as fonts, images, embedded data, audio, video, and so on. In just a few clicks, you can see where the elements are in the file and accomplish tasks such as embedding fonts; exporting images, audio, and video; or removing embedded data. If you have ever struggled with trying to find odd fonts in a file and replace them, this is a great feature to have to hand.

- **Slide Masters (2)**: This view allows you to view all the masters and layouts in your file and find out which slides use them. The beauty of this view is having features that allow you to consolidate masters, remove unused masters and layouts, and even reassign slides between layouts. This removes all the manual work usually required to clean up a file that is cluttered with too many masters and layouts.

- **Notes and Metadata** (**3**): Getting easy access to all your speaker notes and review comments in a presentation file usually requires many steps. In this view of the Slidewise task pane, you can easily see which slides have notes or comments made by the speaker, and then quickly export or delete them.

- **Hidden Content** (**4**): This view helps you find empty placeholders and hidden slides so that you can delete them. Be careful with deleting all empty placeholders because it can make your file less accessible to screen readers. What you could do is use this feature to find empty placeholders and navigate to each slide to make sure you have at least a Title placeholder on each slide.

- **Image Audit** (**5**): This view allows you to scan for images that are too large or that might be of poor quality in your file. The feature is **Off** by default to avoid slowing down the add-in. What you might want to do is turn the toggle to **On** to see which slides contain images bloating your file and which images are poor quality. You can then make any image changes as needed. For oversized images, you would not have to do anything if you were using NXPowerLite.

- **Transitions** (**6**): Figuring out whether all your slides have the right transition can take a long time if your file contains many slides. With this view, you can see the transition applied to each slide and easily select slides in the pane before going to the **Transitions** tab and applying the one you need.

- You will see the name of your file and its size below the icons of the views when you are in the **Fonts and Media** view (**7**).

- Clicking on one of the arrows on the left (**8**) expands the list of elements found in the category. This is where you will see font names, image types, slide numbers, and so on.

- Clicking on the arrow on the right (**9**) opens a list of actions you can take, such as embedding or replacing fonts, using the **Show** option in a PowerPoint action to navigate to a slide, and so on.

- At the bottom of the pane, you have the **Inspector** tool (**10**), showing the details of an object that you have selected on a slide, the name of the Slide Master, and the name of the layout used for the selected slide.

Do not fear having problems with this add-in just because I have not covered every feature individually. When you install Slidewise, it opens a `Slidewise Get Started Guide.pptx` file (**1**) (see *Figure 10.14*):

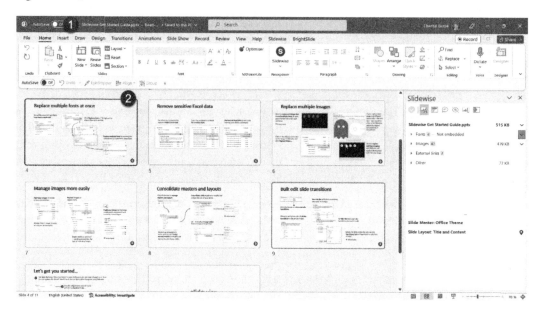

Figure 10.14 – Slidewise Get Started Guide

As you can see from **Slide Sorter** view (**2**), the Neuxpower team has ensured that you have access to all the important information to get you started – whether it's replacing fonts, removing sensitive data, or replacing images, you will be able to follow the simple steps. They even have an exercise on replacing your first font with Slidewise.

You really should go to Neuxpower's products page (see *Further reading*) and download Slidewise so that you can try it for free for 30 days. That's the best way to see whether it is worth the investment in the kind of presentation work you need to do regularly. However, being a one-time purchase add-in, even if you use it only a few times per year, it will pay for itself with only one use.

So far, we have covered productivity, presentation management, and clean-up tools. Let's move on to an add-in that will help you create or access graphics to express yourself more visually.

Billion Dollar Graphics

Billion Dollar Graphics was founded by Mike Parkinson, a very talented visual communicator I have known for many years. Leveraging his 25 years of expertise, he has created how-to books, training workshops, and an amazingly useful add-in called **Build-a-Graphic**. It allows users to build their content using any of the thousands of graphics available within the add-in or use prebuilt graphics to speed up the process.

Using Build-a-Graphic (paid)

Build-a-Graphic is an add-in with a yearly subscription model – it also offers a PowerPoint Asset Library yearly subscription for bigger organizations. Since my target readers for this book are smaller organizations or individuals within organizations that don't have a creative team to help them, I will focus on the add-in, but you can find all the information at the Build-a-Graphic website listed in *Further reading*.

You can use the Build-a-Graphic add-in in two ways:

1. Starting with your own bullet lists or text slides, build your own visuals with the help of the thousands of creative assets provided by the add-in
2. Search the library for prebuilt graphics tagged with keywords and add your own text content into the text boxes

Whether you choose to build your own or use a prebuilt graphic, the great advantage is that everything is fully customizable. Everything you add is a vector graphic, making it 100% editable. You can change the colors, remove the fill colors, keep outlines, and ungroup shapes. Anything you can do in the **Shape Format** tab with PowerPoint's native shapes can be used for Build-a-Graphic assets. If you feel you lack the skills to build your own graphics, and especially if you want to work wisely by not putting so much time into creating your own graphics, you should consider investing in this add-in.

It is worth mentioning that at the time of writing this book, the Build-a-Graphic add-in is being rebuilt from the ground up. Also, by the way, this effort was a collaboration with the Neuxpower people. If you have used or are using this add-in, you will be impressed by the new version, which has two major improvements:

*   It is compatible with Windows, Mac, and web versions of PowerPoint.
*   It is always connected to the complete library of graphics.

After installing the add-in, you will have a new **Build-a-Graphic** button (**1**) available in the **Home** tab (*Figure 10.15*):

Figure 10.15 – The Build-a-Graphic button in the Home tab of the ribbon

Clicking on the button will open the **Build-a-Graphic** pane (**1**) (*Figure 10.16*):

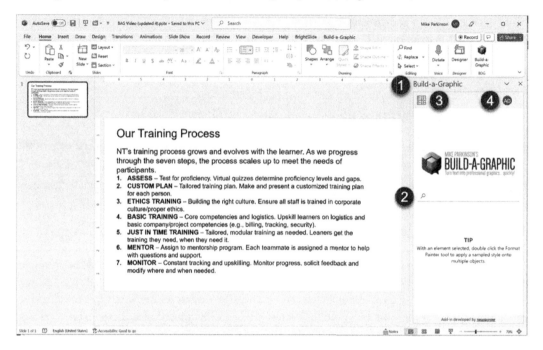

Figure 10.16 – The Build-a-Graphic pane

From there you will be able to search from over 10,000 graphics (**2**), use the tool to chunk your text (**3**), and **Manage your account** (**4**), and have access to tutorials, FAQs, license agreements, and a way to contact support.

Let's start by showing an example of how you can create your own graphics from a bullet list on a slide in the next section.

Creating your graphic from a text slide

This is an example provided by Mike in the documentation on his website. The text details a training process, from assessment to monitoring success, in seven steps on the slide (**1**) in the selected placeholder (see *Figure 10.17*):

Figure 10.17 – Using the Chunk Text tool with a bulleted list

When clicking on the **Chunk Text** button (**2**), you see three options to help you separate your list into individual text boxes:

- **Chunk Text by Sentence** (**3**)
- **Chunk Text by Bullet** (**4**)
- **Chunk Text by Paragraph** (**5**)

So, it does not matter how the text is formatted on the slide because those three options cover everything.

For my example, I used **Chunk Text by Paragraph** (**1**) and the resulting slide looks like *Figure 10.18*, with the standard content placeholder now empty and eight new content placeholders containing the divided text (**2**):

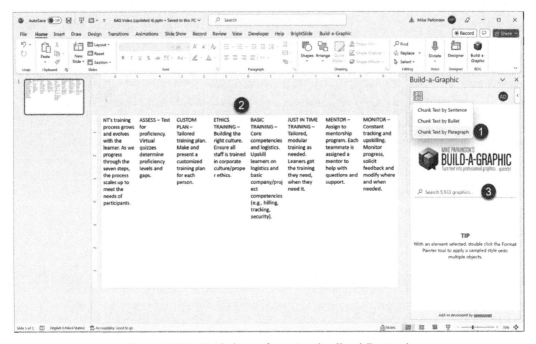

Figure 10.18 – Divided text after using the Chunk Text tool

To continue without having to deal with the empty placeholders, you need to go to **Home | Layout** and select **Blank layout**. Deleting the placeholders without changing the layout is not the best practice and can cause problems with editing.

Before starting to insert graphics on the slide, I also reduced the font size and the size of the text boxes while aligning them below the middle of the height of the slide and distributing them evenly. Then, I used the search box (**3**) with the keyword **Assess**.

When you see the search results, clicking on a graphic takes you to the detail page where you have a preview (**1**), the associated list of **KEYWORDS** (**2**), and the **Insert Graphic** button (**3**) (*Figure 10.19*):

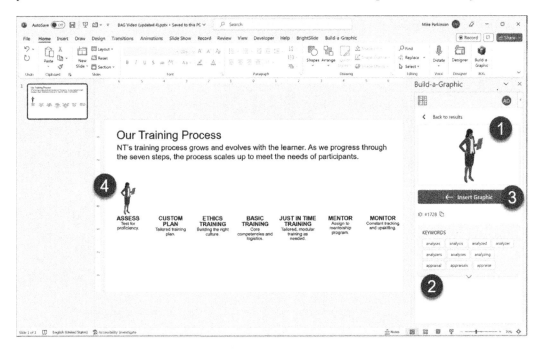

Figure 10.19 – Searching for and inserting graphics

After inserting a graphic, you can resize it and position it close to the text box you want to illustrate (**4**).

As you can see in *Figure 10.20*, the inserted graphic is a group of shapes that can be formatted with any of the tools in the **Shape Format** tab:

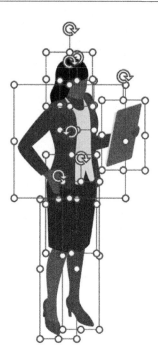

Figure 10.20 – The inserted graphic is fully editable with formatting tools

You can repeat the process and include as many graphics as you need for your slide, moving and resizing them to your needs. If you have very specific needs, this might be a great way to assemble a professional-looking slide without spending days searching online libraries, purchasing many licenses, or creating everything from scratch.

Figure 10.21 shows the final slide produced using this method:

Figure 10.21 – Final slide using graphic elements

You have access to thousands of graphic elements you can use to make almost any graphic you can imagine. Think of it as a kit of parts to build your perfect graphic (*Figure 10.22*):

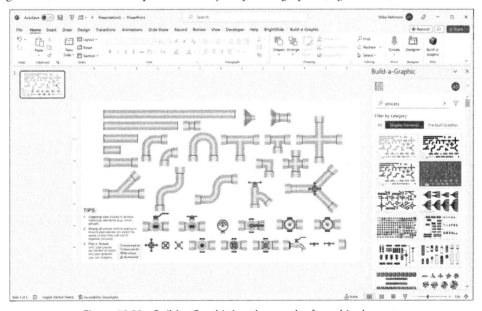

Figure 10.22 – Build-a-Graphic has thousands of graphic elements

But you might also want to just search the Build-a-Graphic library and use a complete graphic, which is the topic of the next section.

Using the Build-a-Graphic library

If you are creating content for a common business topic, you might find exactly what you need in the Build-a-Graphic library. To find a graphic, search as you normally would, click on the **Filter** tool (**1**), and choose **Pre-built Graphics** (**2**) from the menu (*Figure 10.23*):

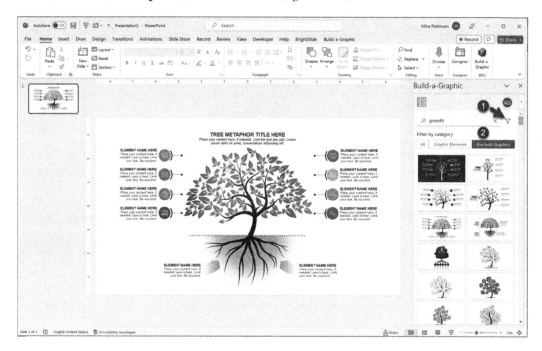

Figure 10.23 – Using Pre-built Graphics

In the list of graphics, you can then click on the one you want to insert on your slide.

As you can see, you get a lot of value for your investment. I would even say that if you ever have paid a talented graphic designer, what you will have paid for an hour or 2 hours of their time is similar to what you would invest in Build-a-Graphic per year to have thousands of assets available just a few clicks away.

Now, we will move on to the last section on add-ins in this chapter, looking at two productivity add-ins from PPTools.

PPTools

Why come back to productivity tools after discussing a design add-in? Simply because the man behind PPTools is highly respected in our industry. Steve Rindsberg has been creating PowerPoint add-ins and help articles since 1997! I made a great friend when I first met him in 2005 during a conference.

His add-in site (see *Further reading* for the link) has many add-ins that have been created over the years to help users with specific needs that remain unmet by the native PowerPoint features. Instead of trying to figure out which ones to include in this chapter myself, I simply asked Steve to tell me his two most popular add-ins, one free and one paid. We'll cover the free one first in the next section.

Using THOR (free)

The **THOR** add-in has one simple focus: memorize the size and position of an object on a slide so you can apply it – or hammer it, as Steve would say – to one or multiple selected objects elsewhere in your presentation. As for the name, yes, he is referring to the hammer-wielding god in Norse mythology, reflecting his great sense of humor and how cultured he is.

To install the add-in, simply navigate to the **Free PPTools Add-ins** section of the site (see *Further reading*) and select **THOR - The Hammer** from the list. Then, follow the instructions in the **Download and install THOR** section. Once installed, you will see a new **PPTools** tab (**1**) in the ribbon (see *Figure 10.24*):

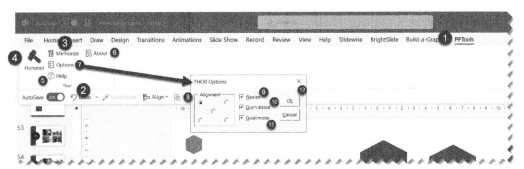

Figure 10.24 – The PPTools tab with the Hammer tool

As you can see, the **Thor** group (**2**) has a simple set of buttons. Here is a brief description of each:

- **Memorize** (**3**): This is the button to click on first when you want to memorize the size and position of a slide object.

- **Hammer** (**4**): This is the button to click after selecting one or many other objects to which we want to apply the same size and position.

- **Help** (**5**): This button opens a `.pdf` file, providing all the information you need about the add-in without having to go back to the website.

- **About** (**6**): This provides access to regular licensing information, a link to the support, and a diagnostics feature.

- **Options** (**7**): This button allows you to configure how THOR will work by changing the options in the **THOR Options** dialog box:

  - **Alignment** (**8**): Simply click on the radio button to choose which reference point to use. In this example, THOR will remember the position of the upper-left corner of an object.

  - **Resize** (**9**): This option allows you to simply remember the position of an object – if the checkbox is unchecked – or remember how to resize objects, as well as how to move them into the same position.

  - **Don't distort** (**10**): This option is important when you decide to resize slide objects to avoid distortion.

  - **Quiet mode** (**11**): This option simply avoids bringing up a dialog box giving you the exact position and size of the memorized object. If you want to know more about this, please refer to the **Help** document.

  - **OK** (**12**): This button confirms your settings.

Let's see how THOR works with the following example in which we want to memorize the size and position of the hexagon on slide **58** (**1**) and apply it to the image on slide **59** (**2**) (see *Figure 10.25*):

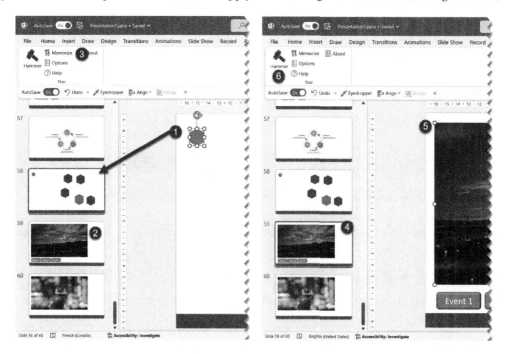

Figure 10.25 – Using THOR to memorize the position and size of an object

I make sure the shape is selected and click on **Memorize** (**3**) – then, I change the view to slide **59** (**4**) and select the image (**5**). The only thing left to do is click on the **Hammer** button (**6**).

The final result is an image (**1**) that was moved on slide **59** (**2**) and resized. The **Don't distort** setting was on, so we still have a rectangular image (see *Figure 10.26*):

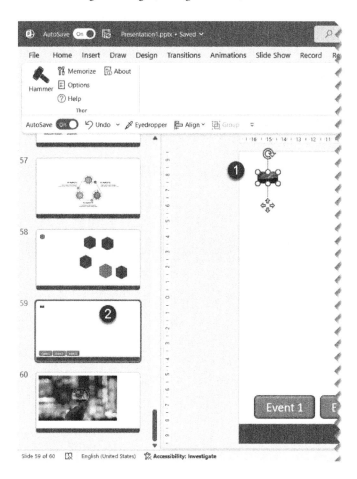

Figure 10.26 – The result of using Hammer on an image

As you can see, THOR is a very simple but also very powerful add-in. If you ever have to quickly resize and position many objects on several slides in your presentation, this is the tool to have in your toolkit, and it will not cost you anything.

Let's now move on to the last add-in I will discuss in this chapter, which will help you merge data in a PowerPoint file just like Mail Merge would work in Word.

Using PPTMerge (paid)

The **PPTMerge** add-in is a great tool to help you merge data from an Excel file to create customized individual slides or complete presentations. If you are wondering how that can be helpful, here are a few examples:

- Creating a presentation file that includes the names of specific people on each slide.
- Using a certificate PowerPoint template, you can then merge the list of names to show on each certificate.
- Creating your social media posts by merging some key elements into a visual template created in PowerPoint. The credit for this amazingly creative idea goes to Catharine Richardson from My TechGenie (see *Further reading*).

This is a paid add-in available on the PPTools website and it can save you so much time. One testimonial on Steve's PPTMerge page is from a client saying they only use it once a year and it is still well worth the cost.

After it has been installed, you can find PPTMerge in the **PPTools** tab in the ribbon (**1**) (*Figure 10.27*):

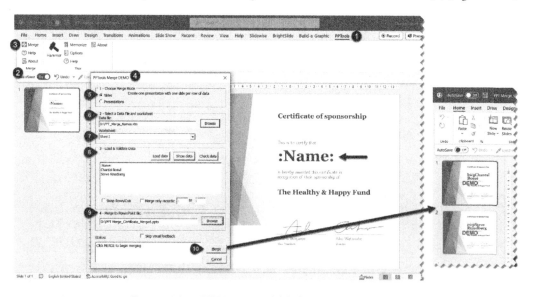

Figure 10.27 – PPTMerge available from the PPTools tab

We can see a simple **Merge** group (**2**) and since I already have the THOR add-in installed, it is also available in the same tab. The **Help** and **About** buttons work the same way as described for our other PPTools add-in.

Let's say we want to create a certificate with the name of each person receiving it – before using the **Merge** button (**3**), you need to make sure you have gone through the following steps:

1. Create the PowerPoint slide that will be used as a template and add :Name: to the text box where the name should be added.

2. Create your Excel file where cell **A1** has the same :Name: title so that the add-in will know what to look for in the data file. Add all the names you need in the following rows.

3. You are now ready to click on the **Merge** button (**3**).

4. The **PPTools Merge** dialog box opens (**4**):

   • In the **1 - Choose Merge Mode** section (**5**), we can keep the **Slides** setting selected so that we create only one presentation file with one slide per row of data.

   • In the **2 - Select a Data File and worksheet** section (**6**), use the **Browse** button to select your Excel file. If you decide to use an Excel workbook that contains many worksheets, you can select which one to use from the **Worksheet** drop-down list (**7**).

   • In the **3 - Load & Validate Data** section (**8**), click on the **Load data** button and then the **Show data** button to see your field and data displayed. In my example, you can see that my name and Steve's name will be added to the certificates.

   • In the **4 - Merge to PowerPoint file:** section (**9**), click on the **Browse** button to choose a place and name for your merged file.

Important note

Choose a local drive to avoid error messages. SharePoint and OneDrive for Business storage can cause error messages.

   • Click on the **Merge** button (**10**) to create your file.

Your merged file is quickly created and easy to use, whether you need to print the slides as certificates or present slides with custom fields. When you are using the trial version, the word *DEMO* is added, and a few extra letters show in the merged fields. You need to purchase your license to get a perfectly merged file.

It might not be an add-in everyone will need, but it is worth the investment if you do need to merge information into a PowerPoint file. Just think of how much time you will save!

Summary

This chapter focused on PowerPoint add-ins that can boost your efficiency either by helping you be more efficient during your content creation phase, cleaning up your presentation file and reducing its size, creating beautiful graphics in a fraction of the time, or adding valuable functions to your PowerPoint application.

If you have struggled with repetitive tasks or ever thought that you were spending way too much time on content creation, it is probably time to take a closer look at the add-ins that can help you boost your PowerPoint efficiency. I only covered a few add-ins from people I know well and a sample of their features, but there are many more add-ins available on the market for you to discover. Search for your specific needs and make sure you inquire about other users' experiences with any new add-in or tool you might be considering.

If you would like to connect with others and discuss anything and everything about presentation design, PowerPoint, and any other tools to help you create your content, I suggest that you have a look at the Presentation Guild website (see *Further reading*) and even consider becoming a member. I am one of the founding members and presently a board member, and I can assure you it is a dynamic and helpful community.

In the next chapter, we will be discussing how to practice your presentation delivery using tools available within PowerPoint because presentations cannot be impactful if you don't practice.

Further reading

- BrightCarbon add-ins: https://www.brightcarbon.com/products/
- Neuxpower add-ins: https://neuxpower.com/products
- Billion Dollar Graphics (Build-a-Graphic): https://billiondollargraphics.com/build-a-graphic/
- PPTools add-ins: http://www.pptools.com/products.htm
- The PowerPoint FAQ: https://www.rdpslides.com/pptfaq/
- Catharine Richardson: http://mytechgenie.ca/
- The Presentation Guild: https://presentationguild.org/

11
Practicing Your Presentation Delivery

You learned how to plan and structure your content in the first part of this book. Then, we discussed how to create better visuals with tools and functions available in PowerPoint or with third-party add-ins. We are now entering the delivery part.

Creating a memorable experience for your audience requires much more than planning the content and creating professional visuals. You need to practice.

Luckily, the PowerPoint development team at Microsoft has been adding tools to help presenters with their delivery in the past years. Here are the topics that will be covered in this chapter:

- Viewing and adapting **Slide Show** options
- Leveraging **Speaker Coach** to help you practice your talk
- Rehearsing timings and creating a recorded practice run
- Using the new **Record** feature to practice

Technical requirements

Some features discussed in the chapter require a **Microsoft 365 (M365)** subscription. They will be identified as such when they are explained. Be aware that since the subscription version of PowerPoint is being updated on an ongoing basis, it is possible that screenshots shown in this chapter might differ from your version of the application.

Viewing and adapting Slide Show options

Many users are not aware of all the PowerPoint options they have control over, and there are a few specific to presentation delivery. To access those options, you need to go to **File | Options | Advanced** (**1**) and scroll down to the **Slide Show** section (**2**) (*Figure 11.1*):

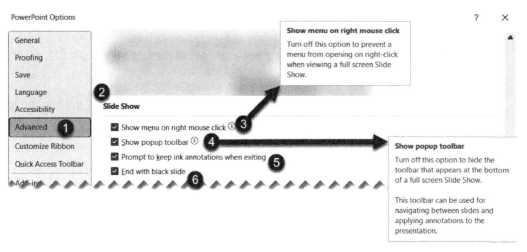

Figure 11.1 – Advanced Slide Show options in PowerPoint

- All options are turned on by default, so you might want to adapt what you want to make available according to how you plan to deliver your presentation.

- The **Show menu on right mouse click** option (**3**) can be turned off by unchecking the box if you want to avoid getting the contextual menu by clicking the right mouse button by mistake. It is not necessarily bad, but I do think using **Presenter View** features—the topic of the next chapter—is much better.

- The **Show popup toolbar** option (**4**) is related to the semi-transparent toolbar that can be seen in the bottom-left corner of the screen during your presentation. Even though it hides itself after a few seconds, I usually find it distracting because I use **Presenter View** most of the time. Therefore, my personal preference is to turn it off.

- If you are a regular ink user, you might want to make sure the **Prompt to keep ink annotations when exiting** option (**5**) is turned on. It allows you to keep them for reference after your presentation is finished.

- The last option of the section, **End with black slide** (**6**), is supposed to be used to avoid ending your slideshow by mistake. If you use **Presenter View**, the slide will be black, but when you are not using **Presenter View**, it unfortunately displays the text **End of Slide Show, click to exit** at the top of the black screen, which I find distracting. I usually advise my clients to have their last slide always be one listing their contact information, making it an obvious reminder that they are on the last slide of their presentation.

> **Tip**
>
> Even if I shared some personal preferences for the **Slide Show** options, I suggest that you practice your presentation with them turned on and then off, to see what makes more sense to you. The main goal is to make you more comfortable delivering your presentation, so maybe my preferences will not be what works best for you.

Let's now move on to a great practice feature right in your PowerPoint application in the next section.

Leveraging Speaker Coach to help you practice your talk

The **Speaker Coach** feature is part of Microsoft's cloud-enhanced features, which means you need to be connected to the internet for it to work. It was first launched in PowerPoint for the web and is now also available in the desktop version if you have an M365 license. While in the free preview stage, anyone using a Microsoft account (for example, an `outlook.com`, `hotmail.com`, `live.com`, or `msn.com` email) without an M365 subscription can access it in PowerPoint for the web.

Another important element, at the time this book is being written, is that **Speaker Coach** only understands English and is available only when your Office user interface is also in English. If you don't know how to change the language of your user interface, have a look at the *Microsoft support* article in the *Further reading* section.

Microsoft always tests **Speaker Coach** enhancements in the web version first, adding them to the desktop version after gathering feedback from PowerPoint for the web users. This means that if you want to practice with the latest features, you need to open your presentation in PowerPoint for the web.

Starting Speaker Coach

To start using **Speaker Coach** in PowerPoint for the web (**1**) or in the desktop application (**2**), you can go to the **Slide Show** tab (**3**) (*Figure 11.2*):

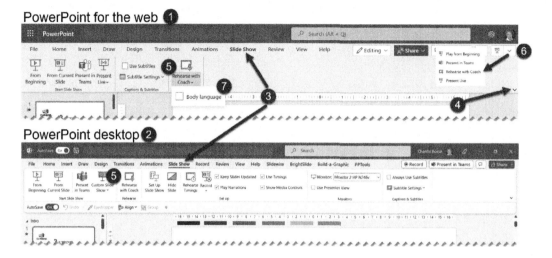

Figure 11.2 – Starting Speaker Coach from the web and desktop applications

When in the web version, if you don't see the feature icons in the ribbon, you can click on the **Ribbon Display Options** arrow (**4**) and choose the **Classic** ribbon. Both versions of the application will have a **Rehearse with Coach** button (**5**) to start the application. In the web version, you can also find the feature in the **Present** dropdown (**6**). At the time this book is being written, PowerPoint for the web has started to test an optional **Body language** analysis feature (**7**) that requires having your camera turned on while practicing your presentation.

After clicking the **Rehearse with Coach** button, your presentation goes into slideshow view, and a dialog box opens on top of your slides (**1**) in the bottom-right corner (*Figure 11.3*):

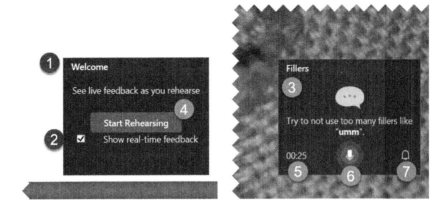

Figure 11.3 – Speaker Coach dialog box

By default, the **Show real-time feedback** feature (**2**) is turned on, meaning you can see comments in the **Fillers** section (**3**) regarding filler words, repetitive words, or lack of inclusiveness in your language as you practice. You will need to test whether you find it too distracting or not. When you are ready to start, make sure your microphone is turned on and click on the **Start Rehearsing** button (**4**). You will see the timer (**5**), a blinking microphone icon (**6**) that can be used to pause the rehearsal, and a bell icon (**7**) allowing you to turn off real-time feedback while you are rehearsing. When you are finished, simply hit the *Esc* key to end your slideshow, ending the rehearsal at the same time.

If you are using PowerPoint for the web, you can also use your camera and try the **Body language** feedback. It can give you insight into your distance from the camera (**1**) and whether you are making eye contact (**2**) (*Figure 11.4*):

Figure 11.4 – Speaker Coach feedback for body language in PowerPoint for the web

This feature is quite new at the time this chapter is being written and still in preview. It will probably keep improving a lot in the upcoming months. When you end your rehearsal, whether in the web or desktop version, you get your rehearsal report—the topic of our next section.

Analyzing your rehearsal report

The rehearsal report (**1**) gives you very interesting insights into how well your practice run went (*Figure 11.5*):

Figure 11.5 – Speaker Coach rehearsal report

- You get a summary (**2**) of the total time spent rehearsing and the number of slides you rehearsed.

- It has a **Fillers** section (**3**) letting you know whether you were using filler words often or not. This is a big challenge for many presenters I have worked with through the years. Knowing you are using too many filler words is the first step to help you reduce their use.

- The AI can even analyze repetitive language (**4**) in your presentation. This feature is new at the time I of writing this, and the word **sure** suggested to replace **really** was not appropriate in the context of the spoken words. This will get better as more users try **Speaker Coach**.

- Inclusiveness (**5**) of the language is also analyzed, helping presenters realize where they could improve. An example that comes to mind is the use of the expression *you guys* by many people, which is not considered gender-neutral. It could be replaced by *you all* or *everyone*, depending on the context.

- The **Pace** section (**6**) and the following **Your average pace over time** (**7**) section are great indicators to help you adjust how fast or slow you talk. The shaded area between 100 and 150 words per minute in the chart (**8**) indicates the optimal pace you should have to keep your audience engaged.

- The report also includes information on your voice pitch (**9**). A lack of variation in pitch when you speak will inevitably make your audience tune out. In other words, you will become boring for the audience! The more you work on your variations, such as increasing the tone of your voice for important points, the better it will be to keep your audience engaged.

- In the **Originality** section (**10**), **Speaker Coach** will pick up if you are reading every word on your slides. If you started using text and bullet points alternatives (as we discussed when we covered best practices or visual alternatives), you should not see many suggestions in this category of the report. There are times when I think it is still okay to read text on a slide—for example, when you are using a quotation. The way to do it is to read it slowly and clearly, then give the audience a few seconds to absorb it.

- To help Microsoft developers and engineers fine-tune **Speaker Coach**, you should take the time to rate your experience (**11**).

- And finally, if you are ready to start over, just click on the **Rehearse Again** button (**12**).

At the time this book is written, there are two other features available when using **Speaker Coach** in PowerPoint for the web: **Pronunciation** (**1**) and **Body Language** (**2**) (*Figure 11.6*):

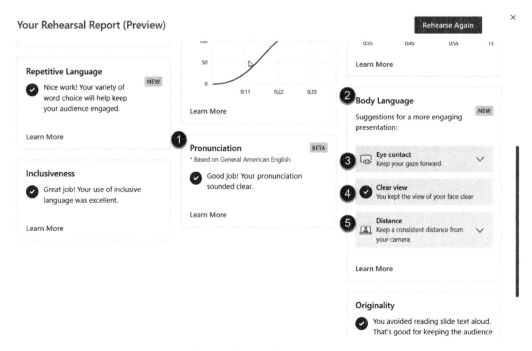

Figure 11.6 – Two new features for Speaker Coach in PowerPoint for the web

The **Pronunciation** feedback is based on American English and will evolve as more languages become available. Microsoft has already mentioned it is working on expanding **Speaker Coach** to new languages, including Spanish, French, and Japanese. The **Body Language** feature will give you feedback on eye contact (**3**), whether your face was always visible in **Clear view** (**4**), and whether your distance (**5**) from your camera was consistent. This type of feedback would be useful if you are delivering mostly virtual presentations, helping you get into the habit of controlling how you interact with your camera.

Speaker Coach should be your go-to feature to practice your presentations, helping you improve your pacing and choice of words, while reducing filler words, and even helping with your body language. Practice with **Speaker Coach** as long as needed to help you become more in control of your delivery. *At the moment, you cannot save your reports, so you need to take a screen capture if you want to keep track of how you improve.*

If you need to have a better sense of how much time you spend on each slide and keep track of your improvement, you need to leverage the **Rehearse Timings** feature—the topic of the next section.

Rehearsing timings and creating a recorded practice run

If you struggle to keep on topic for some of your slides, making you run over time for most of your presentations, you should consider practicing with the **Rehearse Timings** feature (**1**) available in the **Slide Show** tab (**2**) (*Figure 11.7*):

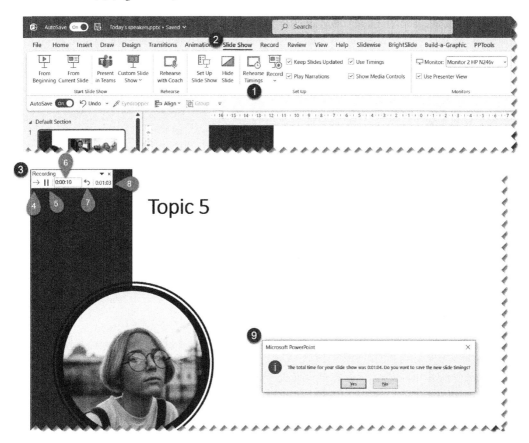

Figure 11.7 – Starting and using Rehearse Timings

When you click on **Rehearse Timings**, it starts your presentation in **Slide Show** mode (**2**) and records how much time you spend on each slide. You will see the small **Recording** tool (**3**) in the upper-left corner of the screen. You can click through your slides with your mouse, use your keyboard, or click on the small arrow in the **Recording** tool (**4**). If you need to stop, just click the **Pause** button (**5**) in the toolbar.

The first timer (**6**) shows you how much time you have spent on a slide. If you need to repeat the recording, you can click on the small **Repeat** arrow (**7**). The second timer (**8**) shows you how long you have been talking. If you want to end the **Rehearse Timings** tool quickly, just hit the *Esc* key on your keyboard. It will prompt a dialog box (**9**) showing you how long your slideshow was and asking whether you want to save the slide timings.

If you keep the slide timings, you will then have **automatic transitions** added to the slides you rehearsed (*Figure 11.8*). The easiest way to view the timings is to switch to **Slide Sorter** view (**1**) to see them underneath each thumbnail (**2**). You can also see them when you go to the **Transitions** tab (**3**) and look at **After** (**4**) in the **Timing** group:

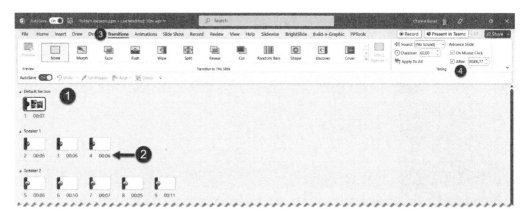

Figure 11.8 – Viewing slide timings added by Rehearse Timings

Every time you practice and use the feature, you will see how you improve your timing per slide. Use the speaker notes to add keywords to help you stay on track. In *Chapter 12*, *Using Presenter View*, we will discuss how to use those notes while you are delivering your talk.

You could decide to use the timings to have a self-running presentation for your next delivery, but I would suggest you avoid doing that so that you can go with the natural flow of audience interactions without being stressed that your slides will change automatically. To make sure you are not stuck with your timings, simply go to the **Slide Show** tab (**1**) and remove the check mark for **Use Timings** (**2**). You will regain full control over the timing of your presentation (*Figure 11.9*):

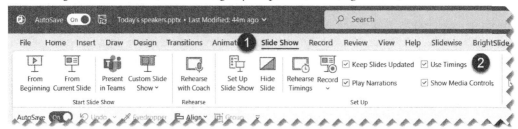

Figure 11.9 – Removing the timings for your slideshow

If you are already relying on notes, you might find that **Rehearse Timings** is not as convenient because it does not allow using **Presenter View**. Microsoft introduced an improved, feature-rich **Record** feature in early 2022 that might just help you, and this will be discussed in the following section. Take note that this improved feature is available in M365. In previous versions, users will have the classic **Record** experience that has fewer features.

Using the new Record feature to practice

Although recording a slideshow has been available as early as Office 2013, the new **Record** feature introduced by Microsoft has many great tools to help you practice. Yes—its main goal is to help presenters create videos of their content for distribution, but using it to see how you look and hear how you talk is the best way to improve your delivery. You will probably hate seeing and hearing yourself the first few times—we all do!—but this type of feedback is even more realistic than just using **Speaker Coach**. Using both is the best practice you can have.

I will review the **Record** feature, but it will be shown under the angle of practicing your delivery, not producing your content to be distributed as a video file. This means not all features will be explained. If you want to follow along, make sure to open a PowerPoint file that contains notes, and have your microphone and camera ready. My example will use presentation content I use in French often, so you can see the notes.

There are three ways to start the **Record** feature and access what the PowerPoint developers have been calling the **recording studio**. You can either click on the **Record** tab (**1**) and decide whether you want to start recording **From Beginning** (**2**) or **From Current Slide** (**3**). You can also click on the **Record** button (**4**) on the right of the tabs to start recording from your current slide, or you can access it from the **Slide Show** tab (**5**) and click on the **Record** button (**6**) to choose **From Current Slide…** (**7**) or **From Beginning…** (**8**) (*Figure 11.10*):

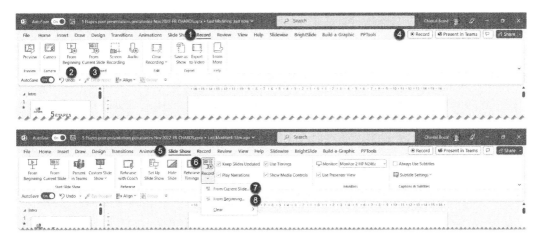

Figure 11.10 – Accessing the Record feature

Whatever the method you choose, it starts your slideshow and opens the recording studio, where we will go over the features most relevant to practice your presentation (*Figure 11.11*):

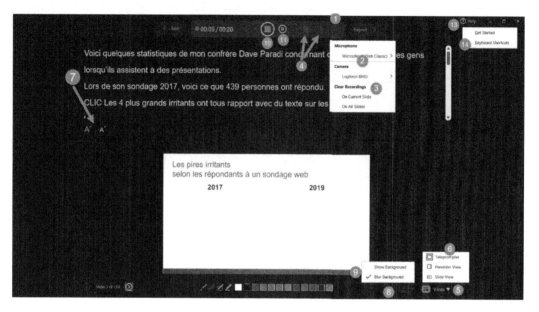

Figure 11.11 – Recording studio features

- The **Select more options** ellipsis (**…**) in the toolbar (**1**) opens a menu to access your **Microphone** and **Camera** settings (**2**). The **Clear Recordings** section (**3**) will be discussed later in this section.

- You can turn your camera and microphone on and off using their respective icons (**4**)

- When you start the **Record** feature, by default, **Views** (**5**) is set to **Teleprompter** view (**6**). This is how you see the notes above your slide (**7**) to help you keep your eyes toward your camera. You can increase or decrease the size of your notes to help you read them during your recording. If you have more notes than the pane allows you to see, scrolling down with your mouse wheel is probably the best thing to do, even if there is a scroll bar on the right.

- The **Select the camera mode** icon (**8**) allows you to choose between **Blur Background** and **Show Background** for your camera setting (**9**).

- The **Start recording/Stop recording** button (**10**) is used when you are ready to record your rehearsal. You can also use the **Pause recording** button (**11**) during the recording.

- You can go through your slides by clicking your mouse, using any keyboard keys available during the slideshow, or by using the arrow icons (**12**) at the bottom of the studio. You might want to have a look at the **Help** icon (**13**) and choose **Keyboard Shortcuts** (**14**) for a refresher on keys you can use.

> **Tip**
>
> When you are recording your rehearsal, you need to keep in mind that it is done on a per-slide basis. This means you need to stop talking during slide transitions. Microsoft also mentions there is a brief buffer of silence at the beginning and the end of each slide, meaning you should wait 1 or 2 seconds before you start the narration on a slide and wait 1 or 2 seconds before changing your slide after you have finished talking.

After clicking the **Stop recording** button or hitting the *Esc* key on your keyboard, the **Slide preview** (**1**) becomes a video with playback option (**2**) with your camera feed in the bottom-right corner (*Figure 11.12*):

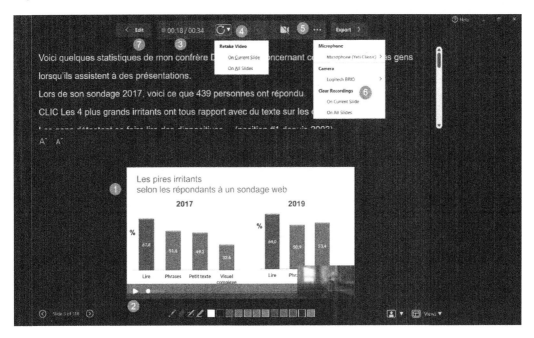

Figure 11.12 – Using studio features after recording a slide

You can also see how long your script for the slide was and the total duration of your recorded session (**3**). If you click on the **Retake Video** button (**4**), you can decide where you want to apply this option with **On Current Slide** or **On All Slides**. If you click on **Select more options** (**…**) (**5**), you can use the **Clear Recordings** section (**6**) to remove recordings, choosing from **On Current Slide** or **On All Slides**. This is very convenient to make sure you don't have to remove videos manually before delivering your presentation to your audience. To go back to your slides, you can click on the **Edit** button (**7**) or hit *Esc* on your keyboard.

Since we are talking about recording a presentation for rehearsal purposes, having the camera feed block information on the slide is not a problem. But if you ever decide to use the feature to create narrated videos of your presentation with the intention of distributing or posting them, you need to plan ahead of time how your content will be displayed on your slides to avoid having it blocked by the video feed.

When you are back in **Normal** slide view, you will see the recorded video as an object on your slide (**1**), and you can play it (**2**) from there too (*Figure 11.13*):

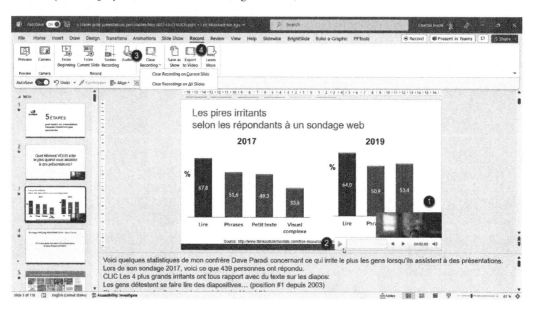

Figure 11.13 – Rehearsal recording video available on the slide

If you click the **Clear Recording** button (**3**), you also get **Clear Recording on Current Slide** and **Clear Recordings on All Slides** possibilities. Unless you decide to use your recordings to produce a narrated video, remember to use this feature before delivering your presentation. If you are curious about how you would do that, you just need to click the **Export to Video** button (**4**) and follow the information provided in the export window.

Even though the **Record** feature was probably intended to help users produce narrated videos more easily, I would recommend it to all presenters to help them improve their presentation delivery. Seeing and hearing ourselves helps us improve even more.

Of course, being in front of an audience in a meeting room or a large venue requires moving on stage to help keep people engaged, something that is difficult to practice with **Record** since you need to be close to your screen to use the various tools in the studio. That is when you should rely on **Presenter Coach** instead so that you can set your camera in a way that you are framed from head to the waist at a minimum, and see the feedback you receive.

Summary

In this chapter, we have discussed how to adapt the various **Slide Show** options available in PowerPoint and how to leverage the **Speaker Coach**, **Rehearse Timings**, and **Record** features to help you rehearse your presentations and improve your delivery skills.

Of course, relying solely on technology to rehearse might not be enough depending on what is at stake. If your next presentation might win you a million-dollar project, start by allowing enough time to plan, create, and rehearse your presentation with the tools you have learned about in this chapter. Then, choose a few people you can count on to be good critics and deliver your presentation in front of them, more than once if possible. Technology can accomplish a lot, but human feedback is priceless!

In the next chapter, we will be discussing how to use **Presenter View** during your presentation delivery to help you increase your confidence and leverage tools to help you navigate your content even if no navigation elements were planned.

Further reading

- Change your Office user interface language: `https://support.microsoft.com/en-us/office/change-the-language-office-uses-in-its-menus-and-proofing-tools-f5c54ff9-a6fa-4348-a43c-760e7ef148f8`

12
Using Presenter View

I often hear from presenters that they want to have all their text on slides because they fear forgetting what to say. Lack of practice is often a problem, but some presenters fear public speaking so much that they need to have more support when using mostly visual slides.

That is why speakers need to learn how to leverage technology to help them ease their fears. PowerPoint has been providing Presenter View for some time now, helping presenters see their notes while the audience sees only their slides. Now is the time to learn how to leverage all its power with the help of the topics discussed in this chapter:

- Defining and starting Presenter View
- Using the display and navigation tools
- Using the annotation tools
- Using other tools
- Making your presentation more accessible with live subtitles

Technical requirements

The Presenter View feature is available in all versions of PowerPoint, but there could be differences in the tools available depending on the version you are using. Be aware that since the subscription version of PowerPoint is updated on an ongoing basis, it is possible that screenshots shown in this chapter might differ from your version of the application.

Defining and starting Presenter View

Presenter View is a PowerPoint feature allowing presenters to see their speaking notes and various tools on their computer while the audience only sees the slides in their presentation. We'll see how easy it is to set it up and describe the various parts of the Presenter View window.

If you are using any version of PowerPoint from 2013 to the latest ones, as soon as you connect your computer to a second monitor, a projector, or a TV screen, PowerPoint should automatically set up Presenter View for you. When you are working with two monitors permanently connected to your computer, there might be times when you don't want to use it, so let's see where Presenter View can be turned on or off.

From the **Slide Show** tab (**1**), go to the **Monitors** group (**2**) and uncheck the **Use Presenter View** box (**3**) (*Figure 12.1*):

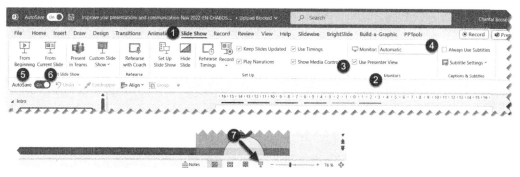

Figure 12.1 – Activating or deactivating Presenter View in the Slide Show tab

The **Monitor** drop-down list (**4**) allows you to choose on which display you want to see Presenter View. The **Automatic** setting is usually the default one, allowing PowerPoint to choose the display automatically. We will see an option in Presenter View to change the display if it is not appropriate.

Starting the slide show can be done directly in the **Slide Show** tab by using the **From Beginning** button (**5**) in the ribbon, starting your presentation on the first slide, the **From Current Slide** button (**6**) in the ribbon, or the **Slide Show** button in the status bar (**7**), if you want to continue from another slide you selected in normal view. You can also use the following keyboard shortcuts to start your slide show:

- From the first slide: *F5*
- From the current slide: *Shift + F5*

Once you start the slide show, you will see Presenter View on your main monitor and the slide displayed on the second monitor. If you want to practice your presentation with Presenter View but don't have access to a second monitor, projector, or TV, you will need to first start your slide show and then right-click your mouse to get the contextual menu with the **Show Presenter View** option (**1**) (*Figure 12.2*):

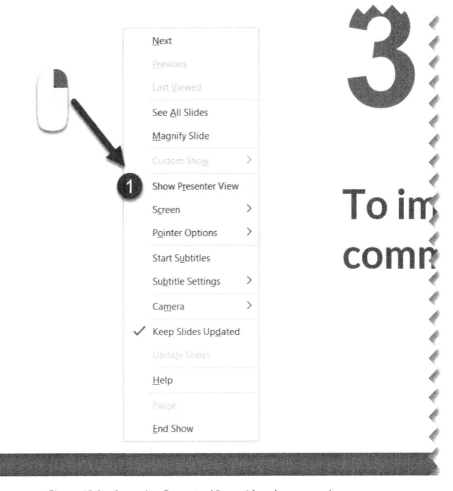

Figure 12.2 – Accessing Presenter View with only one monitor

Now that we have seen how to start Presenter View, let's go over the main sections of the window (*Figure 12.3*):

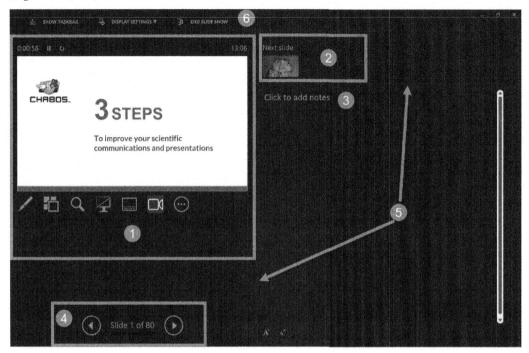

Figure 12.3 – Exploring Presenter View's sections

1. The first section shows you your actual slide and the various delivery tools you can access (**1**).

2. The second section shows a preview of your next slide (**2**), allowing you to see where you are moving to next.

3. In the third section, you will see your speakers notes (**3**), if you added any during your content creation phase. In the latest version of PowerPoint, you can also add notes in this section during your presentation. There'll be more on that later in the chapter.

4. You also have navigation buttons (**4**) underneath your actual slide preview, showing you the slide number of your current slide and the total number of slides in your presentation.

5. The main sections in the window can be resized by clicking and dragging the lines between **Actual slide** and **Next Slide/Notes**, or **Next Slide** and **Notes** (**5**).

6. At the top of the window, you have a section to manage your displays (**6**).

The previous example shows my own resized sections display. The default display usually shows a much bigger **Next slide** thumbnail, which can be confusing for most presentations because it is right above the speaker notes for the current slide. Many times, when I've helped speakers rehearse with

Presenter View, I found that have been were confused because their notes did not match the slide right above them. I suggest that you resize the **Next slide** section and make it much smaller, so your eyes can make sense of the upcoming visual and you have even more space for your notes.

Now that we know about the various sections in Presenter View, let's move on to using the display and navigation tools.

Using the display and navigation tools

When you start your slide show with Presenter View, you might need to change how it is displayed, so we will first have a look at the display tools (*Figure 12.4*):

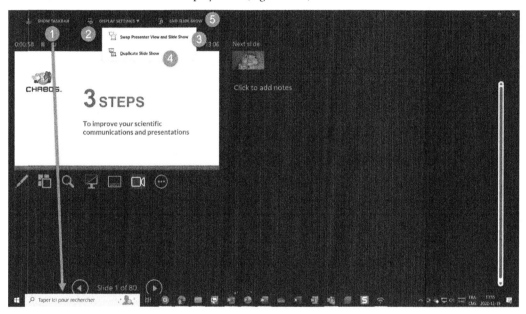

Figure 12.4 – Using the display tools in Presenter View

If you need to look for something in another window on your computer while in a slide show, you will quickly realize you don't see your taskbar when using Presenter View, so using the **SHOW TASKBAR** tool (**1**) could be helpful. It works like a toggle that you click to show or hide your taskbar.

The **DISPLAY SETTINGS** tool (**2**) allows you to change the device on which you want Presenter View displayed by using the **Swap Presenter View and Slide Show** setting (**3**). You might have a need for it if you realize the display is not right when starting your presentation on a computer that is not yours. I have used it many times during training sessions so that people would see Presenter View on a big screen to help them learn about the feature. The **Duplicate Slide Show** setting (**4**) will show only the slide on your computer and the audience's screen.

You can select **END SLIDE SHOW** (**5**) from the display tools too, or simply use *Esc* on your keyboard.

To help you deliver your presentation, let's now have a closer look at the actual slide section with its tools to help you keep on track and navigate through your slides (*Figure 12.5*):

Figure 12.5 – Presenter View tools to keep you on track and navigate your slides

Right above the slide preview, you can see a timer (**1**) displaying the duration of your presentation. It starts counting as soon as you open Presenter View, meaning that it will keep counting while you are getting ready to start your presentation with the audience. That is why you might appreciate the **Pause the timer** and **Restart the timer** tools (**2**) right next to it if you want to rely on the timer to know how long you have been presenting. This is unless you want to rely on the time of day (**3**), which is displayed above the upper-right corner of the slide preview. For example, during training sessions, I find the time of day convenient to keep track of when I need to give people a break.

To navigate through your slides, you can use the **Advance to next animation or slide** button (**4**) or **Return to previous animation or slide** button (**5**), although I think a much more efficient way is to use keyboard keys and shortcuts or a presentation remote. If you need a refresher on keyboard shortcuts, click on the **More slide show options** button (**6**) and select **Help** to access the whole list.

The final navigation tool you should know about is the **See all slides** button (**1**), allowing you to access all your slides in a new window (**2**) (*Figure 12.6*):

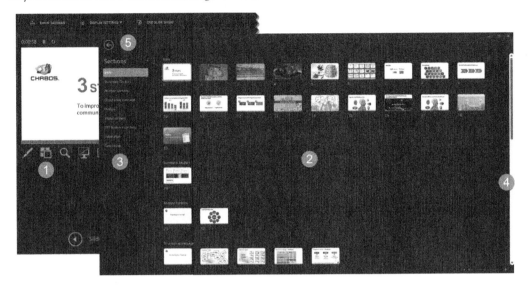

Figure 12.6 – Using the See all slides tool in Presenter View

In my example, the sections created in the file are shown in the left pane of the window (**3**), which can be helpful to find specific content more quickly than just using the scroll bar on the right (**4**). Clicking on any slide thumbnail brings you back to Presenter View. If you decide you don't want to change to another slide, simply click on the **Back** arrow (**5**).

As you can see, using Presenter View helps you manage your displays more easily and improves your flexibility with audience questions or comments by being able to navigate your whole presentation quickly, even if you have not planned any navigation elements in your presentation. Let's now move on to another set of tools that can help you deliver more engaging presentations – the annotation tools.

Using the annotation tools

When you click on the **Pen and laser pointer tools** button (**1**) below the slide preview in Presenter View, you get access to nice annotation tools that can be easily used directly on the slide preview thumbnail (*Figure 12.7*):

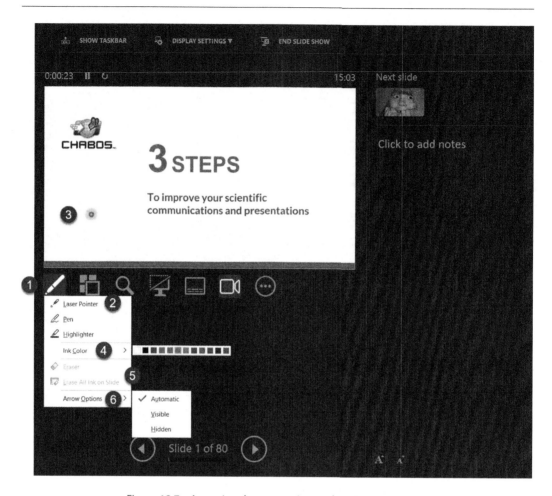

Figure 12.7 – Accessing the annotation tools in Presenter View

Selecting either the **Laser Pointer**, **Pen**, or **Highlighter** tool options (**2**) changes your mouse cursor to the selected type, such as **Laser Pointer** in my example (**3**), making it much easier for the audience to follow your cursor. If you are using **Pen** or **Highlighter** tool, you will be able to draw over your slide to bring attention to some content.

After changing your cursor to any of the tools, you can change its color (**4**) before using it on your slide. And if you drew anything on a slide, you can use **Eraser** and **Erase All Ink on Slide** (**5**) tools to remove part of your annotations or all of them at once.

Arrow Options (**6**) is helpful only if you plan on moving your mouse cursor over what is displayed to the audience. When you are in slide show mode using Presenter View, what it does in the background is extend the view of your screen as if you had a very large monitor, on which the left part is used to display your speaker view, while the right part is used for the full-screen slide for the audience. I suggest that you leave the setting as **Automatic** and use the annotation tools if you need to highlight something on your slide for the audience. It will make things easier to follow than just having a regular mouse pointer moving over the slide.

If you used any of the annotation tools, you need to go back to the list and click on the one you activated to turn it off. When you end your presentation, any annotations left on your slides will trigger a dialog box, asking you whether you want to keep or discard them. If you need to refer back to them after your presentation is over, keep them and they will show as editable ink objects on your slides.

Now that we have seen how to annotate slides during a presentation, we will see other tools you might find helpful while presenting in the next section.

Using other tools

We will not necessarily go through all the remaining tools and settings available in Presentation View. Instead, we will focus on **Zoom into the slide** (**1**), **Black or unblack slide show** (**2**), and **Click to add notes** (**3**) while you are presenting (*Figure 12.8*):

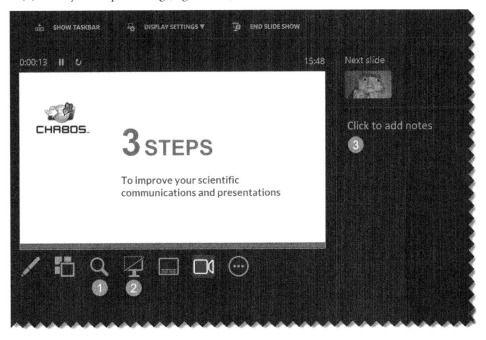

Figure 12.8 – Extra useful tools in Presenter View

If you want the audience to have a closer look at a specific element on your slide, using the **Zoom into the slide** feature (**1**) is an excellent way to do it (*Figure 12.9*):

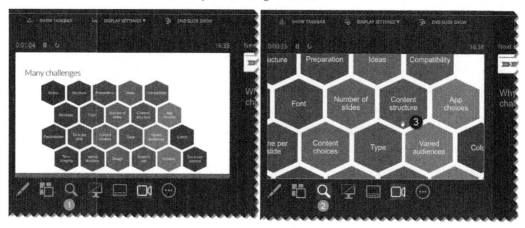

Figure 12.9 – The Zooming into the slide feature in Presenter View

After clicking on the **magnifying glass** icon (**1**), it is now highlighted to show it is selected (**2**), and the slide preview is zoomed in (**3**), showing a hand instead of the regular mouse cursor. If you left-click your mouse and maintain it, you can drag the image to move the zooming effect around your slide. When you want to go back to your whole slide view, simply click on the **magnifying glass** icon again (**2**).

This feature is easy to use and creates a simple but effective zooming effect to help improve your audience's understanding. Sometimes, helping our audience understand what we are saying means helping them focus on us without distractions, and this is when you can leverage the **Black or unblack slide show** feature (**1**) (*Figure 12.10*):

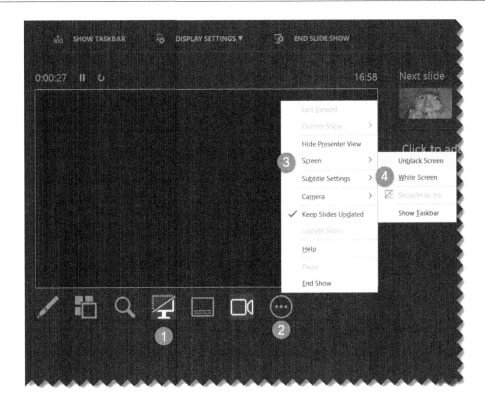

Figure 12.10 – Using the Black or unblack slide show feature to improve audience focus

When you click on the monitor icon (**1**), it becomes highlighted, and the slide preview becomes black. I would suggest using this feature when you need to talk and the slide visual is not relevant to what you have to say. You will see people's eyes focus back on you, helping them concentrate on what you say.

While your slide is black, you can leverage a setting in **More slide show options** (**2**). Go to **Screen** (**3**), and select **White Screen** (**4**). Your slide preview then turns white, allowing you to use the annotation tools if you need to sketch something to help the audience understand. If you try this trick, just be aware that your annotations cannot be saved, as you are drawing over the hidden slide.

When you want to resume your presentation, click again on the **Black or unblack slide show** icon (**1**). If you have used the white screen, it will not stay for the next time. You will need to go back to the options settings to change it again.

If you need to take some notes while you are presenting, Presenter View has received a nice upgrade, allowing M365 users to add their notes. At the time of writing, it is available on **Beta Channel, Version 2204, Build 15225.20000 or later**.

The first clue that lets you know whether this feature is available in your version is seeing the **Click to add notes** text (**1**) when you don't already have speaker notes for your slide (*Figure 12.11*):

Figure 12.11 – Adding notes to your slide in Presenter View

You will also see a highlighted scroll bar on the right (**2**). To add notes, simply click in the notes section and type in your text (**3**). You will also see a white outline (**4**) for the section. When you end your presentation, your notes will be in the notes pane available under your slides.

Now that we have covered many of the tools that can help you with your delivery, let's see one last feature that will help you deliver presentations that are more accessible.

Making your presentation more accessible with live subtitles

If you are an M365 user, you can use a good microphone connected to your computer and make sure to have access to an internet connection to deliver your presentation. You should also consider using live subtitles to make your presentation easier to understand for your audience.

While in Presenter View, you can click on **Toggle Subtitles** (**1**) to start the feature. In the slide preview, your words will be captured and then added under your slide (**2**) (*Figure 12.12*):

Figure 12.12 – Using subtitles during your presentation

You can decide to show subtitles in your spoken language or make them available in another language. All you have to do is click on **More slide show options** (**3**) and then on **Subtitle Settings** (**4**). The first two options (**5**), **Bottom (Overlaid)** and **Top (Overlaid)**, will add captions at the bottom or top of your slides respectively on a semi-transparent shape. I suggest you avoid those options because they require extra planning when you are creating your content to avoid covering important information; it also means less space on the slide for your content.

The following two options, **Below Slide** and **Above Slide** (**6**), are the best choices. Yes, it reduces the size of your projected slide, but you will be sure that your content will never be hidden by subtitles. If you are presenting in a large room and the bottom of the projection screen could be obscured by people, whether sitting at the front of the room or on a stage, you might want to consider using the **Above Slide** setting instead of the default **Below Slide** setting.

Under **More Settings…** (**7**), there is the **Captions & Subtitles** dialog box (**8**) where you have a **Position** section (**9**), giving you the same options as in the previous list of settings. The **Language** section (**10**) is where you need to make changes depending on the spoken language (**11**) of your talk, and choose the subtitle language (**12**) you want to use. Take note that if your spoken language is identified as **Preview**, it means the AI will not be as precise as it is for the fully supported languages.

> **Tip**
>
> When using subtitles during your presentation, you will need to be mindful of your speech pace and pronunciation to get more precise subtitle results.

If you want to use subtitles during all your presentations, you can simply change the setting in the **Slide Show** tab (**1**) by checking the **Always Use Subtitles** box (**2**). You can also access **Subtitle Settings** (**3**) from the ribbon (*Figure 12.13*):

Figure 12.13 – Using subtitles for all your presentations

Using subtitles might require extra equipment, depending on whether you are presenting online or in a venue. Don't hesitate to ask technology experts questions if you don't know what equipment is required. It is worth the time and investment to greatly improve the impact you will have on your audience.

Summary

In this chapter, you have seen how to use Presenter View and leverage many of its great tools to improve your presentation delivery, and how to make your presentations more accessible and inclusive by using subtitles.

Using Presenter View to help you reduce your fear of forgetting what to say is a great way to improve your presentation delivery. Just make sure that you don't put very long scripts in the notes. Doing so might increase your stress level because you have to scroll through the notes, or may even make your eyes focus on your computer instead of on your audience. Also, if you have a long script, reading it might make you sound unprepared and unnatural. The best advice I can give you is to aim to reduce your notes to very short sentences or keywords so that they are a reminder of the points you have to discuss.

As wonderful as I think Presenter View can be, if you think it will solve all your delivery problems, you are wrong! No tool can ever replace quality practice time; it can only help improve your performance because you have practiced your talk.

In the final chapter of this book, we will be discussing how to use the PowerPoint Live feature in Microsoft Teams. If you are doing remote or virtual presentations with Teams on a regular basis, it will help you manage your presentation more efficiently.

13

PowerPoint Live and Interactive Features in Microsoft Teams

If you present mostly virtually, you might run into challenges while trying to figure out the best way to share your PowerPoint presentation. Yes, you could simply share your whole screen and use **Presenter View**, as discussed in the previous chapter. But then you might have a hard time seeing your meeting controls, especially if you are working with only one monitor.

With virtual presentations being widely used and, I'm quite sure, here to stay, I wanted to include a chapter on leveraging Microsoft Teams' PowerPoint Live, and other features that help you create more interactions and engagement. Why Teams and not another virtual meeting tool? Simply because it is the application I have been using and have seen evolve since its introduction in 2017, and its ability to leverage many more features included in Microsoft 365.

To help you take your presentations to a new level using PowerPoint Live within Teams, here are the topics discussed in this chapter:

- Getting started with and using PowerPoint Live
- Creating and using breakout rooms
- Using Q&A and Polls to create more interactions
- Improving the camera, lighting, and microphone setup

Technical requirements

You need access to Microsoft Teams with a Microsoft 365 work or school license to have access to PowerPoint Live. Be aware that since Microsoft Teams, just like the subscription version of PowerPoint, is updated on an ongoing basis, it is possible that screenshots shown in this chapter might differ from your version of the application.

Getting started with and using PowerPoint Live

Trying to manage your PowerPoint presentation, participants, reactions, and the chat pane in Microsoft Teams can be quite challenging, especially if you only have one monitor connected to your computer. Even when you do have two monitors, handling the various overlapping windows can be overwhelming.

That is when the PowerPoint Live feature can help you. You will find it when clicking on the **Share** button (**1**) in your Teams meeting window (*Figure 13.1*):

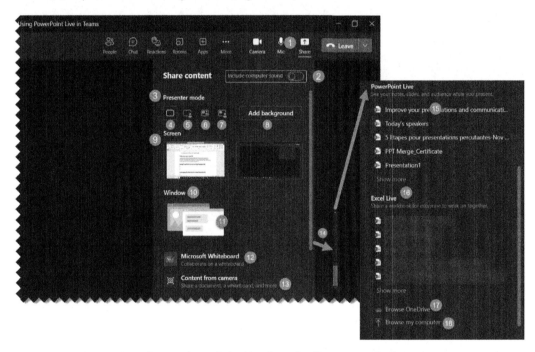

Figure 13.1 – Starting PowerPoint Live from the Share screen feature in Teams

Let's start by defining a few settings you have in the sharing options:

- **Include computer sound** (**2**): Make sure you toggle this option on if your presentation includes sound. This is the only way attendees will hear it.

- The **Presenter mode** section (**3**): This allows you to share your content only (**4**), use **Standout** mode (**5**) to overlap your video feed on top of your slides, use **Side-by-Side** (**6**) to have your video feed next to your slides, or use **Reporter** (**7**) so your slides are positioned at an angle to the left of your video feed, just as we see for news reporters. The **Add background** button (**8**) gives you access to either blur or choose a background image.

- The **Screen** (**9**) section: This allows you to share your whole screen so you can easily switch from one window to another while sharing the screen. If you only have one monitor, only one thumbnail view will be available. One important warning with this type of screen share is that everything you do on your screen is visible to your attendees. Make sure you have closed any confidential content before you start your meeting.

- The **Window** (**10**) section: This allows you to show only one window at a time. The number in parentheses shows you how many single windows are available to choose from. When you click on the window illustration (**11**), you will see previews of all your windows so you can choose the one you need.

- You can also choose to share a whiteboard with **Microsoft Whiteboard** (**12**) so everyone can sketch and brainstorm on a virtual board, or use **Content from camera** (**13**), allowing you to share external content with your camera or from a more complex equipment setting.

- If you scroll down the list of sharing options (**14**), you will get to the **PowerPoint Live** section (**15**) where you may have a list of PowerPoint files opened recently from your OneDrive for Business or SharePoint sites. Clicking on one of the files starts sharing your content with PowerPoint Live, which we'll describe soon.

- A new feature rolling out to users is **Excel Live** (**16**), a way to share and collaborate on a workbook while in a Teams meeting.

- If you did not have any files in the PowerPoint Live list, or the one you need is not there, you can use **Browse OneDrive** (**17**) or **Browse my computer** (**18**) to load your presentation and use it.

> **Important note**
>
> If you browse your computer or a network drive to upload a presentation file, it gets added to the meeting files. If you create a personal meeting, the file is made available to meeting participants when they open the Teams meeting details in their calendar and it is saved in your OneDrive space. If you create a channel meeting, the file is available to all team members in the team files.

After selecting a PowerPoint file that you want to share during your meeting, your Teams meeting screen will be adjusted to include PowerPoint Live features (**1**), which has a similar layout to Presenter View, seen in the previous chapter, while keeping your meeting management tools available (*Figure 13.2*):

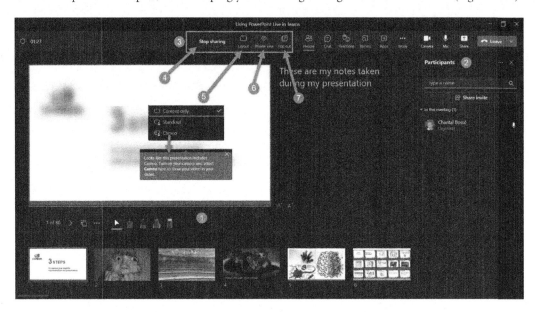

Figure 13.2 – PowerPoint Live features integrated into your Teams meeting window

I also opened the **Participants** pane (**2**) to show you how easy it becomes to manage the presentation and your attendees. You now have a new category of tools (**3**) available in the meeting toolbar at the top of the meeting window:

- **Stop sharing** (**4**): This is the button you need to click when you want to stop sharing your presentation.

- **Layout** (**5**): This button allows you to change the type of **Presenter mode**, described in the **Share** settings in the previous figure. The rectangular icon indicates we are only sharing the content. If you click on it, you will see a list of **Content only** and **Standout**, and if **Cameo** is detected on your slide, it will also be available. Teams will show you a callout when Cameo is detected, reminding you to turn on your camera and select this mode to make it work.

- **Private view** (**6**): PowerPoint Live has a special feature allowing attendees to navigate your slides while you are presenting. If you want to restrict the navigation to the slides that have been already covered, then you need to click this button to avoid attendees browsing through your upcoming slides.

- **Pop out** (**7**): This button allows you to have PowerPoint Live in a separate window. I suggest you avoid using it if you have only one monitor, as it will make your meeting management more complex.

PowerPoint Live makes it easy to navigate through your slides because most tools are similar to the ones we have described in **Presenter View** in the previous chapter. Let's review what you have available (*Figure 13.3*):

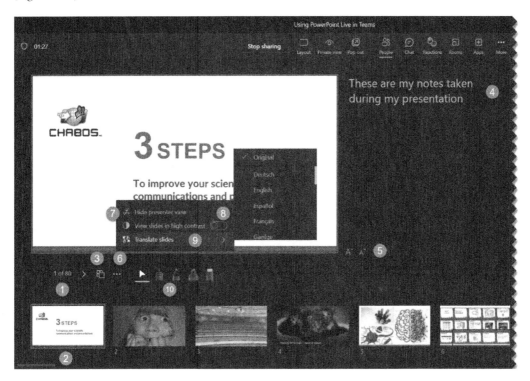

Figure 13.3 – Slide management tools in PowerPoint Live

- You have arrows, the current slide number, and the total number of slides here for navigation (**1**).

- The slide thumbnail strip (**2**) allows you to quickly access another slide.

- **Grid view** (**3**) gives you access to a list of all your slides to easily show one on demand.

- The notes pane (**4**) allows you to follow your notes and tools to increase or decrease the font size (**5**). At the time this book is being written, it is not possible to edit or add any notes in this pane during your presentation.

- In **More actions (…)** (**6**), you can remove your notes and the strip of slide thumbnails with **Hide presenter view** (**7**) while keeping the line of tools below the slide preview. The two other tools can be used as accessibility features on the attendees' side. **View slides in high contrast** (**8**) helps people with visual contrast or color issues. As for **Translate slides** (**9**), attendees can choose the language of their choice to machine-translate the text on your slides.

- The annotation tools (**10**) are like the ones discussed for Presenter View. Click on one of them to change your mouse cursor into a laser pointer, pen, or highlighter. Clicking on the icon a second time brings up settings such as color or thickness, when applicable. Use the eraser to remove an annotation or click a second time to access the setting to erase all the annotations on the slide.

In previous figures, you have seen a meeting window without any attendees. When you do have attendees and their cameras are on, you can adjust how the video feeds are displayed in your window. You can have the videos on the right of your slide (**1**) or use the **More (…)** option (**2**) to select **Gallery at top** (**3**) and move the video cameras above your slide (**4**) (*Figure 13.4*):

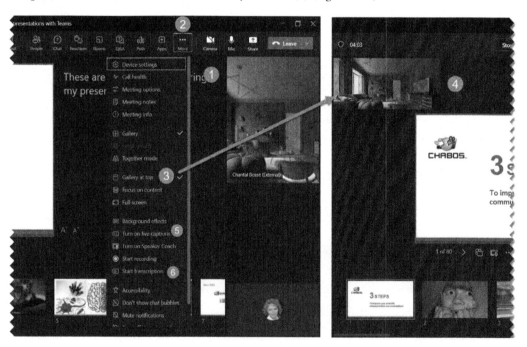

Figure 13.4 – Changing how video cameras are displayed while using PowerPoint Live

There are other options from the list I want to point out that you should consider when presenting in a Teams meeting:

- First, you have **Turn on live captions** (**5**). Just as we mentioned when discussing **Presenter View**, live captions can also be added during a Teams meeting. They can help you make your presentations much more inclusive and accessible. With the regular Microsoft 365 license, captions will display in the spoken language. A Teams Premium license is required to get access to translated live captions. Have a look at the Microsoft Support article available in *Further reading* for more information.

- The other option you should consider for more accessible and inclusive presentations is **Start transcription** (**6**). Starting the feature opens a pane on the right of your meeting screen and captures what each participant is saying, either with their name or anonymously depending on the Teams settings they chose. It can be a productive feature for meetings, capturing your discussions as you go. Transcriptions can also help you repurpose your virtual presentations because you can download the transcript as a Word file or `.vtt` file to add captions to your videos. The feature is limited to the desktop version of Teams and to a select set of licenses. See the support article in *Further reading* for details.

- The last feature I want to point out in **More (…)** (**1**) is **Turn on Speaker Coach** (**2**) (*Figure 13.5*):

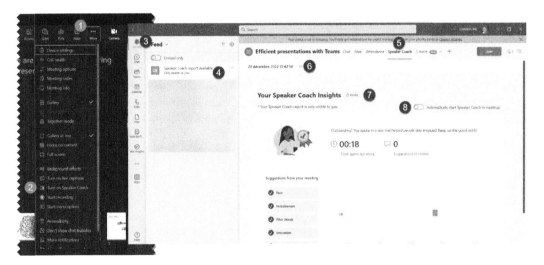

Figure 13.5 – Using Speaker Coach in a Teams meeting

Being able to use **Speaker Coach** in Teams is brand new and still in preview at the time this book is being written. Depending on how the feature rollout is going, it might take a while before it is widely available publicly. Also, it is only available when the Teams interface is in English.

When you turn on the feature, Speaker Coach will be running in the background. When your meeting is over, a notification will point you to your **Activity** feed (**3**) and you will see the **Speaker Coach report available** notification at the top (**4**) if you are consulting it before any new activity is logged in by Teams; click on it to view the report. You can see a new **Speaker Coach** tab (**5**), the date and time list (**6**) where you could view more reports if you have practiced several times with this scheduled meeting, and the report itself, **Your Speaker Coach Insights** (**7**), where you can see it is **Private**. The report information will be similar to what we discussed in *Chapter 11, Practicing Your Presentation Delivery*. I think it is a great way to practice your virtual presentations ahead of time, or even use it every time you present with Teams to help you improve, so you might consider turning on the toggle for the **Automatically start Speaker Coach in meetings** feature (**8**).

Now that we have seen the most important features that can be used while sharing a presentation with PowerPoint Live, let's see how to use breakout rooms from your meeting window to create more engagement.

Creating and using breakout rooms

There are many scenarios in which you can use breakout rooms during a Teams meeting. And there are many ways to create and use those rooms too! Since I want to keep my focus on how using this feature can be helpful to keep your presentation attendees engaged, I will discuss only one scenario in the following example. If you want to learn more about the various ways to create and use breakout rooms, have a look at the support article listed in *Further reading*.

Let's say you are delivering a workshop using Teams meetings. If you were in a room with your attendees, you would probably ask them to work in small groups to discuss a specific topic that each team would present to the whole group after. To reproduce this team exercise from your meeting window, you need to click on the **Rooms** icon (**1**) to access the **Create breakout rooms** pane (**2**) (*Figure 13.6*):

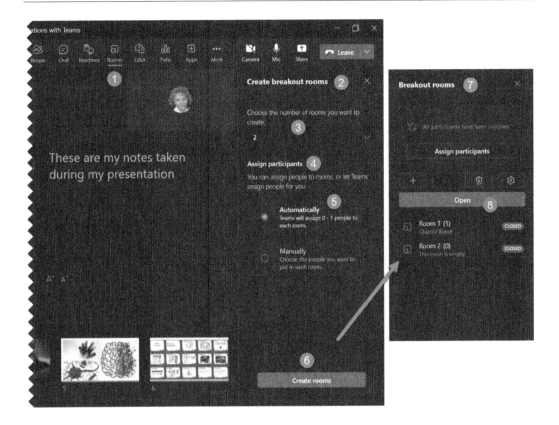

Figure 13.6 – Creating and using breakout rooms in Teams

The first section, **Choose the number of rooms you want to create.** (**3**), has a drop-down list to choose the number of rooms you want to create; you can create up to 50. For our example, I will keep **2** as the number of rooms to create.

In the **Assign participants** section (**4**), the default option is **Automatically** (**5**). To be efficient during our workshop example, this is what I suggest using when creating breakout rooms on the fly. If you need to assign specific people to certain groups, consult the Microsoft Support article in *Further reading* to see how you can create your breakout rooms before your event.

The only thing left to do is to click on the **Create rooms** button (**6**) to change the right-hand pane to **Breakout rooms** (**7**) with its own tools and **Open** button (**8**).

When rooms are open (**1**), you see it in your **Breakout rooms** pane. In the common scenario in which you have more attendees than the number of rooms you have created, all your rooms will be open with the number of people assigned to them in parentheses, such as **Room 1 (1)** (*Figure 13.7*):

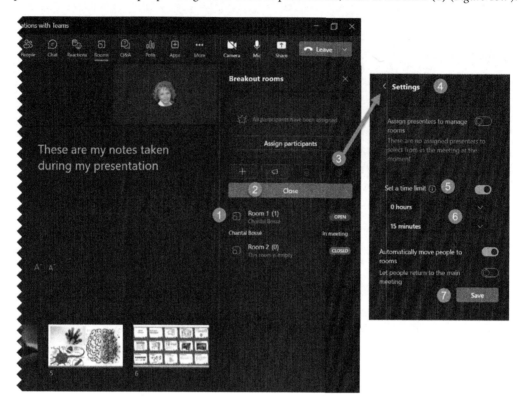

Figure 13.7 – Manage open breakout rooms

In the context that you want to allow your workshop attendees to discuss a topic in small groups, you can time it yourself, then click on the **Close** button (**2**) to bring back everyone to the main meeting. Or you can click on the gear icon (**3**) to open the **Settings** pane (**4**) and configure **Set a time limit** (**5**) by toggling the feature on and selecting the duration in the hours and minutes lists (**6**), then clicking on the **Save** button (**7**). Your attendees will return automatically to the main meeting room at the end of the set time limit, usually seeing a warning one minute before closing.

Using breakout rooms can help change the pace during your presentation while helping attendees interact more with one another, energizing them before you continue with your presentation. Get familiar with the various breakout room features and settings so you can try a scenario that works for your type of content.

Let's now move on to two other interactive features you can use in a Teams meeting to help increase interactions with your attendees while getting their feedback to help you adapt your talk.

Using Q&A and Polls to create more interactions

Virtual presentations require more interaction to keep your audience engaged. The reason is simple: you are competing with emails, news feeds, text messages, and social media so you absolutely need to find ways to grab everyone's attention.

When using Microsoft Teams, you have nice tools that can help you and we will discuss two of them in the following sections.

Using Q&A

Q&A is a recent addition to Teams meetings allowing you to separate questions and important discussions from the regular chat pane. To have **Q&A** (**1**) available in your meeting toolbar, you first need to make sure it is turned on in your meeting's options by clicking **More (…)** (**2**) | **Meeting options** (**3**) to open the **Meeting options** pane (**4**). Make sure to look at the bottom of the pane for **Enable Q&A** (**5**) to check that the toggle is on (*Figure 13.8*):

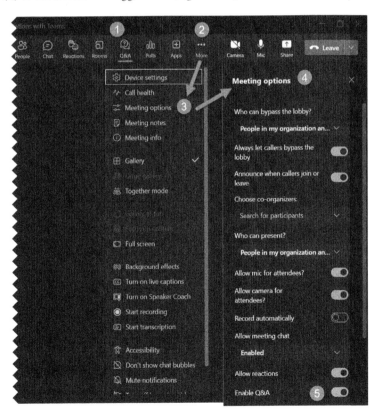

Figure 13.8 – Checking meeting options to enable Q&A

The previous steps are only available if you are the Teams meeting organizer, or if you were made a co-organizer for the meeting. If the meeting was scheduled by someone else for you and they did not make you a co-organizer, you need to ask them to make the changes. They can go back to their meeting in their calendar and make changes to the meeting options, or they can start the meeting and change the options by following the previous steps. If you are not familiar with the different roles in Teams meetings, have a look at the Microsoft Support article in *Further reading*.

When you do have Q&A available in your meeting window toolbar, click on its icon (**1**) so the **Q&A** pane (**2**) shows on the right (*Figure 13.9*):

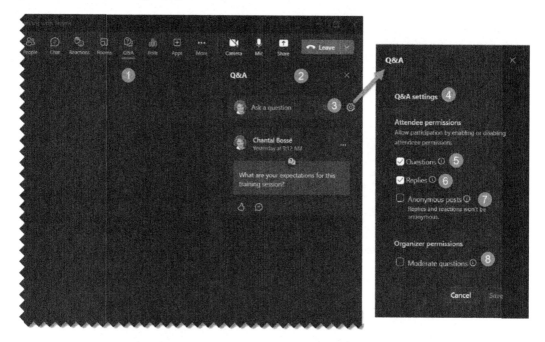

Figure 13.9 – Opening Q&A and managing its settings

The first thing you should do if you have never used this feature is to click on the gear icon (**3**) to access the **Q&A settings** pane (**4**). You can then decide what permissions you give your attendees, such as asking questions (**5**) or adding replies (**6**). Since our goal is to improve interactions with attendees, allow them to ask questions and reply instead of using Q&A solely for your own questions. The next setting is for allowing attendees to use anonymous posts (**7**) – there is an important note mentioning that replies and reactions won't be anonymous. Finally, you can check the **Moderate questions** checkbox (**8**), making them available only after reviewing them. Clicking the **Save** or **Cancel** button (**9**) brings you back to the **Q&A** pane. If you are running your meeting alone, I would advise you not to use it to avoid overwhelming you with many extra tasks.

You or your attendees can quickly enter a question by clicking **Ask a question** (**1**) to access the dialog box (**2**), enter a question, and click **Post** (**3**) (*Figure 13.10*):

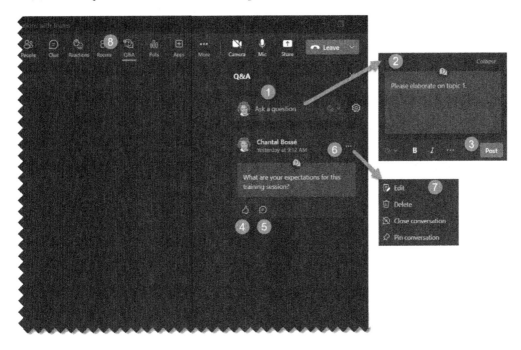

Figure 13.10 – Adding and managing questions in Q&A

When a question is posted, people can add a reaction (**4**) or a comment (**5**). And if you want to manage the Q&A list of messages, you can click on the ellipses (**…**) (**6**) to access features (**7**) to edit, delete, close, or pin a conversation. When you have a new activity in Q&A during your meeting, you will see a small circle over the Q&A icon (**8**) to notify you. The best way to get comfortable with this feature is to plan a practice meeting with a few people.

The advantage of using Q&A for any formal question is to avoid having to search the chat pane when it is used for everything. To make this work, you do need to tell your attendees when starting your meeting what your expectations are when they have questions.

Even though Q&A could be a nice place to add your own questions for attendees, you might want to consider Polls instead, the topic of the next section.

Using Polls in a meeting

Polls is an application that can quickly be added to your Teams meetings so that you can ask various questions and get attendees to participate. You will find the **Polls** icon (**1**) in your Teams meeting toolbar, or you will need to add it by clicking the **Apps** icon (**2**) and using the **Find an app** search box (**3**) with the `Polls` keyword if you don't see it in the list. When you see **Polls** in the list, click on it (**4**) (*Figure 13.11*):

Figure 13.11 – Finding and adding the Polls app

During your presentation, you can quickly launch the Polls application by clicking on its icon (**1**) to open the **Polls** pane (**2**) and view **Suggestions** (**3**) (*Figure 13.12*):

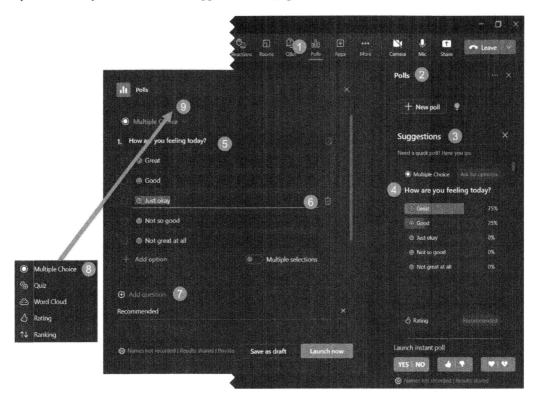

Figure 13.12 – Launching Polls and using Suggestions

This list has many quick-start polls you can easily customize on the fly. For example, if we click on **How are you feeling today?** (**4**) it opens a new window where you can edit the question or answers simply by clicking on any of the fields (**5**). If you want to remove one of the choices, click on the field and then choose the delete icon (**6**). Your poll could have more than one question; just click on **Add question** (**7**) and select the type of question you want to create from the list (**8**). This list is also available when you click on the arrow beside a question type (**9**) if you want to change it.

Next, you should have a look at the poll settings (**1**) available from the link at the bottom of the Polls creation window (*Figure 13.13*):

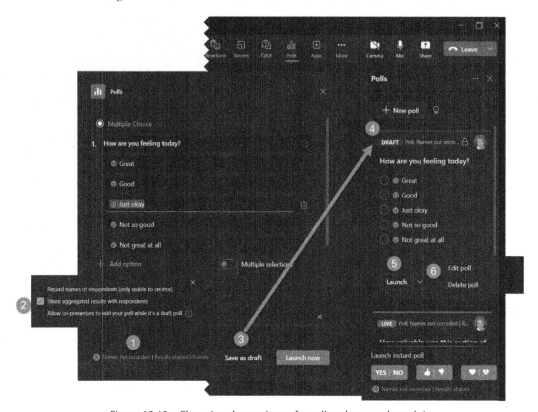

Figure 13.13 – Changing the settings of a poll and save or launch it

By default, the poll's aggregated results are shared with your attendees (**2**) but you could decide to record their names for your own use, or allow your co-presenters to edit polls that have been saved as drafts. When you click on the **Save as draft** button (**3**), your poll is now visible in the **Polls** pane and labeled as a draft (**4**). You can click the **Launch** button (**5**) when you are ready to make it live, or the arrow beside it (**6**) if you want to edit or delete your poll.

When you launch a poll with **Launch now** (**1**), it becomes available in the **Polls** pane and is labeled as **LIVE** (**2**). Your attendees will see a poll window appear at the top of their meeting window to invite them to answer your questions. The other way your polls are made available is in the **Meeting chat** pane (**3**), where anyone can click the **View poll** button (**4**) to answer (*Figure 13.14*):

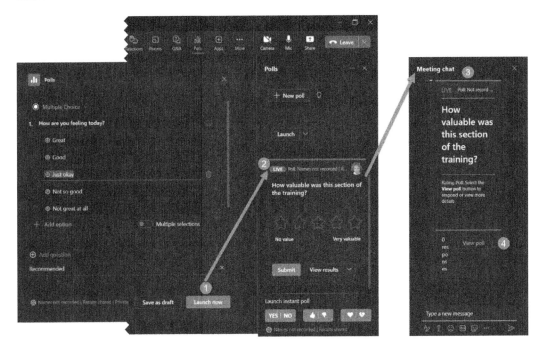

Figure 13.14 – Launching a poll and retrieving it in the meeting chat

Using Polls on the fly might be helpful at times, but it would be much better for you to plan those polls, or interactions, before your presentation date. In the first chapter of this book, we discussed how important planning is for your presentation content. For your delivery, it is as important to plan the types of interactions you will involve.

For Polls, you could start your presentation before the day of your presentation to plan your polls and save them as drafts. A better way would be to go to your Teams calendar (**1**) and double-click on the meeting you planned so you can access the **Polls** tab (**2**) (*Figure 13.15*):

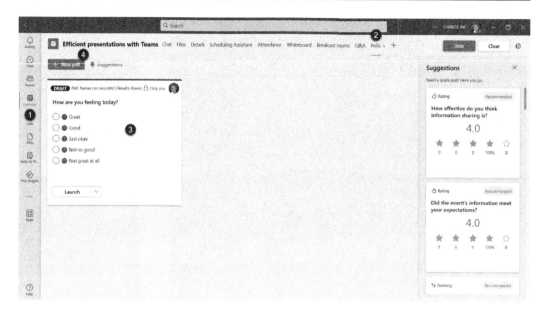

Figure 13.15 – Planning your polls from the Polls tab in your meeting details

If you have created any **DRAFT** polls already (**3**), you will see them in the window. You will also be able to easily use the **+ New poll** button (**4**) to create all your polls in advance. Just leave them in draft mode and you will be able to launch them when you need them during your Teams meeting. If you want more information on Polls, have a look at the Microsoft Support article in *Further reading*.

You have now seen a few tools to help you improve interactions during your virtual presentations. When you share your presentation file with PowerPoint Live, you can easily access them directly in the same meeting window.

In the final section of this chapter, we will discuss a few ways you can improve how you look and sound during a virtual meeting.

Improving the camera, lighting, and microphone setup

My goal with this section is not to cover all the greatest and latest equipment available on the market, but to share some features and tips that can help you even when you don't have access to fancy gear.

Checking Microsoft Teams device settings

The first place to start is by showing you hidden device settings available in Microsoft Teams. You first need to click on **More (…)** (**1**) | **Device settings** (**2**), to access the **Device settings** pane (**3**) (*Figure 13.16*):

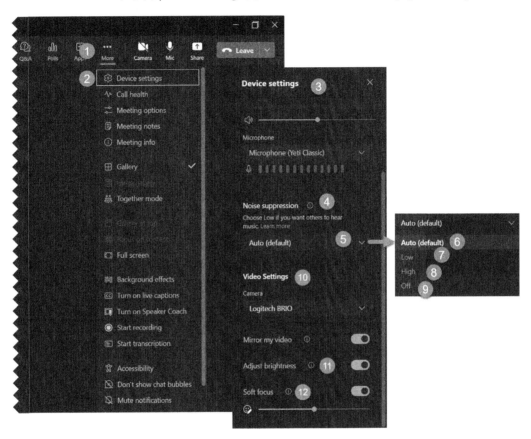

Figure 13.16 – Accessing Device settings in Teams

Scroll down to the **Noise suppression** section (**4**). If you were not aware of its existence, it is an AI-based feature analyzing background noises. Here is a description of each setting:

- **Auto (default)** (**5/6**): Teams monitors your background noise and turns suppression up or down to remove noise not recognized as your voice. Do you need to search for a piece of paper on your desk? No one should hear you. Is the dog barking? You should be covered too. I have seen it in action with someone vacuuming during the meeting or crumpling a bag of chips near the microphone, and we could not hear it at all. But I would add that the reliability of the feature might depend on which type of microphone you are using because I have experienced moments where other noises could still be heard. Test it with your own equipment.

- **Low** (7): Microsoft suggests using this setting if you want people to hear background music. Any other persistent background noise, such as a fan, will be removed.

- **High** (8): This is the highest level of noise suppression, removing everything that is not considered to be speech.

- **Off** (9): There is no noise suppression with this setting. If you can hold Teams meetings without any noise suppression, I'm impressed at how quiet your environment is!

There are two other interesting settings in the **Video Settings** section (**10**), and they only need to be toggled on. The **Adjust brightness** setting (**11**) enhances the quality of your video when the lighting is poor. The **Soft focus** setting (**12**) applies a smoothing effect to your appearance, which you can adjust with the slider when it is turned on. Just be careful not to overdo it, because it can make you look unnatural.

Now that we have seen what Teams settings can help you improve how you look and sound during a meeting, let's see some best practice tips in the next section.

Tips to help you improve how you look and sound

Even though I will not discuss any specific equipment, it is clear that if you want to look more professional for your virtual presentations, you need to avoid using the built-in camera and microphone of your laptop. You simply cannot control them well.

Try looking for a separate webcam, and ideally for quality headphones with a microphone. When you add that equipment, small applications are usually supplied by their manufacturer that can help you adjust the settings.

To help you look your best, make sure your webcam is in front of you at eye level. This also helps you look toward your attendees, which is much more engaging (*Figure 13.17*):

Figure 13.17 – Position your webcam in front of you at eye level

For lighting, you should ideally try to present from a room where you have natural light in front of you or where you can use LED or ring lights if you don't have a window. Never present with lighting coming from behind you because you will look like a silhouette with no face (*Figure 13.18*):

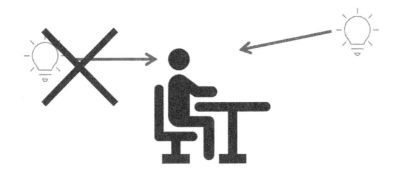

Figure 13.18 – Position yourself so the light is in front of you

If the room you are using to deliver your virtual presentation is rather dark, try adding light sources at an angle on each side of your face to avoid shadows (*Figure 13.19*):

Figure 13.19 – Adding light sources on each side when you are in a dark environment

Of course, improving how you look when delivering your virtual presentations means cleaning up what you have in your background. There is also the possibility to use features such as blurring your background or adding a virtual background. Be aware that if you risk having people walk behind you during your presentation, it will look as if you have human body parts floating behind you if they walk close enough. In my case, virtual backgrounds are just not up to par yet because of my curly hair; I usually end up having part of my face disappear when I move. So, I decided to purchase meeting backdrops that I clip to a pole behind me. My face now stays intact for the duration of my classes or meetings.

The tips I shared in this section are what I would call quick fixes. If you are going to present virtually on a regular basis, you should invest in good equipment and lighting. Your best bet in terms of knowing what to choose is to ask other presenters what they use and what they would recommend.

Summary

This chapter was all about using tools in Microsoft Teams to help you deliver better virtual presentations. We discussed how PowerPoint Live can help you manage your presentation and your meeting in the same window. We also learned about a few features that can help you keep your attendees engaged, such as breakout rooms, Q&A, and Polls. We finally discussed how to improve your camera, lighting, and microphone setup, sharing quick tips you can easily try.

My wish is that you realize that virtual presentations need as much practice as the ones you do in meeting rooms or large venues. In my opinion, they are even more complex to manage because often you have to learn more about the features that will help you keep people engaged, and handle technology problems by yourself. Make sure you continue learning about the virtual tools you can use because remote presentations will certainly not disappear.

Conclusion

If you have read this book from start to finish, you probably remember from our content structure in the chapters that your content should have an introduction, your main key points, and a conclusion.

In this book, my introduction was all about the challenges encountered while creating your content. I then proceeded to help you learn how to plan, create, and deliver more impactful presentations with the help of the many advanced tools and features in PowerPoint. And my conclusion on this one: now that you have more knowledge on how to create better presentations, will you plan more time in your schedule to put your learnings into practice?

Wishing you much success in your upcoming presentations!

Further reading

- Microsoft Support article on sharing slides in Teams meeting: `https://support.microsoft.com/en-us/office/share-slides-in-a-teams-meeting-with-powerpoint-live-fc5a5394-2159-419c-bc59-1f64c1f4e470`

- Microsoft Support article on live captions: `https://support.microsoft.com/en-us/office/use-live-captions-in-a-teams-meeting-4be2d304-f675-4b57-8347-cbd000a21260`

- Microsoft Support article on live transcription: `https://support.microsoft.com/en-us/office/view-live-transcription-in-a-teams-meeting-dc1a8f23-2e20-4684-885e-2152e06a4a8b`

- Microsoft Support article on Speaker Coach in Teams: `https://support.microsoft.com/en-us/office/preview-speaker-coach-in-a-teams-meeting-30f50d15-5f62-4e09-b3bf-cadeb806386a`

- Microsoft Support article on breakout rooms in Teams: `https://support.microsoft.com/en-us/office/use-breakout-rooms-in-teams-meetings-7de1f48a-da07-466c-a5ab-4ebace28e461`

- Microsoft Support article on the different roles in Teams meetings: `https://support.microsoft.com/en-us/office/roles-in-a-teams-meeting-c16fa7d0-1666-4dde-8686-0a0bfe16e019`

- Microsoft Support article on Polls in Teams meetings: `https://support.microsoft.com/en-us/office/poll-attendees-during-a-teams-meeting-9923b7d4-ea97-4aa2-b8b8-b45fefe7d454`

Index

Packtpub.com

Subscribe to our online digital library for full access to over 7,000 books and videos, as well as industry leading tools to help you plan your personal development and advance your career. For more information, please visit our website.

Why subscribe?

- Spend less time learning and more time coding with practical eBooks and Videos from over 4,000 industry professionals

- Improve your learning with Skill Plans built especially for you

- Get a free eBook or video every month

- Fully searchable for easy access to vital information

- Copy and paste, print, and bookmark content

Did you know that Packt offers eBook versions of every book published, with PDF and ePub files available? You can upgrade to the eBook version at packtpub.com and as a print book customer, you are entitled to a discount on the eBook copy. Get in touch with us at customercare@packtpub.com for more details.

At www.packtpub.com, you can also read a collection of free technical articles, sign up for a range of free newsletters, and receive exclusive discounts and offers on Packt books and eBooks.

Other Books You May Enjoy

If you enjoyed this book, you may be interested in these other books by Packt:

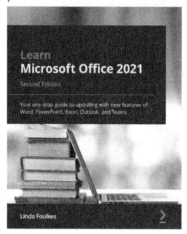

Learn Microsoft Office 2021 - Second Edition

Linda Foulkes

ISBN: 978-1-80323-973-6

- Uncover OneDrive features and Word enhancements such as dictation, co-authoring, embedding, styles, referencing, and media tools
- Manage Word document layouts, online forms, recording document automation, and track, compare, and combine
- Create engaging PowerPoint presentations using Presenter Coach, Auto Fix, Record, and drawing tools
- Explore Excel functions such as XLOOKUP, LET, XMATCH IFS, arrays and IFERROR, and VLOOKUP
- Work with database and COUNTIF functions, Advanced Filter, clean data, and PivotTables and Dashboards
- Explore Outlook enhancements

Work Smarter with Microsoft OneNote

Connie Clark

ISBN: 978-1-80107-566-4

- Understand how to create and organize notes in your notebooks
- Discover how to turn handwritten notes into typed text
- Explore how to access your content from anywhere even if offline
- Uncover ways to collaborate with your team or family and stay in sync
- Understand how to insert your emails, documents, or articles from the web
- Find out how to integrate with other Microsoft products such as Outlook or Teams

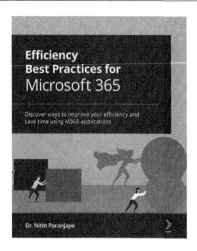

Efficiency Best Practices for Microsoft 365

Dr. Nitin Paranjape

ISBN: 978-1-80107-226-7

- Understand how different MS 365 tools, such as Office desktop, Teams, Power BI, Lists, and OneDrive, can increase work efficiency

- Identify time-consuming processes and understand how to work through them more efficiently

- Create professional documents quickly with minimal effort

- Work across multiple teams, meetings, and projects without email overload

- Automate mundane, repetitive, and time-consuming manual work

- Manage work, delegation, execution, and project management

Packt is searching for authors like you

If you're interested in becoming an author for Packt, please visit `authors.packtpub.com` and apply today. We have worked with thousands of developers and tech professionals, just like you, to help them share their insight with the global tech community. You can make a general application, apply for a specific hot topic that we are recruiting an author for, or submit your own idea.

Share Your Thoughts

Now you've finished *Microsoft PowerPoint Best Practices, Tips, and Techniques*, we'd love to hear your thoughts! Scan the QR code below to go straight to the Amazon review page for this book and share your feedback or leave a review on the site that you purchased it from

`https://packt.link/r/1-839-21533-X`

Your review is important to us and the tech community and will help us make sure we're delivering excellent quality content.

Download a free PDF copy of this book

Thanks for purchasing this book!

Do you like to read on the go but are unable to carry your print books everywhere? Is your eBook purchase not compatible with the device of your choice?

Don't worry, now with every Packt book you get a DRM-free PDF version of that book at no cost.

Read anywhere, any place, on any device. Search, copy, and paste code from your favorite technical books directly into your application.

The perks don't stop there, you can get exclusive access to discounts, newsletters, and great free content in your inbox daily

Follow these simple steps to get the benefits:

1. Scan the QR code or visit the link below

https://packt.link/free-ebook/9781839215339

2. Submit your proof of purchase
3. That's it! We'll send your free PDF and other benefits to your email directly